P9-CMY-707

	117–18	119	123	134	141–42	144	145	146	153	155	158	159	162	1890	177	178	179	181	182	184–87	188	193–95	200	201	202	206	207	209–11	220	221–22	224	225	226	229	230	231	232–34	235	242–45

Demographic Characteristics

	117–18	119	123	134	141–42	144	145	146	153	155	158	159	162	1890	177	178	179	181	182	184–87	188	193–95	200	201	202	206	207	209–11	220	221–22	224	225	226	229	230	231	232–34	235	242–45	
Aggregate Population	●			●	●				●	●					●	●			●					●			●		●	●	●		●	●	●			●	●	
Historic from 1790					●				●						●										●				●	●	●								●	
Age									●						●	●	●	●	●				●	●			●		●	●	●		●	●			●		●	
Race and Condition					●				●						●	●								●	●	●	●		●	●	●	●	●	●			●		●	
Sex					●				●						●	●	●	●	●				●	●			●		●	●	●	●	●	●			●		●	

Social and Economic Characteristics

	117–18	119	123	134	141–42	144	145	146	153	155	158	159	162	1890	177	178	179	181	182	184–87	188	193–95	200	201	202	206	207	209–11	220	221–22	224	225	226	229	230	231	232–34	235	242–45	
Citizenship															●	●			●								●		●	●	●	●							●	
Crime							●		●									●	●								●		●	●		●							●	
Disabilities				●			●		●								●	●											●	●		●							●	
Education				●					●							●		●	●				●				●		●	●		●	●	●					●	
Employment and unemployment	●	●		●	●		●	●	●		●	●		●			●	●		●	●	●		●			●	●	●	●	●	●	●			●			●	
Families							●		●					●			●	●					●		●		●		●	●	●								●	
Farms																				●			●	●	●	●	●			●			●						●	
Housing			●					●	●					●									●		●	●	●		●				●		●				●	
Immigration																											●													
Income and property		●				●			●			●										●					●		●										●	
Institutionalized population							●		●					●		●		●	●								●		●	●		●							●	
Language									●					●	●	●		●	●				●		●				●	●			●			●			●	
Literacy									●						●	●	●	●	●				●		●				●	●			●			●			●	
Military															●	●	●	●	●						●				●			●							●	
Nativity				●					●					●	●	●	●	●	●				●			●		●	●	●	●	●	●				●		●	
Occupations					●				●						●	●	●	●	●				●	●	●	●			●	●			●		●	●			●	
Paupers							●		●										●										●		●								●	
Publications and Libraries									●																														●	
Religion																							●	●	●				●	●	●								●	
Slavery																																							●	
Transportation				●				●				●												●					●	●	●				●				●	

Apportionment, Density, Geography

	117–18	119	123	134	141–42	144	145	146	153	155	158	159	162	1890	177	178	179	181	182	184–87	188	193–95	200	201	202	206	207	209–11	220	221–22	224	225	226	229	230	231	232–34	235	242–45	
Apportionment									●						●															●	●							●	●	
Density								●							●											●		●		●	●				●					
Geography			●					●				●		●										●			●		●	●								●		

Vital Statistics

	117–18	119	123	134	141–42	144	145	146	153	155	158	159	162	1890	177	178	179	181	182	184–87	188	193–95	200	201	202	206	207	209–11	220	221–22	224	225	226	229	230	231	232–34	235	242–45	
Births	●															●	●	●			●			●															●	
Deaths	●	●							●						●			●						●		●	●			●				●			●		●	
Marriages and Divorces															●		●	●	●				●		●			●	●			●				●		●		

Foreign Data

	117–18	119	123	134	141–42	144	145	146	153	155	158	159	162	1890	177	178	179	181	182	184–87	188	193–95	200	201	202	206	207	209–11	220	221–22	224	225	226	229	230	231	232–34	235	242–45
	●			●												●							●		●		●									●			

Population Information in Nineteenth Century Census Volumes

by Suzanne Schulze

Ref
HA
214
.S25

NOV 8 1984

457826

 ORYX PRESS
1983

The rare Arabian Oryx is believed to have inspired the myth of the unicorn. This desert antelope became virtually extinct in the early 1960s. At that time several groups of international conservationists arranged to have 9 animals sent to the Phoenix Zoo to be the nucleus of a captive breeding herd. Today the Oryx population is over 400 and herds have been returned to reserves in Israel, Jordan, and Oman.

Copyright © 1983 by Suzanne Schulze
Published by The Oryx Press
2214 North Central at Encanto
Phoenix, AZ 85004

Published simultaneously in Canada

All rights reserved
No part of this publication may be reproduced or transmitted in any form or by any means, electronic or mechanical, including photocopying, recording, or by any information storage and retrieval system, without permission in writing from The Oryx Press

Printed and Bound in the United States of America

Library of Congress Cataloging in Publication Data

Schulze, Suzanne.
   Population information in nineteenth century census
volumes.

   Bibliography: p.
   1. United States—Census—Indexes.   2. United
States—Population—History—19th century—Sources—
Indexes.   I. Title
Z7164.D3S44   1983   [HA214]   304.6′0973   83-17380
ISBN 0-89774-122-6

TABLE OF CONTENTS

PREFACE AND ACKNOWLEDGMENTS

This publication was supported by a grant from the National Foundation for the Humanities. I want to thank the Foundation, and particularly Mary Beth Norton, chair of the reading committee, and William K. Wallach, the Foundation staff member assigned to my application for a grant under the Research Resources program. The grant made possible a leave from my position as documents librarian at the University of Northern Colorado for three months in the summers of 1981 and 1982. Dr. Claude J. Johns, Jr., Dean of the University Libraries, generously allowed one month of library time to work on this volume. I wish to thank him as well.

My interest in historical census information arose through a number of reference questions on the development of communities in Weld County Colorado, where the University is located. Geography and history students and faculty members, city and county planners, and community developers made frequent requests for population statistics of Weld County communities from their earliest days. I found myself locating the old census volumes and duplicating pages to have them available for the next time census information was requested.

Michener Library, I began to realize, had an excellent census collection, apparently better than other neighboring libraries. When I learned this, I obtained a small grant from the Faculty Research and Publications Committee to compile Colorado population counts for the first century of the State's existence, and to make the volume available to the other depository libraries in Colorado. With a somewhat larger grant under the Library Services and Construction Act, I was able to publish a revised volume with some 3,000 additional pages on microfiche. These pages included the details on age, sex, race, nativity, occupation and other social and economic statistics. Both editions published at the Library in 1976 and 1977, are entitled A Century of the Colorado Census.

Government document librarians have their own organization within the American Library Association which in turn has a Census Work Group. At a meeting in 1980, it was suggested that I develop a new publication which would enable those in other states to compile a volume similar to the one for Colorado. One of the purposes of this volume is to meet that suggestion. Members of the Census Work Group deserve many thanks for their suggestion and for their willingness to search their own collections for those volumes still eluding Michener Library and to lend their volumes for this index. Through their efforts, particularly those of Pat Sloan of the Nebraska Library Commission and Bob Shaklee of the Denver Public Library, I have been able to borrow and copy virtually every missing piece referred to in this volume.

My original intent with this index was to include only population volumes. In fact, that is what the Foundation reading committee approved. But in a rather casual conversation with Basil Zimmer, an old friend from Ann Arbor, of the Brown University Sociology Department, when I was explaining what I planned to do, his immediate reply was, "What have you found on the size of farms?" That question completely changed the project. It was quite apparent, as perhaps it should have been from the beginning, that information on population is not limited to population volumes alone. The size of farms was, of course, an important aspect of the life of the people in the Nineteenth Century. And the size of farms is found in the volumes on agriculture, as is information on employment in the volumes on manufactures, and a number of other population related subjects such as disabilities, vital statistics and transportation in single subject census volumes. Anyone using this publication will note that very vew census volumes have no population data at all.

Because of the expansion of this index to include so many more volumes than originally anticipated, and because its final reports are quite different from those of the Nineteenth Century, I have not included the 1900 Census. I believe that an index to the 1900 volumes would more properly belong with those of 1910, 1920, 1930, and 1940.

This publication is based on the work of Henry J. Dubester, who was chief of the Census Library Project, a joint endeavor of the Library of Congress and the Bureau of the Census in the 1940's. The numbers he assigned to the volumes in his Catalog of Census Publications: 1790 to 1940 are the base numbers used in this volume. I was fortunate to be able to meet Dr. Dubester in April 1982 and to discuss this project with him. Although documents librarians have come to use his name in the term "Dubester numbers" to identify census volumes, that was a surprise to him when he first learned of the fact some years ago. I am most appreciative of his interest in this project.

In our efforts to build up the census collection at Michener Library, Peggy Swanson, the other original member of the government publications staff, and I had found it necessary to cross reference various methods of classification of census documents when searching for them on gift and exchange lists from other libraries. From these efforts, we developed the page used in this volume to identify census publications according to Dubester numbers. I am very much indebted to her and to Elmer Bachenberg, now also a member of the government publications staff for his assistance in verifying the various classifications. As a University of Illinois Library School graduate, he had been aware that Illinois had used the Dewey system for its large documents collection. Gary Golden, documents librarian there, generously annotated our list with the Illinois Dewey citations. I am most appreciative of his assistance, and have tried to assign Dewey numbers to those volumes which Illinois did not have in accordance with Illinois usage.

I was fortunate to have three consultants on this project. Mary Redmond, then of the Illinois State Library and now of the State Library of New York, gave valuable assistance in developing the subject categories for indexing the volumes. Dr. Robert Larson of the University of Northern Colorado History Department who specializes in late Nineteenth Century American history has given weekly, if not sometimes daily

assistance. Dr. Robert Markham of the Michener Library Micrographics
Laboratory and author of the <u>National Lands Index</u> also served as con-
sultant on the indexing aspect of the project. I wish to thank each of
them for their aid and support.

During the course of developing this volume, I was fortunate to be able
to visit a number of libraries and to see their census collections. I
would like to thank each of the following librarians for their
assistance and interest:

    Grace Waibel and Jeffrey King of the Bureau of the Census
    Library, in Suitland, Maryland

    Maryellen Trautman, Paul Guite and Jerry Hess of the National
    Archives in Washington and Suitland

    Kay Ihlenfeld of the Chicago Public Library

    Ellen Holroyd of the Illinois State Library

    Ellen Isenstein of the Boston Public Library

    Doris Detweiler of the Detroit Public Library

This is a good time to say a word for the gift and exchange system which
operates among libraries, and particularly among depository libraries.
The collection at Michener Library is greatly indebted to the librarians
at South East Missouri State Teachers College, to John R. Walker of the
Riverside California City and County Library, and to Virginia Schwartz
of the Milwaukee Public Library for gifts to Michener Library which
helped complete our collection.

I would also like to thank several other persons who have given valuable
advice and assistance on this project: Jeanne Clare Ridley of the
Center for Population Research at Georgetown University, Gerry O'Donnell,
Denver Regional Coordinator for Data Services of the Census Bureau,
Catharine Reynolds, Regional Documents Librarian at the University of
Colorado at Boulder, Maxine Haggerty of the University of Utah Library,
and Gail Nichols of the University of California at Berkeley. Michael
Gebhart assisted me in verifying the table guides and in typing much of
the next-to-final draft, Theresa Solis and Elaine Schmidt of the government publications staff have taken on more than their share while my
mind was strayed to the Nineteenth Century. JoAnn Herrick has had the
thankless task of final typing. I am most appreciative of all their
work.

Needless to say, my husband and daughter will be glad to see the end of
this project. I must thank them for their patience, their housekeeping,
and their willingness to put up with amended vacation dates and a car
trunk frequently full of census tomes in place of summer clothes.

A major part of the work in developing this volume has been to try to make consistent what is itself inconsistent. Quite naturally, the Census has changed over the decades. Between 1790 and 1890 many new subjects were added, most of them were revised, and the terminology changed. It was necessary to develop a single set of terms to apply to all the subjects in the eleven censuses, and to make sure that the terms were meaningful to those more familiar with the Censuses of 1970 and 1980. The decisions on the terminology were my own, the format was my own, and the tables I constructed myself. I must take complete responsibility and all the blame for errors which surely exist. I would welcome their being called to my attention and suggestions for improvement.

The Nineteenth Century Census is a wonderful beast, full of surprises. For those searching for information about the people and the communities of that period, there are wonderful things in store. If I have teased anyone into looking into volumes they would have passed by, this volume has surely been worth the effort.

Michener Library
University of Northern Colorado, Greeley   Suzanne Schulze
October 1982

HOW TO USE THIS BOOK

To search for population information for a certain period:

First consult the table inside the covers. Note the subjects listed in the left hand column. All population information is shown under the categories listed there. Choose the category you need.

Note the decennial dates listed across the top of the page. These indicate the eleven census years from 1790 through 1890 included in this reference. Many census volumes carry information from prior years. Many census volumes also carry information which would not be apparent from the title.

Entries in the table below the decennial years refer to census volumes numbered under the system developed by Henry J. Dubester. The Dubester number for each volume which carries information on a given subject is shown on the table.

Next turn to the page which carries that Dubester number in the upper right hand corner. There will be at least one page with the identifying information about the volume. For those volumes which carry considerable information on population, there will be additional pages with table finding guides on successive pages. This should lead you to the proper volume and table.

Note the various classifications under which a census volume might be found in any one library. Libraries sometimes have census materials in several collections under different classifications. For example, some volumes might be with Congressional materials, others in the reference collection, some with the rare books, and others in the stacks. In some libraries census materials may be in a microform collection. Be sure to check each possibility in the library you are using before attempting to obtain the material on interlibrary loan.

Consult the union list at the back of this book for any notation as to the Dubester number of a volume the library might show as being held by another library. If there is such a notation, that would probably be the best place to request your information.

Determine the exact volume and tables and pages you need, then make your request through interlibrary loan.

SUMMARY OF SUBJECTS OF CENSUS INQUIRIES
1790-1890

Following is a list of inquiries made in 1790 and those added for each decennial census. Generally, but not always, an inquiry once added was continued in similar form in future censuses.

Decennial Census	Subject of inquiry or question as stated	Terminology used in this volume
1790	Name of head of household	Aggregate population
	Number of free white males 16 and over	Age
	Number of free white males under 16	Race
	Number of free white females	Sex
	Number of all other free persons	
	Number of slaves	Condition
1800	Additional age groups of males: under 10, 10-15, 16-25, 26-45, 45 and over	Age
	Age groups stated for females as well as males	Age
1810	Same inquiries as 1800	
1820	Age groups and sex of free colored persons as well as of white persons	Age, Sex
	Persons engaged in three categories of employment or occupations: agriculture, commerce, manufactures	Employment Occupations
	Foreigners not naturalized	Citizenship
1830	Additional age groups for white persons: each 5 years to age 20	Age
	Each 10 years to age 100	
	Age groups for slaves	Age
	Sex of slaves	Sex
	Blind, deaf and dumb persons	Disabilities
1840	Persons employed in seven categories: mining, agriculture, commerce, manufacturing and trade, navigation of the	

2

Decennial Census	Subject of inquiry or question as stated	Terminology used in this volume
1840-- continued	ocean, navigation of canals, lakes and rivers, and learned professions and engineers	Employment Occupations
	Pensioners for revolutionary or military services	Military
	Insane and idiotic, and whether at public or private charge	Disabilities
	Schools--universities and colleges, academies and grammar schools, primary and common schools; number of students, and number at public charge	Education
	Number of persons 20 years and over who cannot read and write	Literacy
1850	Color: white, black or mulatto	Race
	Profession, occupation or trade of each person over 15 years of age	Occupation
	Value of estate owned--real estate	Property
	Place of birth--state, territory or country	Nativity
	Married within the year	Vital statistics
	Whether pauper	Paupers
	Whether convict	Crime
	Persons who died within the year (special schedule)	Vital statistics
	Slaves (special schedule: name of owner, age, sex and color of slaves, fugitives, manumitted slaves, deaf and dumb, blind, insane, idiotic)	Disabilities
1860	Value of estate owned--personal property	Property
	Slaves (special schedule: number of slave houses)	
1870	(No further questions on slavery)	
	Age--if under one year, month of birth	Vital statistics
	Color--white, black, mulatto, Chinese, Indian	Race

Decennial Census	Subject of inquiry or question as stated	Terminology used in this volume
1870--continued	Parentage--father, mother of foreign birth	Nativity--parental nativity
	Constitutional relations--male citizens of 21 years; same, whose right to vote is denied or abridged	Citizenship Age--voting age
	Literacy--cannot read, cannot write as separate questions	Literacy
1880	Relationship to head of family--whether wife, son, daughter, servant, boarder or other	Family
	Single, married, widowed or divorced	Marital status
	Profession, occupation or trade of each person, male or female (not limited to person 15 and over)	Occupation
	Number of months unemployed during year	Employment and un-employment
	Health--sick or temporarily unable to attend to ordinary business or duties	Disabilities and health
	Maimed, crippled, bedridden or otherwise disabled	Disabilities
	Place of birth of father, mother	Nativity--parental nativity
	Homeless children (special schedule)	Family
	Blind, deaf mutes, idiots, insane (special schedules for each)	Disabilities
	Inhabitants in prison (special schedule)	Crime
	Paupers and indigents in institutions (special schedule)	Paupers, institutional population
	Indians (special schedule)	Race
1890	(First census with separate schedule for each family)	
	Whether a soldier, sailor or marine during the Civil War (U.S. or Confederate) or widow of such person	Military
	Whether white, black, mulatto, quadroon, octaroon, Chinese, Japanese or Indian	Race

Decennial Census	Subject of inquiry or question as stated	Terminology used in this volume
1890--continued	Mother of how many children, and number of these children living	Family
	Number of years in the United States	Nativity
	Whether naturalized, whether naturalization papers have been taken out	Immigration citizenship
	Able to speak English; if not, the language or dialect spoken	Language
	Whether suffering from acute or chronic disease	Disabilities
	Whether a prisoner	Crime
	Is the home you live in hired or owned by a member of the family?	Housing
	If owned, is it free from mortgage encumbrance?	Property
	If the head of the family is a farmer, is the farm hired or owned?	Farms
	If owned, is it free from mortgage encumbrance?	Property
	If the home or farm is mortgaged, give p.o. address of owner (special schedule on mortgaged farms and homes) (Several special schedules for disabled, on crime, pauperism, soldiers' homes, veterans and widows, Indians, and institutionalized populations)	Institutional population

Note: Information published in the census volumes 1790 through 1890 does not exactly correspond to the above inquiries. Some data in the published reports was obtained by direct inquiry to institutions, commercial or government establishments or from published records. This includes information on crime, education, employment and unemployment, immigration, institutionalized population, publications and libraries, religion, transportation, and of course all foreign data. Likewise, not all population inquiries appear to have resulted in publication in the final reports of the Census.

Eleventh Census of the United States
Robert P. Porter, Superintendent.

1790

POPULATION.

MAP
SHOWING IN FIVE DEGREES OF DENSITY THE DISTRIBUTION
WITHIN THE TERRITORY EAST OF THE 100TH MERIDIAN
OF THE
POPULATION OF THE UNITED STATES
excluding Indians not taxed.
Compiled from the Returns of Population at the First Census 1790.

NOTE
Center of Population   39 16.5 N.
76 11.2 W.

LEGEND.

Under 2 inhab to the Sq. Mile	
2 . 6	I
6 . 18	II
18 . 45	III
45 . 90	IV
90 and over	V

Cities over 8000 inhabitants in solid color
in circles proportionate to population.

LITH. A. HOEN & CO. BALTIMORE.

1790

VOLUMES OF THE FIRST DECENNIAL CENSUS

Volume Title	Dubester Number
Return of the whole number of persons within the several districts of the United States	Dubester 1, 2, 3, 4
By order of the House of Representatives. Philadelphia: Printed by Joseph Gales, 1791	Dubester 1
Philadelphia: Printed by Childs and Swaine, 1791	Dubester 2
Philadelphia: Reprinted in London and sold by J. Phillips, 1793	Dubester 3
Washington City: Printed by William Duane, 1802	Dubester 4
Heads of families at the First Census of the United States taken in the year 1790. Washington: twelve volumes printed in the years 1907 and 1908	Dubester 5
List of Free Black heads of families in the First Census of the United States. Washington: 1973	Dubester 6

States listed in the following order:

Vermont
New Hampshire
Maine
Massachusetts
Rhode Island
Connecticut
New York
New Jersey
Pennsylvania
Delaware
Maryland
Virginia
Kentucky
North Carolina
South Carolina
Georgia

Territories:

S. Western Territory
N. Western Territory

1790

THE FIRST DECENNIAL CENSUS

The First Decennial Census of the United States was taken according to an act providing for "The Enumeration of the Inhabitants of the United States," passed March 1, 1790. The results of the First Census were published in a small pamphlet of some 56 pages entitled Return of the Whole Number of Persons Within the Several States of the United States.

Since the federal marshals who took the census in each state made up their own forms, there is variation in the amount of detail provided for the sixteen states and the two territories, the South Western Territory and the North Western Territory. No population data at all was published for the North Western Territory.

As in the following several decades, state enumeration results are shown not in alphabetical order, but from north to south. Counts for the New England states, and the states of New York, New Jersey, and Maryland are shown by towns, with summaries for counties. The other states show totals only for counties.

This original enumeration established the pattern still used in censuses in the United States, that is a count by households. The "head of family" whether male or female was listed first, by name and other members of the household simply counted after him or her. In 1790, age was determined for free white males only--either as 16 years of age and upwards, or below 16 years. Free white males and females, all other free persons, and slaves were counted for each household. Sex was listed for free white persons only.

It should be noted that the Return was published by Joseph Gales and also by Childs and Swaine, both Philadelphia printers, in 1791. It was also reprinted in London in 1793, and again in Washington by William Duane in 1802. The table finding guide in the following pages is from the Childs and Swaine publication of 1791, shown by the designation assigned by Dubester as number 2. There was no government printing office until after the 1860 census was taken, and reports for censuses taken before that time were printed by private printers, often designated by the House of Representatives or the Senate.

Early in the Twentieth Century, the Bureau of the Census published nine volumes entitled "heads of Families . . . " taken from the original census returns for those states for which the original census rolls still existed. Rolls for five of the states had been burned when the Capitol was destroyed during the War of 1812. Some data were reconstructed from state census rolls. The nine volumes list

the names of the heads of families and the number of free white males
and females, all other persons, and slaves for each household. Families are listed by name in an alphabetical index at the end of each
volume.

In 1973, the National Archives published a small volume entitled
List of Free Black Heads of Families in the First Census of the United
States, 1790. Like the earlier Library of Congress volumes, this
publication contains the actual names listed. Names are shown alphabetically by state, and for most states, the number in the family is
also indicated.

Decennial year	1790	Dubester 1

Census   First Census

Volume   Book 1

Title   Return of the Whole Number of Persons within the several districts of the United States, according to "An Act providing for the enumeration of the inhabitants of the United States, passed March the first, one thousand seven hundred and ninety.

Publication   Printed by order of the House of Representatives. Philadelphia: Printed by Joseph Gales, no 23 South Third Street

Date   1791

Congress   1st Congress, 2d Session, Act of March 1, 1790

Classifications

     Supt. of Documents   I 2.5: Bk 1

     Library of Congress   HA201.1790

     card   9-19547

     Dewey   317.3 Un301

Microforms

     National Archives   Film T825   Reel 1

     Research Publications   Film 1790   Reel 1

     Evans Microcard   34905

Pages   56 pages

Notes   Page 3: "Truly stated from the original returns deposited in the office of the Secretary of State. Th: Jefferson."
See Dubester 2 for table guide.

<u>Decennial year</u>	1790	Dubester 2
<u>Census</u>	First Census	
<u>Volume</u>	Book 1	

<u>Title</u> Return of the Whole Number of Persons within the several districts of the United States, according to "An act providing for the enumeration of the inhibitants of the United States," passed March the first, one thousand seven hundred and ninety-one. (Incorrect date; act was March 1, 1790.)

<u>Publication</u> Philadelphia: Printed by Childs and Swaine

Date 1791

<u>Congress</u> 1st Congress, 2d Session

<u>Classifications</u>

Supt. of Documents I 2.5: Bk 1^2

Library of Congress HA 201.1790 A^3

  card 8-20182

Dewey 317.3 Un301

<u>Microforms</u>

National Archives Film T825 Reel 1

Research Publications Film 1790 Reel 1

Evans Microcard 23916

Sabin 11662

Sowerby 3160

<u>Pages</u> 56 pages

<u>Notes</u> South Carolina totals omitted in U.S. totals and page missing in some copies

<u>Reprints and facsimiles</u> Luther M. Cornwall, New York City
Wolcott Pamphlets, vol. 37, no. 11
(AC901.W7)

1790   Dubester 2
Return of the Whole Number of Persons--
Childs and Swaine

Contents   Tables   Pages

Whole number of persons, for the United States, each
   State and for South Western Territory. North
   Western Territory listed, but no population shown   D,Dr   3

Whole number of persons by Districts. States shown
   as districts, with tables for counties, and in
   some cases, towns and cities   W   5-55

Towns--Towns shown for Vermont, New Hampshire, Maine, Massachusetts,
   Rhode Island, New York, New Jersey, North Carolina and South
   Carolina. Most distinguish some cities.

Cities--For those states which show counties as the smallest
   districts, Pennsylvania, Maryland and Virginia show the population
   of cities, or "principal towns." Kentucky cities are shown.

Territory--Territory South of the River Ohio includes Washington and
   Mero Districts, the latter of which has a count for Tennessee county.

 W - Whole number of persons

 D - District pages. Within districts, counties are the smallest
       units shown for Connecticut, Pennsylvania (except for
       Philadelphia), Delaware, Maryland (except Baltimore), Virginia
       (except principal towns or cities), South Carolina and Georgia

DR - District recapitulation by counties

	United States	States and Territory	Counties	Towns and Cities
Demographic Characteristics				
Aggregate population	W	W, DR	DR, D	D

Age
   Free white males only,
   16 and upwards, under 16
	W	W, DR	DR, D	D

Race and condition
   Free white males and females
   All other free persons
   Slaves
	W	W, DR	DR, D	D

1790
Return of the Whole Number of Persons--
Childs and Swaine

	United States	States and Territory	Counties	Towns and Cities
Sex				
Free white persons only	W	W, DR	DR, D	D

Social and Economic Characteristics

Slavery--see "Race and condition" above

Decennial year	1790	Dubester 3

Census   First Census

Volume   Book 1

Title   Return of the Whole Number of Persons
                  within the several districts of the United
                  States, according to "An act passed March
                  the first, one thousand seven hundred and
                  ninety-one." (Incorrect date)

Publication   Philadelphia printed; London: Reprinted
                  and sold by J. Phillips

Date   1793

Congress   1st Congress, 2d Session

Classifications

  Supt. of Documents   I 2.5: Bk 1^3

  Library of Congress   HA 201.1790 A^4

    card   8-20291

  Dewey   317.3 Un301

Microforms

  National Archives   Film T825 Reel 1

  Research Publications Film 1790 Reel 1

Pages   56 pages

Notes   South Carolina totals omitted in U.S.
                  totals and page 54 missing in some copies
                  See Dubester 2 for table guide.

<u>Decennial year</u>	1790	Dubester 4

<u>Census</u>   First Census

<u>Volume</u>   Book 1

<u>Title</u>   Return of the Whole Number of Persons
within the several districts of the United
States, according to "An act passed March
the first, one thousand seven hundred and
ninety-one." (Incorrect date)

<u>Publication</u>   Washington City: Printed by William Duane

  Date   1802

<u>Congress</u>   1st Congress, 2d Session

<u>Classifications</u>

  Supt. of Documents   I 2.5: Bk 1^4

  Library of Congress   HA 201.1790.B

    card   8-20292

  Dewey   317.3 Un301

<u>Microforms</u>

  National Archives   Film T825   Reel 1

  Research Publications   Film 1790   Reel 1

  Sabin   70145

  Sowerby   3288

<u>Pages</u>   52 pages

<u>Notes</u>   Title page same as Dubester 2 printed by
Childs and Swaine
See Dubester 2 for table guide.

Decennial year	1790	Dubester 5
Census	First Census	
Volume	--	
Title	Heads of Families at the First Census of the United States taken in the year 1790.	
Publication	Department of Commerce and Labor, Bureau of the Census, Washington: Government Printing Office	
Date	1907-1908	
Congress	Not a Congressional publication	

Classifications

Supt. of Documents	C 3.11: 790/nos.1-12
Library of Congress	E 302.5 U57
card	7-35273
Dewey	312.73Un3h

Microforms

National Archives	Film M637, 12 rolls
Research Publications	Film 1790

        Reel 1 - Maine, New Hampshire, Vermont, Massachusetts, Rhode Island, Connecticut
        Reel 2 - New York, Pennsylvania, Maryland, Virginia
        Reel 3 - North Carolina, South Carolina

Pages	Variable-first 8 pages identical
Maps	Map for each state on inside cover
Notes	12 separate volumes for the following states; indicated by Cutter letters.

C 76 Connecticut	N 81c North Carolina
M 28 Maine	P 38 Pennsylvania
M 36 Maryland	R 34 Rhode Island
M 38 Massachusetts	So 86 South Carolina
N 42h New Hampshire	V 39 Vermont
N 42y New York	V 81 Virginia

16

___

Volumes for all states have identical first 8 pages
Schedules for enumeration generally included five categories:
   Free white males of 16 and upwards, including heads of families
   Free white males under 16 years
   Free white females, including heads of families
   All other free persons
   Slaves
References are to page numbers

Contents   Pages

	United States	States and Territory	Counties	Towns and Cities
Demographic Characteristics				
Aggregate population	8	8	9-	9-

Age
  Free white males only,
  16 and upwards, under 16
	8	8	9-	9-

Race and condition
  Free white males and females
  All other free persons
  Slaves
	8	8	9-	9-

1790
Heads of Families--Separate volumes for
twelve states

	United States	States and Territory	Counties	Towns and Cities
Sex				
Free white persons only	8	8	9-	9-
Social and Economic Characteristics				
Family			9-	9-
Number of families, name of head of each family, male and female, number in family				
Slavery--see "Race and condition" above			9-	9-

States	Volume Cutter Symbol	Volumes for these states printed from original schedules	Returns for these states destroyed during the War of 1812
Connecticut	C76	x	
Delaware			x
Georgia			x
Kentucky			x
Maine	M28	x	
Maryland	M36	x	
Massachusetts	M38	x	
New Hampshire	N42h	x	
New Jersey			x
New York	N42y	x	
North Carolina	N81c	x	
Pennsylvania	P38	x	
Rhode Island	R34	x	
South Carolina	So86	x	
Tennessee			x
Vermont	V39	x	
Virginia	V81	x*	x

*Virginia volumes were printed from state enumerations taken in the years 1782, 1783, 1784 and 1785 in 39 of the 78 counties in the State.

Decennial year	1790	Dubester 6

Census   First Census

Volume   --

Title   List of Free Black Heads of Families in the
                  First Census of the United Stats, 1790.

Publication   National Archives and Records Service
                  General Services Administration (Special
                  List No. 34)

Date   Washington: 1973 (Not published by the
                  Government Printing Office)

Congress   Not a Congressional publication

Classifications

  Supt. of Documents   GS 4.7:34

  Library of Congress   E 185.96 N47

    card   73-600195

  Dewey   929.373

Microforms

  National Archives   National Archives Publication

Pages   v, 44 pages

Notes   Compiled by Debra L. Newman
                  This volume, compiled many years after
                  publication of the Dubester Catalog, does
                  not have a Dubester number. The number
                  here, 6, has been supplied by the author.

1790   Dubester 6
Free Black Heads of Families

States included in this volume: Connecticut, Delaware, Maine,
Massachusetts, New Hampshire, New York, North Carolina, Pennsylvania,
Rhode Island, South Carolina, Vermont and Virginia

                                                              States

---

Demographic Characteristics

Race and condition
  Names of heads of families, and number in family.   Names listed
    Publication is restricted to the names of those   alphabetically
    heads of families which are not designated as   by states, with
    "white." Indians not taxed were excluded from   page number for
    the enumeration. Anyone who makes use of this   the census
    volume should read the introductory pages care-   volume for each
    fully.   state.

Social and Economic Characteristics

Family
  Publication is restricted to heads of families.
  Number in family is shown for all states except
  Delaware.

Eleventh Census of the United States
Robert P. Porter, Superintendent.

1800

POPULATION.

B R I T I S H

P O S S E S S I O N S

Lake of the Woods

LAKE SUPERIOR

LAKE MICHIGAN

TERRITORY N.W. OF THE RIVER OHIO

INDIANA TERRITORY

SPANISH POSSESSION

TEXAS

NEW YORK

PENNSYLVANIA

MASSACHUSETTS

CONNECTICUT

RHODE ISLAND

VIRGINIA

KENTUCKY

TENNESSEE

NORTH CAROLINA

SOUTH CAROLINA

GEORGIA

MISSISSIPPI TERRY.

SPANISH POSSESSION

A T L A N T I C   O C E A N

G U L F   O F   M E X I C O

BAHAMA ISLDS.

C U B A

CHEROKEE INDIANS

CHOCTAW INDIANS

CREEK INDIANS

CHICKASAW INDIANS

MIAMI INDIANS

POTTAWATOMIE INDIANS

SAC & FOX INDIANS

WHINEBAGOE MENOMONEE INDIANS

OTTAWA & CHIPPEWA INDIANS

DIST. OF MAINE

LEGEND

Under 2 inhab to the Sq. Mile	
2 . 6	I
6 . 18	II
18 . 45	III
45 . 90	IV
90 and over	V

*Cities over 8000 inhabitants in solid color
in circles proportionate to population.*

MAP
SHOWING IN FIVE DEGREES OF DENSITY THE DISTRIBUTION
WITHIN THE TERRITORY EAST OF THE 100TH MERIDIAN
OF THE
POPULATION OF THE UNITED STATES
excluding Indians not taxed.
Compiled from the Returns of Population at the Second Census 1800

NOTE
☀ *Center of Population*   39°16.1' N
76°56.5' W

LITH. A. HOEN & CO. BALTIMORE

Decennial year	1800	Dubester 8

Census   Second Census

Volume   Book 1

Title   Return of the whole number of persons within the several districts of the United States, according to "An Act providing for the Second Census or enumeration of the inhabitants of the United States." Passed February the twenty-eighth, one thousand eight hundred.

Publication   Printed by order of the House of Representatives, Washington

   Date   1801 (A reprint by Wm. Duane & Son, 1802)

Congress   7th Congress, 1st Session

   House/Senate   By order of the House of Representatives

Classifications

   Supt. of Documents   I 3.5: Bk 1

   Library of Congress   HA201 1800 A   HA 201 1800 B (Duane reprint)

    card   8-20293   8-20289

   Dewey   f 317.3 Un302

Microforms

   National Archives   Film T825 Reel 3

   Research Publications Film 1800-1810-1820-1830 Reel 1

   Sabin   70147

   Sowerby   3289

Pages   88 pages, numbered to page 34, followed by letters 2A-R

Reprints and facsimiles   Luther M. Cornwall, New York City: Central Book Company, Brooklyn, N.Y.

1800   Dubester 8
Second Decennial Census--Duane Reprint

_____

All pages have the same format. Column headings are as follows:
   Free white males under 10 years of age
                       10 and under 16
                       16 and under 26, including heads of families
                       26 and under 45, including heads of families
                       45 and up, including heads of families
   Free white females--same age categories as males
   All other free persons except Indians not taxed
   Slaves
   Total

Contents   Tables   Pages

Transmittal letter

Aggregate page, totals for United States, states
   and territories   A   A

District pages--states are designated as districts,   B-2R
   First 34 pages by number and by folio letter   3-34
   Second group of pages by folio letters 2A-2R only D.DR   2A-2R

Maryland revision   2S

States and territories are shown, with varying lesser divisions, as
follows:

                                                Pages   Folio

New Hampshire   Counties, towns   3-7   B
Massachusetts   Counties, towns   8-12
Maine   Counties, towns   13-17   G
Connecticut   Counties, cities and towns   18-20
Vermont   Counties, cities and towns   21-25   L-N
Rhode Island   Counties, towns   26
New York   Counties, cities, towns, townships 27-34 O
                     City of New York by wards
Pennsylvania   Counties, City of Philadelphia by
                     wards, townships, boroughs
                     Eastern District   2A
                     Western District   2D
Delaware   Counties, hundreds   2G
Maryland   Counties, cities, towns, hundreds
                     also see below for revision

1800
Second Decennial Census--Duane Reprint

Dubester 8--
<u>continued</u>

		<u>Pages</u>	<u>Folio</u>

Virginia	Counties, cities towns
	  Eastern District
	  Western District		

			2I
North Carolina	Districts, cities, towns, counties		2K
South Carolina	Districts, cities, towns, parishes, counties		
			2M
Georgia	Counties, cities, towns and captain's districts		
			2N
Kentucky	Counties, cities, towns		2P

Territory of the U.S. Northwest of the Ohio, including   2Q
  the following counties and towns: Jefferson,
  Washington, Adams, Hamilton, Wayne, Ross, Trumbell

Mississippi Territory, including the following counties   2Q
  and townships: Washington, Pickering, Adams

Territory of Indiana, including the following divisions:
  Knox, Randolph, St. Clair
At Michilimackanac on the first of August
Boatmen from Canada, etc.
At Prairie du Chien on the Mississippi
Green Bay on Lake Michigan
Opee on the Illinois River
District of Tennessee, including districts, towns and
  counties
Maryland Revision   2R

  A - Aggregate page, at beginning of volume

  D - District pages for states and territories

  DR - District recapitulation at the end of each district

	United States	States and Territory	Counties	Other
<u>Demographic Characteristics</u>				
Aggregate population	A	A, DR	DR, D	D
Age White persons only	A	A, DR	DR, D	D

1800
Second Decennial Census--Duane Reprint

	United States	States and Territory	Counties	Other

Race and condition
  Free white persons
  All other free persons,
    except Indians not taxed
  Slaves
	A	A, DR	DR, D	D

Sex White persons only	A	A, DR	DR, D	D

Social and Economic Characteristics

	United States	States and Territory	Counties	Other

Family
  Free white males and females
  who are heads of families,
  but families not separately
  designated
	A	A	DR, D	D

Slavery--see "Race and condition" above

Eleventh Census of the United States
Robert P. Porter, Superintendent.

1810

POPULATION.

MAP

SHOWING IN FIVE DEGREES OF DENSITY THE DISTRIBUTION
WITHIN THE TERRITORY EAST OF THE 100TH MERIDIAN
OF THE

POPULATION OF THE UNITED STATES

excluding Indians not taxed.

Compiled from the Returns of Population at the Third Census 1810.

NOTE

✹ Center of Population   39° 11.5 N.
                          77° 37.2 W.

LEGEND.

Under 2 inhab. to the Sq. Mile

2 - 6 ········· I

6 - 18 ········· II

18 - 45 ········· III

45 - 90 ········· IV

90 and over ····· V

Cities over 8000 inhabitants in solid color
in circles proportionate to population.

30

1810

VOLUMES OF THE THIRD DECENNIAL CENSUS

Volume Title	Dubester Number
Book I Aggregate Amount of Each Description of Persons	Dubester 10
Book II A Statement of the Arts and Manufactures United States . . .	Dubester 11

States listed in the following order:

Maine
Massachusetts
New Hampshire
Vermont
Rhode Island
Connecticut
New York
New Jersey
Pennsylvania
Delaware
Maryland
Virginia
Ohio--new state
Kentucky
North Carolina
East Tennessee
West Tennessee
South Carolina
Georgia

Territories:

Orleans
Mississippi
Louisiana
Indiana
Illinois
Michigan (4 civil districts)
District of Columbia (Washington, Georgetown,
  Washington County, Alexandria, Alexandria
  County)

1810

THE THIRD DECENNIAL CENSUS

Two volumes were published as a result of the Third Census: one on
population and one on arts and manufactures. The latter volume,
although extremely interesting for historical purposes, includes no
specific information on population, such as the number of persons
employed in various manufactures.

Population inquiries in 1810 were essentially the same as those of
1800. The same format is used for all tables in the population
volume, which, like the other, is of quarto size. Within states,
counties are listed in alphabetical order, with a recapitulation page
at the end of each state.

It is important to consult the map as to the designation of states
and territories. By 1810, Michigan, Indiana and Illinois Territories
had been set apart, although with boundaries to be changed at later
dates. The present states of Illinois andd Wisconsin were, in 1810,
both parts of Illinois Territory, and the Upper Penninsula of present-
day Michigan was part of Indiana Territory. In the printed volume
the District of Columbia appeared the first time in 1810 and its
population is listed at the end of that of the territories. The
Territory of Orleans, later to become the State of Louisiana, had
been designated from part of the large area that had come to the
United States through the Louisiana Purchase.

<u>Decennial year</u>	1810	Dubester 10

<u>Census</u>   Third Census

<u>Volume</u>   Book 1

<u>Title</u>   Aggregate amount of each description of
                  persons within the United States of
                  America, and the Territories thereof,
                  agreeably to actual enumeration made
                  according to law, in the year 1810.

<u>Publication</u>   Washington: Department of the Treasury

  Date   1811

<u>Congress</u>   Not a Congressional publication

<u>Classifications</u>

  Supt. of Documents   I 4.5: Bk 1

  Library of Congress   HA201.1810 B

    card   8-21063

  Dewey   q 317.3 Un 303

<u>Microforms</u>

  National Archives   Film T825 Reel 3

  Research Publications Film 1800-1810-1820-1830 Reel 1

<u>Pages</u>   90 numbered leaves

<u>Reprints and facsimiles</u>   Luther M. Cornwall, New York City: Central
                  Book Company, Brooklyn, N.Y.

1810   Dubester 10
Aggregate amount of persons within
the United States

All pages have the same format. Column headings are as follows:
   Free white males under 10 years of age
                    10 and under 16
                    16 and under 26, including heads of families
                    26 and under 45, including heads of families
                    45 and up, including heads of families
   Free white females--same age categories as males
   All other free persons except Indians not taxed
   Slaves
   Total

Contents	Tables	Pages
No title page or transmittal letter		
Aggregate amount of each description of persons within the United States of America, and the Territories	A	1
District pages. States referred to as districts; data presented by counties and towns, with totals by county for most states. Recapitulation showing totals for each category at end of each state. Slight variations among states. Territories with variations, including districts, parishes, cities, towns, settlements, townships, counties, divisions and civil districts	D.DR	2-89
Memoranda and errata		90

A - Aggregate page--totals for U.S., States and Territories

D - District pages

DR - District recapitulation, at end of table for each district

---

	United States	States and Territory	Counties	Other
Demographic Characteristics				
Aggregate population	A	A, DR	DR, D	D
Age White persons only	A	A, DR	DR, D	D

1810
Aggregate amount of persons within
the United States

Dubester 10--
continued

	United States	States and Territory	Counties	Other
Race and condition 　Free white persons 　All other free persons, 　　except Indians not taxed 　Slaves	A	A, DR	DR, D	D
Sex 　White persons only	A	A, DR	DR, D	D

Social and Economic Characteristics

Family 　Free white males and females 　who are heads of families, 　but families not separately 　designated	A	A	DR, D	D

Slavery--see "Race and condition" above

Decennial year	1810	Dubester 11

Census   Third Census

Volume   Book 2

Title   A statement of the arts and manufactures of
                          the United States for the year 1810:
                          digested and prepared by Tench Coxe,
                          Esquire of Philadelphia.

Publication   By instruction of Albert Gallatin,
                          Secretary of the Treasury, Philadelphia:
                          Printed by A. Cornman, Junr.

Date   1814

Congress   13th Congress, 1st Session

House/Senate   By resolution of March 19, 1812

Classifications

  Supt. of Documents   I 4.5: Bk 2

  Library of Congress   HA 201. 1810 B2

  Dewey   313.3 Un303s

Microforms

  National Archives   Film T825 Reel 3

  Research Publications   Film 1810-1820-1840 Reel M-1

  Library of American
    Civilization   LAC 10093

Pages   6 leaves, v[lxiv] p, 46, 169 (i.e., 171)
                          pages

Notes   Extensive data on specific products manu-
                          factured, but none on population, such as
                          number of employees

Eleventh Census of the United States
Robert P. Porter, Superintendent.

1820

POPULATION.

MAP
SHOWING IN FIVE DEGREES OF DENSITY THE DISTRIBUTION
WITHIN THE TERRITORY EAST OF THE 100TH MERIDIAN
OF THE
POPULATION OF THE UNITED STATES
excluding Indians not taxed.
Compiled from the Returns of Population at the Fourth Census 1820.

NOTE
Center of Population.   39° 5.7′ N.
78° 25′ W.

LEGEND.

Under 2 inhab. to the Sq. Mile	
2 . 6	I
6 . 18	II
18 . 45	III
45 . 90	IV
90 and over	V

Cities over 8000 inhabitants in solid color
in circles proportionate to population.

LITH. A. HOEN & CO. BALTIMORE.

1820

VOLUMES OF THE FOURTH DECENNIAL CENSUS

Volume Title	Dubester Number
Book I Census for 1820	Dubester 15
Book II Manufacturing Establishments and Manufactures	Dubester 16

States and the District of Columbia listed in the following order:

Maine
New Hampshire
Massachusetts
Rhode Island
Connecticut
Vermont
New York--Northern and Southern Districts
New Jersey
Pennsylvania--Western and Eastern Districts
Delaware
Maryland
District of Columbia
Virginia--District west of the Allegheny Mountains and Eastern
          District
North Carolina
South Carolina
Georgia
Alabama--new state
Mississippi--new state
Louisiana--with county of Opelovsas-new State
Tennessee--East and West Districts
Kentucky
Ohio
Indiana--new state
Illinois--new state

Territories:

Missouri
Michigan
Arkansas

1820

THE FOURTH DECENNIAL CENSUS

Two volumes were published as the result of the Fourth Decennial Census. The first, similar in format to that of the two preceding decades, contained information on population, and the second, information on manufactures.

Population inquiries in 1820 were expanded over those of previous decades. For the first time, data were obtained and published by age for free colored persons as well as for whites. In addition, a column was used for listing the number of "foreigners not naturalized."

The 1820 Census was the first one to make inquiries as to occupation or employment. Except for the next census in 1830, inquiries on one or the other subject have been made in each census following to the present day. Enumerators were to designate the number of persons in each household who were "engaged in agriculture, engaged in commerce, and engaged in manufactures." In the separate schedule for manufactures, inquiries were made as to the "number and names of articles manufactured in manufacturing establishments" and the results were published by county. The number of men, of women, and of boys and girls employed were counted and published for each product in each county.

Several new states had entered the Union by 1820, and once again territorial designations had been changed. Parts of what had been Indiana and Illinois Territories had been designated as Michigan Territory, and what had been known as Louisiana Territory had become Missouri Territory. In addition, Arkansas and Florida Territories had been established, and an area now part of Oklahoma was designated as Indian Territory. No enumeration, however, was made or published for that area.

Decennial year	1820	Dubester 15

Census   Fourth Census

Volume   Book 1

Title   Census for 1820

Publication   By authority of an act of Congress, under the direction of the Secretary of State. Washington: Printed by Gales and Seaton.

Date   1821

Congress   16th Congress, 2d Session
Act of March 14, 1820

Classifications

    Supt. of Documents   I 5.5: Bk 1

    Library of Congress   HA 201. 1820 B1

    Card   4-11778

    Dewey   f 317.3 Un304

Microforms

    National Archives   Film T825 Reel 4

    Research Publications   Film 1800-1810-1820-1830 Reel 1

Pages   80 leaves, unnumbered

Reprints and facsimiles   Luther M. Cornwall, New York City: Central Book Company, Brooklyn, N.Y.

___

All pages have the same format. Age categories are as follows:
   Free white males under 10 years   Free colored persons under 14
               10 and under 16   14 and under 26
               16 and under 26   26 and under 45
               26 and under 45   45 and upwards
               45 and upwards
      Free white males 16 to 18

Contents

Contents presented in the following order without page numbers:
Transmittal letters
Schedules for enumerators
Aggregate table for United States, States and Territories
District tables. States and Territories designated as districts;
   data presented by counties, counties by towns, cities and wards,
   townships, parishes

 A - Aggregate page--totals for U.S., States and Territories

 D - District pages

DR - District recapitulation, at end of table for each district

	United States	States and Territory	Counties	Other
Demographic Characteristics				
Aggregate population	A	A, DR	DR, D	D
Age	A	A, DR	DR, D	D
Free white persons by sex				
Free colored persons by sex				
Race and condition	A	A, DR	DR, D	D
Free white persons by age and sex				
Free colored persons by age and sex				
All other persons (i.e. slaves) except Indians not taxed				

1820
Book I--Population

	United States	States and Territory	Counties	Other
Sex				
White and free colored persons	A	A, DR	DR, D	D
Social and Economic Characteristics				
Citizenship	A	A, DR	DR, D	D
Foreigners not naturalized				
Employment				
See "Occupations" below				
Occupations	A	A, DR	DR, D	D
Persons engaged in:				
Agriculture				
Commerce				
Manufactures				
Slavery				
See "Race and condition" above				
Apportionment, Density Geography				
Representative number	A	A		
Free population plus 3/5 number of slaves, for apportionment of representatives in Congress				

Decennial year	1820	Dubester 16

Census   Fourth Census

Volume   Book 2

Title   Digest of accounts of manufacturing
                          establishments in the United States, and of
                          their manufactures

Publication   Under direction of the Secretary of State.
                          Washington: Printed by Gales and Seaton.

Date   1823

Congress   17th Congress, 1st Session
                          Resolution of March 30, 1822

Classifications

   Supt. of Documents   I 5.5: Bk 2

   Library of Congress   HA 201.1820.B2

      card   1-5859

   Dewey   f 317.3 Un304 M

Microforms

   National Archives   Film T825 Reel 4
                          Also Film M279 - 27 reels - Records of the
                          1820 Census of Manufactures

   Research Publications Film 1810-1820-1840 Reel M-1

Pages   64 leaves

Reprints and facsimiles   Luther M. Cornwall, New York City: Central
                          Book Company, Brooklyn, N.Y.

44

1820   Dubester 16
Book II--Manufactures

The Act providing for the census of 1820 called for an account of "the
several manufacturing establishments and their manufactures" within
each area division. Household manufactures were to be excluded.

A list of items manufactured was provided to each enumerator, but
they were to add other items as found. A schedule for inquiries was
also provided, and it called for the number of men, the number of
women, and the number of boys and girls employed at each establishment.

In the printed report, each manufactured article and each establishment is shown by county. No total numbers of items or establishments
are shown for counties, states, or for the United States. Counties
are listed by state.

D - District pages

                                                              Counties

---

Social and Economic Characteristics

Employment   D
   According to the nature and name of each article
      manufactured, the number of:
         men employed
         women employed
         boys and girls employed

Eleventh Census of the United States
Robert P. Porter, Superintendent.

1830

POPULATION.

MAP
SHOWING IN FIVE DEGREES OF DENSITY THE DISTRIBUTION
WITHIN THE TERRITORY EAST OF THE 100TH MERIDIAN
OF THE
POPULATION OF THE UNITED STATES
excluding Indians not taxed.
Compiled from the Returns of Population at the Fifth Census 1830.

NOTE
☀ Center of Population   38° 57.9' N.
79° 16.9' W.

LEGEND.

Under 2 inhab to the Sq. Mile	
2 - 6	I
6 - 18	II
18 - 45	III
45 - 90	IV
90 and over	V

Cities over 5000 inhabitants in solid color
in circles proportionate to population.

1830

VOLUMES OF THE FIFTH DECENNIAL CENSUS

Volume Title	Dubester Number
Book I Fifth Census; or, enumeration of the inhabitants of the United States . . . schedule of the whole number of persons within the several districts of the United States, taken according to the acts of 1790, 1800, 1810, 1820	Dubester 19
Book II Abstract of the Fifth Census--Blair	Dubester 20
Abstract of the Fifth Census--Duff Green	Dubester 21

States listed in the following order:

Maine
New Hampshire
Massachusetts
Rhode Island
Connecticut
Vermont
New York--Northern and Southern Districts
New Jersey
Pennsylvania--Eastern and Western Districts
Delaware
Maryland
Virginia--Eastern and Western Districts
North Carolina
South Carolina
Georgia
Alabama--Northern and Southern Districts
Mississippi
Louisiana--Eastern and Western Districts
Tennessee
Kentucky
Ohio
Indiana
Illinois
Missouri--new state

Territories:

Michigan
Arkansas
Florida--Eastern, Western, Southern, and Middle Districts
District of Columbia

1830

THE FIFTH DECENNIAL CENSUS

One major folio-size volume and two pamphlet-size abstracts resulted from the 1830 Census. The enumeration was to be made on the first day of June, and was the first one for which printed schedules were provided for the taking down of information by the enumerators. Only population inquiries were made: there were no inquiries as to manufactures as there had been in 1820, nor were there inquiries as to whether persons were engaged in agriculture, commerce or manufactures.

Although the occupation and manufactures inquiries were dropped, the questions were otherwise expanded. For the first time, sex and age of slaves was recorded. There were also for the first time inquiries as to disabilities. Blind, deaf and dumb persons were recorded by age and by race.

The major volume for 1830 contains two separate parts: the first, paginated separately, provides data from all previous censuses; the second provides results from the 1830 Census.

The two abstract volumes, one of 43 and one of 51 pages, were published by two different printers, one of them produced as a Document of the House of Representatives. They both appeared in 1832, the same year as the folio volume. Apparently considerable corrections were made in census counts, and Dubester calls attention to discrepancies between the three volumes.

Unlike preceding decades, few changes were made among states and territories. Missouri had become a state, but the larger portion of Missouri Territory retained that status.

Decennial year	1830	Dubester 19

Census   Fifth Census

Volume   Book 1

Title   Fifth Census; or, enumeration of the inhabitants of the United States, 1830 as corrected at the Department of State. To which is prefixed, a schedule of the whole number of persons within the several districts of the United States, taken according to the acts of 1790, 1800, 1810, 1820.

Publication   By authority of an act of Congress. Washington: Printed by Duff Green.

Date   1832

Congress   22d Congress, 1st Session

Classifications

     Supt. of Documents   I 6.5: Bk 1

     Library of Congress   HA 201.1830 B

       card   4-20566

     Dewey   f 317.3 Un305

Microforms

     National Archives   Film T825 Reel 4; (also corrected edition)

     Research Archives   Film 1800-1810-1820-1830 Reel 1

Pages   vi, 163 pages; corrected edition 165 pages

Reprints and facsimiles   Luther M. Cornwall, New York City: Central Book Company, Brooklyn, N.Y.

1830   Dubester 19
Enumeration of Inhabitants

This volume has two distinct parts. The first part includes all
totals from earlier censuses. The second part includes results from
the 1830 Census. There are two paginations.

Age categories for 1830 are as follows:

Free white persons	Free colored persons and slaves	Disabled deaf and dumb only
Under 5 years	Under 10 years	Under 14 years
5 and under 10	10 and under 24	14 and under 25
10 and under 15	24 and under 36	25 and upwards
15 and under 20	36 and under 55	
20 and under 30	55 and under 100	
ten year periods	100 and upwards	
90 and under 100		
100 and upwards		

Contents	Tables	Pages
--Part I--		
Schedule of the whole number of persons within the several districts of the United States, taken according to the Acts of 1790, 1800, 1810, and 1820	I A	2-27
--Part II--		
Enumeration of the inhabitants by districts, for 1830	IIA, IID	2-161
Epitome for United States--aggregates, by States and Territories	IIA	162-163
Errata		164-165

  A - Aggregate pages at end of:
      Part I 1790-1820 - pages 2-27
      Part II 1830   - pages 162-163 entitled Epitome

  D - District pages
      Part II pages all have the same format

1830
Enumeration of Inhabitants

	United States	States and Territory	Counties	Towns and Cities
Demographic Characteristics				
Aggregate population	IIA	IIA, IID	IID	IID
Historic from 1790	IA	IA		
Age	IIA	IIA, IID	IID	IID
By sex				
Historic from 1790 by				
categories used each				
Census	IA	IA		
Race and condition	IIA	IIA, IID	IID	IID
Free white persons by sex				
and age				
Free colored persons by				
sex and age				
Slaves by sex and age				
Historic from 1790	IIA	IIA		
Sex	IIA	IIA, IID	IID	IID
By age categories, for				
white, free colored,				
and slaves				
Social and Economic Characteristics				
Citizenship	IIA	IIA, IID	IID	IID
Foreigners not naturalized,				
white persons only				
Historic from 1820	IA	IA		
Disabilities	IIA	IIA, IID	IID	IID
Blind by race and age				
Deaf and dumb by race and				
age				

Slavery--see "Race and condition" above

Decennial year	1830	Dubester 20
Census	Fifth Census	
Volume	Book 2	
Title	Abstract of the Fifth Census of the United States, 1830	
Publication	Washington: Compiled at the Department of State. Printed at Globe office by F. P. Blair	
Date	1832	
Congress	22d Congress, 1st Session	

Classifications

Supt. of Documents	I 6.5: Bk 2
Library of Congress	HA 201.1830 D
card	8-20290
Dewey	317.3 Un305a

Microforms

National Archives	Film T825 Reel 4
Research Archives	Film 1800-1810-1820-1830 Reel 1
Pages	43 pages

52

1830   Dubester 20
Abstract printed by F. P. Blair

This publication of the Abstract, printed at the Globe office by
F. P. Blair is at variance with the other Abstract, Dubester 21, as
printed by Duff Green. This copy states that it is done from
corrected totals, and shows a date of July 10, 1832 at the Department
of State. Total persons who are blind and who are deaf and dumb are
shown only for the U.S. as a whole, as is the total of foreigners not
naturalized. These totals do not appear in the Duff Green publication.
That one does show counties for the three territories and the District
of Columbia, and this does not.

Headings for the columns in this publication are:
  Total   Slaves included
  population   in the foregoing   Representative
                                        numbers

Totals at the end of each state are as follows:
  Total aggregate
  Deducting 2/5ths of the number of slaves leaves the   ____
    representative number for the State
  The representative ratio, 47,700, multiplied by 9,   ____
    the number of representatives give
  This, deducted form the whole representative number   ____
    of the States, leaves the residual fraction   ____

Contents   Tables   Pages

  A - Aggregate table

  E - Epitome table

  S - State tables

1830
Abstract printed by F. P. Blair

	United States	States and Territory	Counties
Demographic Characteristics			
Aggregate population	E p43 A p41	A p40 S	S

Age
  Five year age groups to age 20,
    ten year groups after 20 years
	E p42-43		

Race and condition Condition - slaves	A p40-41 E p43 A p40	A p40-41 A p40 S	S
By sex	E p43 A p40	A p40	
Sex	E p42-43 A p40-41	A p40-41	
By age groups	E p42-43		
By race and condition	A p40-41		
Social and Economic Characteristics			

Citizenship
  Foreigners not naturalized,
    white persons only
	E p42		

Disabilities
  Blind by race
  Deaf and dumb by age groups
    (under 14, 14-25, 25 & upwards)
    and by race
	E p42-43		

Slavery--see "Race and condition" above Number slaves			S
Apportionment, Density and Geography			

Apportionment
  Representative numbers - total population
    less 2/5 slaves
		A p41, S	S

Residual fractions		A p41, S	
Representatives in Congress	A p41	A p41	

Decennial year	1830	Dubester 21

Census   Fifth Census

Volume   Book 2^2

Title   Abstract of the returns of the Fifth Census, showing the number of free people, the number of slaves, the federal or representative number; and the aggregate of each county of each State of the United States.

Publication   Prepared from the corrected returns of the Secretary of State to Congress, by the clerk of the House of Representatives. Washington: Printed by Duff Green

Date   1832

Congress   22d Congress, 1st Session

House/Senate   House Document 263

Serial   Serial 221

Classifications

Supt. of Documents   I 6.5: Bk 2

Library of Congress   HA 201.1830.D2

card   10-29400

Dewey   317.3 Un305a

Microforms

National Archives   Film T825 Reel 4

Research Archives   Film 1800-1810-1820-1830 Reel 1

Pages   51 pages

Notes   This is the first census publication which appears as part of the Congressional Serial Set.

Reprints and facsimiles   Luther M. Cornwall, New York City: Central Book Company, Brooklyn, N.Y.

This is the second abstract printed by Duff Green. It contains 51 pages, and has discrepancies in totals from the other two 1830 publications.

Contents   Pages

State pages   3-45
  Totals at end of each state
U.S. epitome pages   46-51

	United States	States and Territory	Counties
Demographic Characteristics			
Aggregate population	p 46-47	p 46-47	S
Age by sex, race and condition	p 48-51	p 48-51	S
Race and condition	p 46-51	p 46-51	S
Sex by race	p 47-51	p 46-51	
Social and Economic Characteristics			
Slavery--see above			
Apportionment, Density and Representation			
Apportionment			
Population for federal representation	p 46	S	S

Eleventh Census of the United States
Robert P. Porter, Superintendent.

1840

POPULATION.

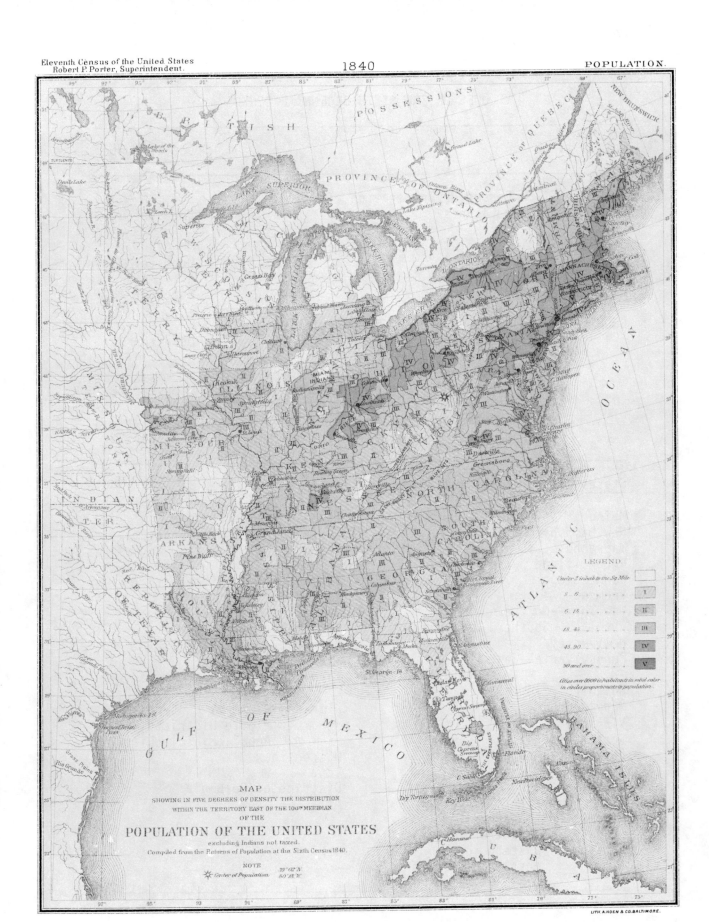

MAP
SHOWING IN FIVE DEGREES OF DENSITY THE DISTRIBUTION
WITHIN THE TERRITORY EAST OF THE 100TH MERIDIAN
OF THE
POPULATION OF THE UNITED STATES
excluding Indians not taxed.
Compiled from the Returns of Population at the Sixth Census 1840.

NOTE
✴ Center of Population   79°02′N.
80°18′W.

LEGEND.

Under 2 inhab. to the Sq. Mile
2.. 6............   I
6.. 18............   II
18.. 45...........   III
45.. 90...........   IV
90 and over.......   V

Cities over 6000 inhabitants in solid color
in circles proportionate to population.

LITH. A.HOEN & CO. BALTIMORE.

58

1840

VOLUMES OF THE SIXTH DECENNIAL CENSUS

Volume Title	Dubester Number
Book I Sixth Census or Enumeration of the Inhabitants	Dubester 24
Book II Statistics of the United States of America	Dubester 25
Book III Compendium	Dubester 26
Book IV A Census of Pensioners for Revolutionary or Military Services	Dubester 27
Report of Department of State on aggregate population of states and territories	Dubester 28
Aggregate amount of each description of persons within the several districts	Dubester 29

States listed in the following order:

Maine
New Hampshire
Massachusetts
Rhode Island
Connecticut
Vermont
New York--Northern and
          Southern Districts
New Jersey
Pennsylvania--Eastern and
          Western Districts
Delaware
Maryland
Virginia
North Carolina
South Carolina
Georgia
Alabama--Northern and
          Southern Districts
Mississippi--Northern and
          Southern Districts
Louisiana--Eastern and
          Western Districts

Tennessee--Eastern and
          Western Districts
Kentucky
Ohio
Indiana
Illinois
Missouri
Arkansas--new state
Michigan--new state

Territories:

Florida--Western, Eastern and
          Middle Districts,
          Appalachiacola District
Wisconsin
Iowa
District of Columbia

1840

THE SIXTH DECENNIAL CENSUS

Four volumes were published with results of the 1840 Census. Numerous additions to the inquiries to be made by enumerators had been made in that year.

Inquiries on the employment of the population, made in 1820 but dropped in 1830, were returned to the questionnaire, and expanded to six categories. The categories themselves provide a flavor of life in 1840: mining, agriculture, commerce, manufactures and trade, navigation of the ocean, navigation of canals, lakes, and rivers, and learned professions and engineers.

For the first time, a question on pensioners for revolutionary and military services was included; pensioners were listed by name and age, and a separate volume was published. Unlike other printed volumes, actual names of pensioners were published. No question on veterans appeared again in census inquiries until 1890, fifty years later.

Inquiries on the disabled were extended to include "insane and idiotic persons" as a single category, and a question as to whether they were supported at public or private charge was added. Age categories were determined, but only for the deaf and dumb.

New questions were added on literacy, of whites only, and on education. Enumerators were to inquire how many of the family twenty years and over could not read and write, and how many were attending school, at what level, and whether at public expense.

Results of all these inquiries were published in Book I of the 1840 Census, and in lesser detail in Book III, the Compendium. The latter also included details of the representative population and of apportionment for the next Congress to be elected in 1842, as well as for the Congresses following the earlier five censuses. Statistics on the six categories of employment were greatly expanded in the Compendium.

By 1840, Michigan and Arkansas had entered the Union, and the Territories of Wisconsin and Iowa had been set out from Missouri Territory, encompassing areas which would later become states by those names, as well as lands to be designated as the Territories of Minnesota and Dakota.

Decennial year	1840	Dubester 24

Census   Sixth Census

Volume   Book 1

Title   Sixth Census or enumeration of the inhabitants of the United States, as corrected at
the Department of State, in 1840

Publication   By authority of an act of Congress, under
the direction of the Secretary of State.
Washington: Printed by Blair and Rives

Date   1841

Congress   26th Congress, 2d Session

Classifications

   Supt. of Documents   I 7.5: Bk 1

   Library of Congress   HA 201.1840 B1

     card   4-11779

   Dewey   f317.3 Un306

Microforms

   National Archives   Film T825 Reels 4 and 5

   Research Publications Film 1840 Reel 1

Pages   476 pages

Reprints and facsimiles Central Book Company, Brooklyn, N.Y.

Each state or portion of a state is shown in a table entitled "Aggregate amount of each description of persons within the district of . . . " in a single large table comprised of two facing pages. Counties include smaller units of cities and wards, towns, townships, hundreds and other named divisions. For each county a total is shown, and at the end of each state, a total by counties is shown in a table entitled "Recapitulation of the aggregate amount. . . " In addition, a table entitled "Epitome" shows the total for each characteristic of the population for each state. The final major table in the volume is entitled "Epitome of the whole population" and shows data for each state and for the United States.

Age categories for the population and for the disabled are as follows:

Free white persons	Free colored persons and slaves	Disabled deaf and dumb only
Under 5 years	Under 10 years	Under 14 years
10 and under 15	10 and under 24	14 and under 25
15 and under 20	24 and under 36	25 and upwards
20 and under 30	36 and under 55	
ten year categories	55 and under 100	
100 and upwards		

Contents   Tables   Pages

A - Aggregate tables for the U.S., for States and Territories
E - Epitome table for the U.S.
D - District tables
DR - District recapitulation tables at the end of each District
DE - District epitome tables

1840
Book 1 Enumeration of Inhabitants

	United States	States and Territory	Counties	Other
Demographic Characteristics				
Aggregate population	E, A	A, DE, DR	DR, D	D

Age
  By race and condition,
    by sex
	E, A	A, DE, DR	DR, D	D

Race and condition
  Free white persons by age
    and sex
  Free colored persons by
    age and sex
  Slaves
	E, A	A, DE, DR	DR, D	D

Sex	E, A	A, DE, DR	DR, D	D
Social and Economic Characteristics				

Disabilities
  Blind by race
  Deaf and dumb by race, with
    whites only by age
  Insane and idiots as a single
    group, by race, and whether
    at public or private charge
	E, A	A, DE, DR	DR, D	D

Education
  Universities and colleges,
    number and number of
    students
  Academic and grammar schools,
    number and number of scholars
  Primary and common schools,
    number and number of
    scholars
	E, A	A, DE, DR	DR, D	D

Employment
  Number of persons employed in
    Mining
    Agriculture
    Commerce
    Manufactures and trades
    Navigation of the ocean,
      of canals, lakes, & rivers
    Learned professions & engineers
	E, A	A, DE, DR	DR, D	D

1840
Book 1 Enumeration of Inhabitants

	United States	States and Territory	Counties	Other
Navigation of canals, lakes and rivers				
Learned professions and engineers				
Literacy Illiterates, by race--white persons only, of 20 years and unable to read and write	E, A	A, DE, DR	DR, D	D
Military Number of pensioners for revolutionary or military services	E, A	A, DE, DR	DR, D	D
Occupations See "Employment" above				

Decennial year	1790	Dubester 25

Census   Sixth Census

Volume   Book 2

Title   Statistics of the United States of America,
                  as collected and returned by the marshals
                  of the several judicial districts, under
                  the thirteenth section of the act for tak-
                  ing the Sixth Census; corrected at the
                  Department of State. June 1, 1840.

Publication   Published by authority of an act of
                  Congress, under the direction of the
                  Secretary of State. Washington: Printed
                  by Blair and Rives

Date   1841

Congress   26th Congress, 2d Session

Classifications

  Supt. of Documents   I 7.5: Bk 2

  Library of Congress   HA 201.1840 B2

    card   6-46445

  Dewey   f317.3 Un306s

Microforms

  National Archives   Film T825 Reel 5

  Research Publications Film 1810-1820-1840 Reel M-1

Pages   409 pages

1840   Dubester 25
Book 2 Statistics of the United States of America

_____

All pages have the same format, with products, number employed and
other such columns listed horizontally and districts listed ver-
tically. States and territories are referred to as "Districts".
Only commercial operations are listed: for example, under agriculture, persons employed in nurseries are the only ones counted as
employed. However, values of home made or family goods are shown.

Most products show men employed; others use the term "persons"
employed, or show males and females employed separately.

Contents   Tables   Pages

  D - District pages

  R - Recapitulation for the United States, States and Territories

_____

	United States	States and Territory	Counties	Other

_____

Social and Economic Characteristics

	United States	States and Territory	Counties	Other
Employment	R	R, D	D	D
Mines				
Men employed in iron, lead, gold and other metals, coal, domestic salt, granite, marble and other stone mines				
Agriculture	R	R, D	D	D
Men employed in nurseries				
Commerce	R	R, D	D	D
Men employed in internal transportation, butchers, packers, etc.				
Fisheries	R	R, D	D	D
Men employed				

66

1840
Book 2 Statistics of the United States of America

Dubester 25--
continued

	United States	States and Territory	Counties	Other
Products of the forest Men employed	R	R, D	D	D
Manufactures Men employed in making: machinery hardware, cutlery cannon and small arms precious metals various metals granite, marble bucks and 1	R	R, D	D	D
Persons employed in manu- facture of wool, cotton				
Number males, number females in manufacture of silk				
Persons employed in manu- facture of flax mixed manufactures tobacco hats, caps, bonnets				
Men employed in manufactures in leather tanneries soap and candles distilled fermented liquor powder mills drugs, medicines, paints, dyes glass, earthenware paper printing and binding cordage musical instruments carriages and wagons mills furniture building of houses				
Income and property Agriculture Value of home made or family goods	R	R, D	D	D

1840   Dubester 25--
Book 2 Statistics of the United States of America   continued

	United States	States and Territory	Counties	Other

Horticulture
  Value of produce of market
    gardens
  Value of produce of nurseries
    and florists
	R	R, D	D	D

Occupations
  See "Employment" above

Decennial year	1840	Dubester 26

Census   Sixth Census

Volume   Compendium

Title   Compendium of the enumeration of the inhabi-
                       tants and statistics of the United States,
                       as obtained at the Department of State,
                       from the returns of the Sixth Census, by
                       counties and principal towns, exhibiting
                       the population, wealth, and resources of the
                       country; with tables of apportionment . . .

Publication   Prepared at the Department of State.
                       Washington: Printed by Thomas Allen;
                       Washington: Also printed by Blair and Rives

Date   1841

Congress   Not a Congressional publication

Classifications

  Supt. of Documents   I 7.2: C73[1] (Allen)
                       I 7.2: C73[2] (Blair and Rives)

  Library of Congress HA201.1840.Ca (Allen)
                       HA201.1840C (Blair and Rives)

    card   6-29060 (Allen) 6-29061 (Blair and Rives)

  Dewey   f317.3 Un306c

Microforms

  National Archives   Film T825 Reel 5

  Research Publications Film 1840 Reel 1

Pages   379 pages (Allen)
                       371 pages (Blair and Rives)

Notes   Dubester states that Blair and Rives edi-
                       tion "includes minor variations in paging
                       of tables." The table guide here is from
                       the Allen edition.

The Sixth Census is the first to have been published with a compendium volume. It contains data from each of the other volumes: data on population, on production of various industries, and on pensioners.

Contents	Tables	Pages
Compendium of the enumeration of the inhabitants and statistics of the population of the United States		
States and territories, with series of columns	D, DR	3-99
Aggregate population of United States by states	A	100-103
Recapitulation of the aggregate volume and produce and number of persons employed in mines, agriculture, commerce, manufactures, etc.		
States and territories, with series of columns	D, DR	105-357
Aggregate produce, employment	AP	358-364
Appendix, containing tables of representative population and apportionment	AR	365-369
Abstract of census of population totals for 1790, 1800, 1810, 1820, 1830	AB	370-375
Index		377-379

 A - Aggregate population - pages 100-103
AP - Aggregate produce - pages 358-364
AR - Apportionment tables - pages 365-375
 D - District tables - states and territories referred to as districts
DR - District recapitulation, of population, at end of each state
DP - District recapitulation by industry, at end of each state
AB - Abstract of earlier censuses

	United States	States and Territory	Counties	Other
Demographic Characteristics				
Aggregate population	A	A, DR	D	D
Historic from 1790	AB	AB		
Age	A	A, DR		
Categories as in Book I				
Historic from 1790	AB	AB		

1840
Book 3 Compendium

	United States	States and Territory	Counties	Other
Race	A	A, DR	D	D
Race - white and colored				
Condition - free white,				
free colored and slaves				
Historic from 1790	AB	AB		
Sex	A	A, DR	D	D
By age categories				
Historic from 1790	AB	AB		

Social and Economic Characteristics

	United States	States and Territory	Counties	Other
Citizenship				
Historic from 1790	AB	AB		
Disabilities	A	A, DR	D	D
Blind				
Deaf and dumb				
Insane and idiotic, by				
whether at public or				
private charge				
Education	A	A, DR	D	D
Federal school lands				
Employment	A	A, DR	D	D
Persons employed in the				
following:				
Agriculture and horticulture				
Commerce Fisheries				
Forest products				
Mines				
Manufactures				
Persons employed in				
production	AP	AP	DP	DP
Literacy	A	A, DR	D	D
Persons 20 years and over				
who cannot read and write				
Military	A	A, DR	DR	D
Pensioners for military and				
revolutionary purposes				

1840
Book 3 Compendium

	United States	States and Territory	Counties	Other
Occupations				
See "Employment" above				
Apportionment, Density, Geography				
Apportionment				
Representative population for 6th Census, 1840 - whole population, 2/5 slaves to be deducted, population to be represented, fractions	AR	AR		
Historic - for 1st-5th Censuses	AR	AR	AR	

Decennial year	1840	Dubester 27

Census   Sixth Census

Volume   Book 3

Title   A census of pensioners for revolutionary or military services; with their names, ages, and places of residence, as returned by the marshals of the several judicial districts, under the act for taking the Sixth Census.

Publication   By authority of an act of Congress, under the direction of the Secretary of State. Washington: Printed by Blair and Rives

Date   1841

Congress   27th Congress, 2d Session

Classifications

  Supt. of Documents   I 7.5: Bk 3

  Library of Congress   E255.U56

    card   3-5267 rev.2

  Dewey   q351.5 U357c

Microforms

  National Archives   Film T825   Reel 5

  Library of American
    Civilization   LAC 14284

Pages   195 pages

Reprints and facsimiles   Central Book Company, Brooklyn, N.Y.
Luther M. Cornwall, New York City, N.Y.
Southern Book Company, (?) 1954

1840   Dubester 27
Book 3 Census of Pensioners

_____

This volume lists pensioners by name, but contains no statistics such
as number of pensioners by state or county.

Contents   Tables   Pages

State lists of pensioners by county, by divisions
    smaller than counties   3-195

State of Kentucky, Carter County, added   195

S/T State and territory pages

_____

	States and Territories	Counties	Other

Demographic Characteristics

	States and Territories	Counties	Other
Age Age of each pensioner is shown	S/T	S/T	S/T

Social and Economic Characteristics

	States and Territories	Counties	Other

Families
   Name of head of family with whom
   each pensioner resided on June 1st
   is given with that of pensioner
	S/T	S/T	S/T

Military
   Name of each pensioner "for revolu-
   tionary or military purposes" is
   given, by state, county, and usually
   by smaller division
	S/T	S/T	S/T

Decennial year	1840	Dubester 28

Census

Seventh Census

Title

Report of Department of State on Aggregate population of states and territories

Publication

Report of the Department of State to the Senate

Date

December 30, 1840

Congress

26th Congress, 2d Session, Volume 2

House/Senate

Senate Document 32

Serial

Serial 376

Classifications

Supt. of Documents

I 7.2: St

Library of Congress

HA 201.1840.D3

Dewey

317.3 306pt

Pages

2 pages

Notes

The report is incomplete, with several states reports not received by the December following the enumeration.

For each State and Territory for which the report was available, totals are shown for the number of white persons, free colored persons, and all other persons.

This report was not included by Dubester and the number has been supplied by the author.

Decennial year	1840	Dubester 29

Census   Sixth Census

Title   Aggregate amount of each description of
                  persons within the several districts

Publication   Message of the President of the United
                  States, John Tyler

  Date   January 6, 1842

Congress   27th Congress, 2d Session, Volume 2

  House/Senate   House Executive Document 76

  Serial   Serial 402

Classifications

  Supt. of Documents   I 8.2: Pr

  Library of Congress   HA 201.1840.B4

  Dewey   317.3 Un306pr

Pages   30 pages

Notes   This message was not included in the
                  Dubester catalog, and the number has been
                  supplied by the author.

1840   Dubester 29
Message of the President

_____

This message of President John Tyler to the House of Representatives
on January 6, 1842 presents the final report of the count of population for the 1840 Census.

All pages have the same format, with states listed in order by counties, with columns for Free white persons by sex, Free colored persons
by sex, slaves, and the total.

Contents   Pages

 R - Recapitulation for the United States - page 30
DR - District recapitulation at end of each State and Territory
 D - District pages, for each State and Territory

_____

	United States	States and Territories	Counties

Demographic Characteristics

Aggregate population	R	R, D	D

Race and condition
  Free white persons
  Free colored persons
  Slaves
	R	R, D	D

Sex	R	R, D	D

Eleventh Census of the United States
Robert P. Porter, Superintendent.

1850

POPULATION.

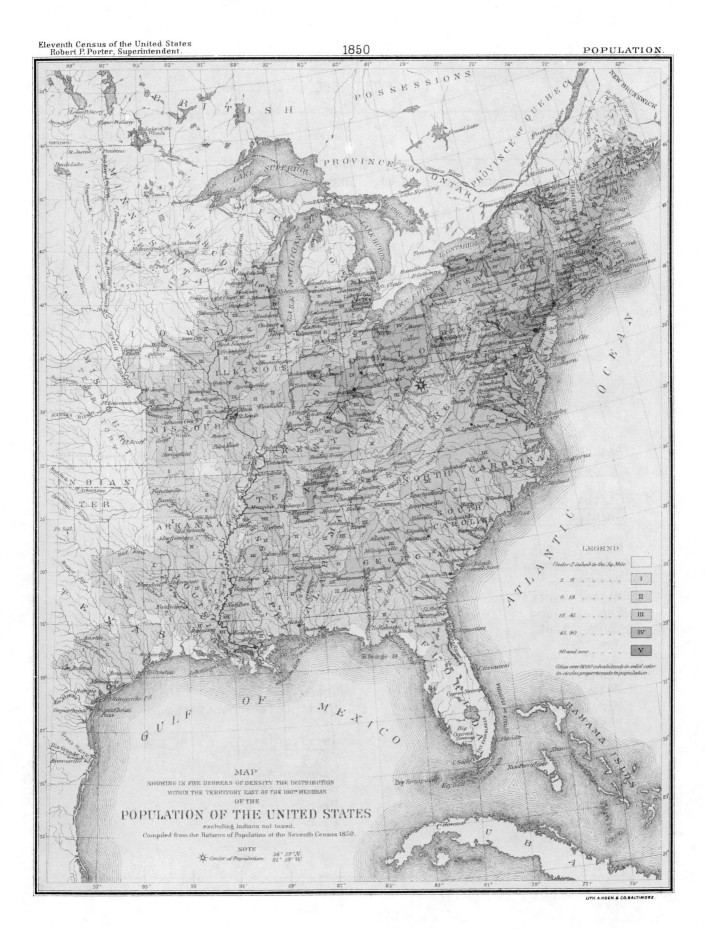

LEGEND.

Under 2 inhab to the Sq Mile

2 . 6   "   "   "   I

6 . 18   "   "   "   II

18 . 45   "   "   "   III

45 . 90   "   "   "   IV

90 and over   "   "   V

Cities over 8000 inhabitants in solid color
in circles proportionate to population.

MAP

SHOWING IN FIVE DEGREES OF DENSITY THE DISTRIBUTION

WITHIN THE TERRITORY EAST OF THE 100TH MERIDIAN

OF THE

POPULATION OF THE UNITED STATES

excluding Indians not taxed.

Compiled from the Returns of Population at the Seventh Census 1850.

NOTE

★ Center of Population   58° 39′ N.
                  81° 19′ W.

LITH. A.HOEN & CO. BALTIMORE.

1850

VOLUMES OF THE SEVENTH DECENNIAL CENSUS

Volume Title		Dubester Number
Book I	Seventh Census of the United States; 1850	Dubester 30
Book II	Message of the President of the United States, communicating a digest of the statistics of manufactures according to the returns of the Seventh Census--United States Department of the Interior	Dubester 31
	Mortality Statistics of the Seventh Census of the United States; 1850	Dubester 32
Compendium	Statistical view of the United States (Senate)	Dubester 33[1]
Compendium	Statistical view of the United States (House)	Dubester 33[2]
Abstract	Abstract of the Seventh Census	Dubester 34

States are listed as follows in Book I and alphabetically in other volumes:

Maine
New Hampshire
Vermont
Massachusetts
Rhode Island
Connecticut
New York
New Jersey
Pennsylvania
Delaware
Maryland
District of Columbia
Virginia
North Carolina
South Carolina
Georgia
Florida--new state
Alabama
Mississippi
Louisiana

Texas--new state
Arkansas
Tennessee
Kentucky
Missouri
Indiana
Ohio
Michigan
Wisconsin--new state
Iowa--new state
California--new state

Territories:

Minnesota
New Mexico
Oregon
Utah

1850

THE SEVENTH DECENNIAL CENSUS

The publications of the Seventh Census consist of a single large main volume and a small abstract, both printed in 1853, two nearly identical 1854 compendium volumes, one published by order of the House, the other by order of the Senate, and a volume of mortality statistics. In addition, a volume of manufacturing statistics was compiled and forwarded to Congress by the President as late as 1859, and is considered a part of the Seventh Census.

This was the first census in which the name and other data about each individual was to be taken. In earlier censuses, only the name of the head of the family was recorded. In this Census, like that of 1860, separate schedules for free inhabitants and for slaves were used. Inquiries on the schedule for slaves were made of the owner, and less information was required than for free persons. Inquiries were made, however, of the number of fugitive slaves and the number of those manumitted during the year.

The 1850 schedule included a question as to marriages during the year, and enumerators were to inquire as to deaths in the household. Where there were any, a separate schedule was used. The answers on that schedule provided the information for the volume on mortality statistics.

Other new questions included an open-ended one on occupations of everyone, male and female, of fifteen years of age. Earlier census schedules had listed a limited number of types of employment such as agriculture, commerce or manufactures for a check to be made by the enumerator. Place of birth by state, territory or foreign country was a new inquiry, as was the value of real estate owned, and whether anyone in the household was a pauper or a convict. Disability questions from the last census were continued in 1850.

In earlier censuses, free inhabitants had been placed in categories as white or colored. For the first time, the 1850 schedule inquired as to "Color: white, black or mulatto," terms which were to change with each census through 1890.

The two compendium volumes, nearly identical, but one done by the House printer and the other by the Senate printer, included all aspects of the results of the census inquiries, as did the abstract. The latter did not, however, include statistics for divisions smaller than states.

The Seventh Census was the first one in which state tables were printed alphabetically rather than by date of entry into the Union, thus making searching for information considerably easier. It is also the first census in which all the volumes were published as Congressional documents, thus becoming part of the Serial Set.

Five new states had entered the Union since the Sixth Census: Florida, Iowa and Texas in 1845, and Wisconsin and California in 1850. California took a state census in 1852, and the results were published at the end of the compendium volumes in addition to the information collected in 1850 by the federal enumerators.

Decennial year	1850 Dubester 30
Census	Seventh Census
Volume	Book 1
Title	The Seventh Census of the United States: 1850. Embracing a statistical view of each of the states and territories, arranged by counties, towns, etc. . .
Publication	Washington: Robert Armstrong, Public Printer
Date	1853
Congress	32d Congress, 1st Session
House/Senate	House Miscellaneous Document unnumbered
Serial	Serial 686
Classifications	
Supt. of Documents	I 8.5: Bk 1
Library of Congress	HA201.1850.B1
card	7-19238
Dewey	q317.3 Un307
Microforms	
National Archives	Film T825 Reel 6
Research Publications	Film 1850 Reel 1
Pages	cxxxvi, 1022 pages
Notes	By J. B. D. DeBow, Superintendent of the United States Census
Reprints and facsimiles	Arno Press, New York. America in Two Centuries, an inventory. 1976

This is the main volume of the Seventh Census. It contains data from
all inquiries in the census, as well as from separate inquiries to
organizations such as churches and schools. It also contains considerable foreign data for comparative purposes.

The volume consists of two distinct parts. The first part consists
of national tables, most of which list data for all states and territories, as well as a total for the United States. This part includes
seventy-three tables numbered in upper case Roman numerals on 136
pages numbered in lower case Roman numerals. At the end of the numbered tables, there is a list of all counties in the country in a
single alphabet, followed by a list of all named places in the
country, also in a single alphabet.

The second part consists of separate groups of 14 tables for each
state and territory, with most data presented alphabetically by counties. These tables, also numbered in upper Roman, are on 1022 pages
numbered in Arabic.

Contents

N - National Tables, pages xxix-xcii
S - State Tables, pages 1-1013

	United States	States and Territory	Counties	Other
Demographic Characteristics				
Aggregate population	N I N XII N LXII N XVIII	N I N XII N XVIII N XXV N LXII S I, SIII S IV	page xcv- cii S I S II S IV	N XXXIV 32 cities N XXXV 56 cities S II county subdivns.
Colonial population 1701, 1747, 1775	N VI N VIII N IX			
Historic from 1790	N I, X N LXII N LXXIII	N I N XXV, XXVI S V		N XXXIV
from 1840				N XXXV
Age				
By race and condition by sex	N XXI	S I	S I	
By white	N XXI	N XXI		
By free colored	N XXII	N XXII		
slave	N XXIII	N XXIII		
Historic	N LXV			
Ratio	N LXXIII			
Race and condition	N I N XII N XVIII	N I N XII N XVIII N XXVI N XXVII N XXVIII S I, S III S IV	page xcv- cii N XXV S I S II	S II
White and free colored, slaves	N XVIII	N XXVI N XXVII		
Ratio	N LX N LXIII N LXIV N LXV			

	United States	States and Territory	Counties	Other
Historic from 1790	N I, XII N XV N XXXVII N LX N LXIII	N I, X N XII N XXV N LXVII S V		
Indian population, by tribe for 1789, 1825, 1853	page xciv	page civ		
Sex		S I	S I, II	S II
By age		S I		
By race and condition		S I, III		
Ratio, by age	N LIX N LXVI	N LIX		
Historic from 1790	N XXXIII			

Social and Economic Characteristics

Disabilities	N XXXI			
See page xlviii				
Blind, deaf and dumb, idiotic and insane				
By race	N XXIX N XXX	N XXIX S VI		
By general nativity	N XXX	S VI		
Multiple disabilities	N XXXII			
Historic from 1830	N XXXIII			

Education

See page lv				
School attendance, by race and sex, and by general nativity	N XLI	N XLI S VIII	S VIII	
Colleges, schools, academies, number, number teachers, students	N XLII N XLIV	N XLII N XLIV S VII	S VII	

Employment

See "Occupations" below				
Number free males employed, ten categories of employment	N LI	N LI		
From 1840	N LII	N LII		

85

1850
Book I--Seventh Census

Dubester 30--
continued

	United States	States and Territory	Counties	Other
Families				
Number families, whites and free colored	N XVIII	N XVIII S IV	S IV	
Number families each county			page xcv	
Farms				
Land in farms	N LV	N LV S XI	S XI	
Housing				
Number of dwellings, whites and free colored	N XVIII	N XVIII S XI	S XI	
Number dwellings each county			page xcv	
Immigration				
Foreign passengers arrived, 1820-1853	N LXVIII			
By sex, 1845, 1847, 1852	N LXX	N LXIX		
By nativity	N LXXI			
By occupation	N XLVII			
Literacy				
Illiterates--persons 20 years and over who cannot read and write, by race and sex, and by general nativity	N XLIII	N XLIII S IX	S IX	
Military				
Militia, by rank	N XI	N XI		
Nativity				
General nativity	N XV	N XV S III	page xcv	
White persons, by sex	N XVI	N XVI		
Free colored, by sex	N XVII	N XVII		
Specific, by state and foreign country	N XV	N XV		

	United States	States and Territory	Counties	Other
Occupations				
See "Employment" above				
Males 15 years and over				
by 325 occupations	N L	N L		
By 100 occupations		S X		
Males employed in manu- factures	page lxxix			
Of immigrants arriving 1845, 1847, 1852	N LIX	N LIX		
Publications and Libraries				
Libraries - by type and number of volumes	N XLVI	N XLVI	S XIII	
	N XLVII	N XLVII		
		S XIII		
Newspapers				
Number, by frequency and circulation	N XLIX	N XLIX		
		S XII		
From 1840	N XLVII	N XLVIII		
Religion				
See page lv				
Number churches, by denomi- nation	N XXXVIII	N XXXVIII	S XIV	
Church property	N XXXIX	N XXXIX		
Accommodations	N XL	N XL		
		S XIV		
Slavery				
See "Race and condition" above				

Apportionment, Density and Geography

Apportionment, from 1790	N XIV	N XIV		
Density	N XII	N XII		
Geography				
Square miles	N II			
Area of North America	N IV, VII			
Shore line	N V			

1850
Book I--Seventh Census

	United States	States and Territory	Counties	Other

Vital Statistics

Events during year ended June 1
See page xxxix

Birth, by race and condition	N XVIII	N XVIII S IV	S IV	
Deaths, by race and condition	N XVIII	N XVIII S IV	S IV	
Persons under one year	page xxxix	page xxxix		
Marriages by race and condition	N XVIII	N XVIII S IV		

Foreign Data

Population				
European nations and Turkey, various historical periods from 1672				N XIII
Principal cities of the world from 1338				N XXXVI
Great Britain, by age 1821 and 1841				N XXIV
Education				
England and Wales 1851, school attendance, by sex				N XLV
Families, Great Britain 1801-1851, number houses, persons				page xix
Literacy - England and Wales, 1839-1844, by marriage records				page lvi
Occupations - Great Britain, 1841 by sex				N LIII

Vital Statisics - England and
  Wales 1841-1850, Prusssia
  1849, births and deaths,
  by sex   page xx

Geography - territorial areas
  of European nations   N III

INDEX TO ALL OF THE SUBJECTS TREATED OF IN THE STATE TABLES.

Decennial year	1850	Dubester 31

Census   Seventh Census

Volume   --

Title   Message of the President of the United
                          States communicating a digest of the sta-
                          tistics of manufactures according to the
                          returns of the Seventh Census. 1859.
                          Running title: Digest of the Statistics of
                          Manufactures.

Publication   U.S. Department of Interior. Washington:
                          William A. Harris, Printer

  Date   1859

Congress   35th Congress, 2d Session, Volume 10

  House/Senate   Senate Executive Document 39

  Serial   Serial 984

Classifications

  Supt. of Documents   I 8.5: Bk 3

  Library of Congress   HA9724. U53 1859 or HA 201. 1850 B3

    card   7-19240

  Dewey   317.3 Un307ma

Microforms

  National Archives   Film T825 Reel 6

  Research Publications   Film 1850-1860 Reel M-1

Pages   143 pages

Notes   By Joseph C. G. Kennedy, Superintendent

1850   Dubester 31
Digest of the Statistics of Manufactures

Contents	Tables	Pages
Message from the President, January 21, 1859		1
Title page		3
Principal manufactures by states and territories, single page for each principal manufactured item, items in alphabetical order	1	5-129
Miscellaneous manufactures - by States and Territories	2	130-136
General survey of manufactures	3	137-142
Condensed table by state and territory, all items	4	143

T - Table number

	United States	States and Territory

Social and Economic Characteristics

Employment

| By sex - male hands, female hands | T 1 | T 1, 2, 4 |
| By manufactured product | T 1, 3 | T 1, 2 |

<u>Decennial year</u>	1850	Dubester 32

<u>Census</u>   Seventh Census

<u>Volume</u>   Book 2

<u>Title</u>   Mortality statistics of the Seventh Census
                of the United States, 1850 . . .

<u>Publication</u>   Washington: A. O. P. Nicholson, Printer

  Date   1855

<u>Congress</u>   33rd Congress, 2d Session

  House/Senate Senate Executive Document 98

  Serial   Serial 805

<u>Classifications</u>

  Supt. of Documents   I 8.5: Bk 2

  Library of Congress HA201.1850.B2

    card   7-19239

  Dewey   317.3 Un307mo

<u>Microforms</u>

  National Archives   Film T825   Reel 6

  Research Publications Film 1850-1880   Reel VS-1

<u>Pages</u>   303 pages

<u>Notes</u>   By J. B. D. DeBow, Superintendent of the
                United States Census

<u>Reprints and facsimiles</u>   Central Book Company, New York City, N.Y.

This is the first decennial census in which a question was asked as
to whether a member of the household had died during the preceding
year. The practice was continued through 1860, 1870, 1880, and 1890.

Questions on the "Schedule regarding persons who died" included name,
age, sex, color, condition, marital status, place of birth, month of
death, occupation, cause of death, and number of days ill. Similar
questions were asked in the following decades.

The volume is divided into two parts. Part I contains statistics for
the United States as a whole, and Part II, those for State and Territories and 38 cities. In Part II there are 49 horizontal columns for
demographic data such as age, race and sex, and 125 vertical columns
listing specific causes of death.

Contents	Tables	Pages
Detailed table of contents		3
Part I Introductory chapter and unnumbered tables		5-16
United States Tables	I-XXVI	17-44
Appendix - Letter re classification of diseases		45-49
Part II State Tables, Territory Tables		50-301
City Tables - a single table with 49 columns		302

Columns

Age groups by sex	18 columns
Nativity	11 columns
Season of decease	4 columns
Duration of sickness	4 columns
Race and condition by sex	12 columns

References are to Table numbers

	United States	Regions	States and Territories	Cities
Demographic Characteristics				
Aggregate population	VIII	VIII		XXIII 29 cities
From 1790	XIX	XXI		

1850
Mortality Statistics

	United States	Regions	States and Territories	Cities
Age	IX, XII		IX	
By race and condition	XIII			
By sex	VIII		VIII	XXIV 27 cities
By race and condition	XIII			
Negro - as black or mulatto	XI		XI	
By sex	X		III, X	XXV 26 cities
Sex	X		X	

Social and Economic Characteristics

Employment
  See "Occupations" below

	United States	Regions	States and Territories	Cities
Nativity				
General nativity		XVI		XIII
White and free colored persons		XVII XVIII	XIV	
White persons			XV	
Specific, by state and county	XX		XX	XXIII
Occupations - free males	XXII		XXII	

Vital Statistics

	United States	Regions	States and Territories	Cities
Deaths				
By age	I		VI, XXVI	page 302
By race	XXVI			
By sex	I		VI	page 302
By race and condition			VI	page 303
By age	XXVI		XXVI	
By sex	V		VI	page 302
By sex			VI	page 302
By race and condition	V		VI	
By nativity				
General nativity	page 13-14		VI	page 302
Specific nativity	II		VI	
By occupation - white and free colored	IV		VI	page 302
By duration of illness	III, page 15		VI	page 302
By season of death	III, page 15		VI	page 302
By cause	I-V		page 11	

1850
Mortality Statistics

Dubester 32--
continued

Foreign data

Deaths - Europe, England,
  number of deaths and
  death rate

page 5

Decennial year	1850	Dubester 33[1]

Census   Seventh Census

Volume   Compendium

Title   Statistical view of the United States,
                          embracing its territory, population--white,
                          free colored and slaves--moral and social
                          condition, industry, property, and revenue;
                          the detailed statistics of cities, towns,
                          and counties . . .

Publication   By resolution of the Senate, July 12, 1854
                          Washington: Beverly Tucker, Senate Printer

  Date   1854

Congress   33rd Congress, 1st Session

Classifications

  Supt. of Documents   I 8.2:C73[1]

  Library of Congress   HA201.1850.C[1]

  Dewey   317.3 Un307s[1]

Microforms

  National Archives   Film T825   Reel 6

  Research Publications   See 33[2]

Pages   400 pages

Notes   By J. B. D. DeBow, Superintendent of the
                          United States Census; see 33[2] for nearly
                          identical volume

Reprints and facsimiles   Central Book Company, New York City
                          Gordon and Breach, Science Publishers,
                          Demographic Monographs v. 5 (1970)

1850   Dubester 33
Statistical View of the United States

_____

Contents	Tables	Pages

* In Dubester 33$_2$, the version printed by A. O.
Nicholson, map faces page 31 and outline faces first page
of Index.

References are to table numbers, except where pages are
indicated.

	United States	Regions	States and Territories	Cities
Demographic Characteristics				
Aggregate population	XII	XIV, XV	XII, XCVI	p. 192-337 counties p. 338-393 cities, towns
Colonial	XI		XI	
From 1790	XII	XIV, XCVII	XII, XCVII	cities CCXVI
annual	XCI			
by race, from 1840			XCIV, XCV XCVIII	
From 1840				counties columns 8, 9
California State Census of 1852			p. 394	p. 394
Age				
Specific ages, individual years	CVII			
Age groups	CIII.CIV		CIII	p. 395-8
by race and condition	CV, CVI			45 cities
School age - 5 to 15 yrs.	CLII		CLII, CLIV	
Voting age - white males of 21 years and over	XXVII		XXVII	
Race and condition, by sex	CV			counties columns 1-5
From 1790 Black and mulatto by condition	LXXI		LXXII LXXIV	
Free colored				
See pages 62-81	XLII		XLII	
From 1790, 1800	XLII	XLIII	XLII, XLV, XLVII, XLVIII	
By age	LV, LVIII, LIX, LXII		LV, LVIII, LXII	

1850
Statistical View of the United States

	United States	Regions	States and Territories	Cities
By sex	XLIX. LVI	LI	XLIX, LV	
From 1800	LII		LVII	
By age	LVII, LX		LVII	
White				
See pages 45-62	XVIII		XVIII, XX, XXI, XXII	
From 1790, by sex	XXIV. XXV, XXVI		XXIII, XXV XXVI	
By age groups	XXIX, XXXI		XXVIII	
From 1830	XXX			
By sex	XXX XXV	XXXIII	XXX	
Rank and proportion by states			XX, XXI	
Slaves				
See pages 82-95, and below				
Aggregate	LXXI LXXII		LXXI LXXII	
From 1790	LXXI		LXXI LXXIII	
Rank and proportion from 1790		LXXX	LXXIV, LXXV	
By age			LXXXII	
By sex	LXXXI-LXXXIII LXXXV-LXXXVI		LXXXI	
Sex	LXXVII-LXXX		LXXVI LXXXI LXXXII LXXXV	
				counties columns 6, 7
Sex	CII			
from 1790	CII			

Social and Economic Characteristics

	United States	Regions	States and Territories	Cities
Crime	CLXXVI		CLXXVI, CLXXVII	
Number convicted during year, Number in prison, June 1				
Number in prison, by type prison			CLXXVVII-CLXXXII	

100

1850
Statistical View of the United States

Dubester 33--
continued

	United States	Regions	States and Territories	Cities
Disabilities				
Blind, deaf and dumb, idiotic and insane	CXIII		CXIII	
By race - all disabilities	CXV		CXV	
By nativity	CXIV		CXIV	
By race -				
white and free colored			XXXVII	
white	XXXIX		XXXIX	
blind and deaf and dumb	XXXVI		XXXVII	
idiotic and insane			XXXVIII	
free colored	LXIII-IV		LXIII-LXV	
By nativity	CXV		CXV	
Education				
See pages 140-151	CXLV-		CXLV-	counties
Number institutions, teachers, pupils, by level; finances	CXLVIII		CXLVIII	columns 14-21
School attendance by race, sex, and general nativity	CXLVII		CXLVII	
Federal lands appropriated for educational purposes	CL		CL	
Families				
Number white and free colored families	XCIX	C	XCIX	
Farms	CLXXXIII		CLXXXIII	counties
Number, acres improved and unimproved, cash value				columns 23-26
Housing	XCIX	C	XCIX	counties
Dwellings, white and free colored; number families to a dwelling			1 (4 states)	column 12
Immigration				
See pages 119-124				
Arrivals 1790-1854	CXIII			
By age and sex	CXXVI			

1850   Dubester 33--
Statistical View of the United States   continued

	United States	Regions	States and Territories	Cities
By sex			CXXV	
By foreign country	CXXIV			
From Great Britain to				
U.S. and Canada	CXXVII			
Income and property				
Average wages, with and				
without board	CLXXV		CLXXV	
Property - real and				
personal estate	CCXIV		CCXIV	
Institutionalized population				
See Crime above				
See Paupers, below				
Literacy				
Persons 20 years and up				
who cannot read and				
write	CXLIX	CLVI	CXLIX	
By race and sex				
By general nativity	CLV		CLV	
Nativity				
General nativity	CXXII	CXVII		Counties
		CXIX		Columns
				10-11
By race--white and				
free colored	CXVI		CXVI	
white, by sex	XLI		XLI	
free colored	LXVI-LXVIII		LXVI-LXVIII	
Specific, by state and				p. 399
foreign country	CXX		CXX	29 cities
Occupations				
See page 125-130				
Seven occupational groups	CXXVIII		CXXVIII	
Specific occupations	CXXX		CXXX	
free males over 15 yrs.	CXXIX		CXXIX	
free colored - 4 states			LXX	
Paupers	CLXXIII		CLXXIII	CLXXII
See page 161			CLXXIV	
Number supported during year				
Number being supported June 1				

1850
Statistical View of the United States

	United States	Regions	States and Territories	Cities
Publications, libraries See pages 155-160				
Newspapers, by frequency and circulation	CLXI- CLXIII	CLXV	CLXI- CLXIII	12 principal cities
Libraries	CLXVII		CLXVII	CLXVI
Religion See pages 132-141				
Number churches by denomination	CXXXVII	CXLIV	CXXXVII	12 cities CXLIII counties column 22
Slavery See pages 82-95 See also Race and Condition, above				
Disabilities of slaves	LXXXVIII LXXXIX		LXXXVIII LXXXIX	
Manumitted and fugitive slaves	XLIV		XLIV	
Mortality of slaves	LXXXVII			
Slaveholders, by number of slaves owned	XC		XC	

Apportionment, Density and Geography

	United States	Regions	States and Territories	Cities
Apportionment From 1790			XVII	
Density From 1790	XII XIII	XV	XII	
From 1840			XII	
Geography Area	III-VI	IV,IX, X	VIII	
Information of states and territories			XVII	

Vital Statistics

	United States	Regions	States and Territories	Cities
Births By race - white and colored	CXI		CXI	
Marriages By race - white and free colored	CXI		CXI, CXII	

1850   Dubester 33--
Statistical View of the United States   continued

	United States	Regions	States and Territories	Cities
Deaths - total	CVIII	CX	CVIII, CX	
By race - white and	CXI		CXI	
free colored slaves	LXXXVII			
By age			p. 400	

Foreign Data

Population and density - European countries	XVI
Crime - prisoners committed, England, Wales, Ireland,	p. 168
by sex, description of convicts, France	p. 168
Education - schools and school laws, Europe	CLI and p. 147
Emigration - from Great Britain	CXVII
Families, housing - Europe	CI
Libraries - Europe	CLXVIII-CLXXI
Nativity - Great Britain	CXVIII
Occupations - Great Britain	CXXIII
Vital Statistics - Births, marriages, deaths,	p. 107
England and Wales	
Deaths, Latin America	XIX, CX
Geography - areas of countries - Europe and Latin	I, II
America	

Decennial year	1850	Dubester 332

Census   Seventh Census

Volume   Compendium

Title   Statistical view of the United States,
                          embracing its territory, population--white,
                          free colored and slave--moral and social
                          condition, industry, property and revenue;
                          the detailed statistics of cities, towns,
                          and counties; being a compendium of the
                          Seventh Census.

Publication   By order of the House of Representatives,
                          January 12, 1854. Washington: A. O. P.
                          Nicholson, Public Printer

  Date   1854

Congress   33rd Congress, 1st Session

Classifications

  Supt. of Documents   I 8.2:C73^2

  Library of Congress   HA201.1850C^2

    card   6-36734

  Dewey   317.3 Un307s^2

Microforms

  National Archives   Film T825   Reel 6

  Research Publications   Film 1850   Reel 1

Pages   400 pages

Map   Map facing index page

Notes   By J. B. D. DeBow, Superintendent of the
                          United States Census; see 33[1] for nearly
                          identical volume

<u>Decennial year</u>	1850 Dubester 34
<u>Census</u>	Seventh Census
<u>Volume</u>	Abstract
<u>Title</u>	The Seventh Census. Report of the Superintendent of the Census for December 1, 1852; to which is appended the report of December 1, 1851. Cover title: Abstract of the Seventh Census
<u>Publication</u>	Printed by order of the House of Representatives. Washington: R. Armstrong, Printer
Date	1853
<u>Congress</u>	32d Congress, 2nd Session
House/Senate	By order of the House of Representatives
<u>Classifications</u>	
Supt. of Documents	I 8.1: 851, 852
Library of Congress	HA201.1850 D
card	6-44893
Dewey	317.3 Un307se
<u>Microforms</u>	
National Archives	Film T825 Reel 6
Research Publications	Film 1850 Reel 1
<u>Pages</u>	160 pages

1850   Dubester 34
Abstract of the Seventh Census

Contents   Pages

Tables and additional statistical data are presented throughout the
text of the two reports. Many references are to foreign data.

References below are to page numbers.

	United States	Regions	States and Territories
Demographic Characteristics			
Aggregate population	160	150	150, 160
From 1790		150	150
Race and condition	129,130, 160		160
From 1790	153		
Social and Economic Characteristics			
Crime	29		
Number of convictions during year			
Number in prison, by general nativity			
Disabilities			
By race and condition, by sex			
Blind	21-22		22
Deaf and dumb	20-21		21
Idiotic	23-26		25
Insane	25-26		24
Employment			
Persons employed in specific	141		154-159
manufacturers, wages	154-159		
Farms			
Land in farms	47-82		49, 84

1850
Abstract of the Seventh Census

	United States	Regions	States and Territories
Immigration	13, 118-121		
Arrivals of foreign passengers, annual 1840-1850, and historic	132-33		
Income and property	154-159		154-159
Value of real estate owned	46		46
Nativity	14-15, 118-121, 131		
Specific by state of birth	16-17		16
Specific by country of birth	18-19		18
Paupers	27-28		28
By general nativity	27		28
Publications, communications, libraries			
Newspapers, circulation by frequency of publication	142		
Telegraph lines and usage	106-115		109, 112
Religion	30-31		30-45
Number of churches by denomination			
Slavery			
See "Race and condition" above			
Manumitted and fugitive slaves	136		136
Transportation	98		
Railroads, locations			

Apportionment, Density and Geography

	United States	Regions	States and Territories
Apportionment, Representative population	160		160
Fractions			
Density		135	134
Geography			
Area, total, and additions since 1840	128		

1850
Abstract of the Seventh Census

	United States	Regions	States and Territories

Vital Statistics

Deaths during census year			140
Death rates, by sex		12	11, 13

Life tables for blacks:
  New England, Maryland,
  Louisiana and Kentucky
	13		

Foreign data

Individual statements comparing conditions abroad are interposed
throughout the reports

Great Britain, Ireland, population housing	6
England - deaths, life tables	11
France - population, life tables	10, 11
Belgium - population, housing	8
Prussia - population, housing	9
Canada - telegraphs	115
Europe - railroads, telegraphs	115

Eleventh Census of the United States
Robert P. Porter, Superintendent.

1860

POPULATION.

LEGEND.

Under 2 inhab to the Sq Mile

2..6 " " " " I

6..18 " " " " II

18..45 " " " " III

45..90 " " " " IV

90 and over " " " " V

Cities over 8000 inhabitants in solid color
in circles proportionate to population.

MAP
SHOWING IN FIVE DEGREES OF DENSITY THE DISTRIBUTION
WITHIN THE TERRITORY EAST OF THE 100TH MERIDIAN
OF THE
POPULATION OF THE UNITED STATES
excluding Indians not taxed.
Compiled from the Returns of Population at the Eighth Census 1860.

NOTE
★ Center of Population   39° 00.4' N.
82° 48.8' W.

1860

VOLUMES OF THE EIGHTH DECENNIAL CENSUS

Volume Title	Dubester Number
Book I Population of the United States in 1860	Dubester 37
Book II Agriculture of the United States in 1860	Dubester 38
Book III Manufactures of the United States in 1860	Dubester 39
Book IV Statistics of the United States, including Mortality, Property, etc.	Dubester 40
Preliminary Report on the Eighth Census	Dubester 41

States listed in alphabetical order:

Alabama
Arkansas
California
Connecticut
Delaware
Florida
Georgia
Illinois
Indiana
Iowa
Kansas--new state
Kentucky
Louisiana
Maine
Maryland
Massachusetts
Michigan
Minnesota--new state
Mississippi
Missouri
New Hampshire
New Jersey
New York
North Carolina
Ohio
Oregon--new state
Pennsylvania
Rhode Island
South Carolina
Tennessee

Texas
Vermont
Virginia
Wisconsin

Territories:

Colorado
Dakota
Nebraska
Nevada
New Mexico
Utah
Washington
District of Columbia

1860

THE EIGHTH DECENNIAL CENSUS

The first results from the Eighth Census were preliminary ones, published as a House Executive Document in 1862. Following in succeeding years, four volumes, each of quarto size, were published. One was on population, one on agriculture, one on manufactures, and the last on miscellaneous statistics. The Eighth Census set a publishing standard, continued into the Twentieth Century, with several major volumes appearing as a set. Like 1850, the volumes were all published as part of the Congressional Series, a practice to be continued through the Eleventh Census in 1890.

Population inquiries in 1860 changed very little from those of 1850. The same basic schedules were used. Only two inquiries were added: to the free inhabitants schedule, one on the value of one's personal estate, and to the slave schedule, one on the number of slave houses. The schedule for "persons who died" was identical to that for 1850, thus permitting easy comparison of data for the two periods.

Publication of the population information developed from the 1860 Census was, however, greatly increased, resulting in the four volume set. The first volume contains an extended essay on population, vital statistics, disabilities, housing, and immigration, together with considerable comparative information from abroad. Age data had been published in each earlier decade, but for the first time, in a practice to be continued in later years, the number of males of militia age, 18 to 45 years, was included.

Numbers of disabled persons were cross tabulated by age, race and sex. Lists of the numbers of persons in various self-described occupations ran to 587 specific occupations. Considerable information taken from immigration records was also included along with census material.

Indians, whom the Constitution had excluded from the need for enumeration, as they were "not taxed" and not represented in Congress, appeared for the first time as a category of "civilized Indians," those living among the general population and paying taxes. Indians "retaining their tribal character" were also estimated in number. The Preliminary Report shows Indians by tribe, and an estimate of the number of those living in Indian Territory.

Also included in the Preliminary Report and Book I is a table of apportionment of representatives for each state.

Statistics of births and deaths were published, and compared with those of European countries. Birth and death rates were calculated for the first time in any census.

Volume II, on Agriculture, provides, in addition to precise data on crop and animal production, information as to the number of farms by counties. It also includes data from the "Schedule of slave inhabitants," showing the number of slave owners, the number of slaves owned, in categories of one to one thousand and over, the number of slave houses, with data down to the county level.

Volume II, on Manufactures, introduces the statistics with an opening chapter of over 200 pages. Discussed is the historical development of individual industries, with the number of "hands employed" for each industry. Manufacturing details were published by product and by county and state. One can learn a great deal about the life of the people in 1860 by noting the articles manufactured for their purchase and consumption. That such items as "Millinery goods and artificial flowers" deserve a separate statement, for example, seems to tell something about the clothing of the period. Places of manufacture of goods eventually important during the Civil War are cited in detail.

The final volume is one of miscellaneous statistics. It includes nearly 300 pages on mortality, developed from the schedule of "People who died", an inquiry made to each family about such an event in the preceding year. The results of the inquiries on ownership of real and personal property, the only census volume to include this subject, became part of this volume.

In addition, information gained from other sources than the population enumeration were included. Data on the public press, banks and insurance, and railroad development during the decade were published. Railroad information included the names of companies, mileage completed by state and city, and the locations of city railroads. Points connected by canals and improved rivers are also presented here.

As to changes in territory, Minnesota had entered the Union in 1858 and Oregon in 1859. Kansas, having been part of Missouri Territory, was admitted in 1861 after the population was enumerated, but before the final volumes were published, and thus appears as a state. New territories included those of Nebraska, Colorado, Dakota and Nevada. New Mexico and Utah Territories, designated in 1850, were to retain their territorial status until after the turn of the century.

<u>Decennial year</u>	1860	Dubester 37
<u>Census</u>	Eighth Census	
<u>Volume</u>	Book 1	
<u>Title</u>	Population of the United States in 1860; compiled from the original returns of the Eighth Census.	
<u>Publication</u>	Under the direction of the Secretary of the Interior. Washington: Government Printing Office	
Date	1864	
<u>Congress</u>	38th Congress, 1st Session	
House/Senate	House Miscellaneous Document, unnumbered	
Serial	1202	
<u>Classifications</u>		
Supt. of Documents	I 9.5: Bk 1	
Library of Congress	HA201.1860 B1	
card	6-44891	
Dewey	Q 317.3 Un308$_r$ v.I	
<u>Microforms</u>		
National Archives	Film T825 Reels 6 and 7	
Research Publications	Film 1860 Reel 1	
<u>Pages</u>	cvii, 694 pages	
<u>Notes</u>	By Joseph C. G. Kennedy, Superintendent of Census	

114

This is the main volume of the 1860 Census. It contains the basic tables of population of the United States, states and territories, counties, cities and towns, as well as tables on age and sex, race and condition, nativity and occupations.

Following an introductory essay of over one hundred pages, with numerous unnumbered tables, there are six tables for each State and Territory, with the latter at the end. These are followed by ninety page recapitulation section, with another series of unnumbered tables with data on population, nativity and occupation. Last is a section on disabilities.

Contents	Tables	Pages
Introductory essays on population change during the decade, on vital statistics, on disabilities, with unnumbered tables for the United States and for foreign countries		iii-cvii
State and Territory tables	T 1-6	1-590
All six tables for each State and Territory are printed together		
Population by age and sex, by counties	T 1	
Population by color and condition by counties	T 2	
Population of cities and towns	T 3	
Nativity of free population	T 4	
Specific, by state and country	T 5	
Occupations	T 6	
Recapitulation of population, nativity and occupation by States and Territories	R	591-680
Appendix - essay on deaf and dumb and blind		681-692
Index		693-694

T - Tables for States and Territories
R - Recapitulation pages

1860
Book I - Population

	United States	States and Territories	Counties	Towns
Demographic Characteristics				
Aggregate population		p iv T 1,2	T 1,2	T 3
Historic 1790 to 1850	R 600	R 600		
Age	R 592	R 592		
By race, condition, and sex		T 1	T 1	
Military age (white males 18-45)	p xvii	p xvii		
Race and Condition			T 1,2	
See pages viii-xv	R 592-607	T 1,2 R 592-607		
By age	R 592	R 592	T 1	
By sex	R 598	T 1,2 R 592, 598	T 1,2	
Historic from 1790-1850	R 600-604	R 600-604		
Slaves by age and sex	R 594-595	T 1,2	T 1,2	
by color and sex	R 599	R 594-595		
Fugitive, manumitted, owned by Indians	p xv			
Indians				
Civilized Indians by sex and age	R 596	R 596		
Retaining tribal character	R 605	R 605		
Sex		T 1,2,4	T 1,2,4	T 3
Prediction for 1870-1900	p ix			
Social and Economic Characteristics				
Disabilities - Mental and Physical				
See pages liv-cvii for essays and tables	R 681-692			
Blind				
See pages lxix-lxxvii				
By race, condition, age, and sex	R 631-3	R 631-3		
By specific nativity	R 634-8	R 634-8		

	United States	States and Territories	Counties	Towns
Institutions for	p lxxiii	p lxxiii		p lxxiii
Publications regarding	R 687			
Deaf and Dumb				
See pages liv-lxxviii	R 686-687			
By age	p lvi			
By race, condition, age, and sex	R 624-	R 624-5		
By sex	p liv, lx			
By specific nativity	R 626	R 626		
Institutions for	p lxiv	p lxiv		p lxiv
Publications regarding	R 681			
Idiotic				
By race, condition, age and sex	R 647-9	R 647-9		
By specific nativity	R 650-55	R 650-55		
Insane				
See pages lxxviii-cvii				
By race, condition, age and sex	R 639-41	R 639-41		
By specific nativity	R 642-6	R 242-6		
By occupation	p lxxxvii			
By cause	p lxxxix			
Institutions for	p lxxxix	p xcvii		p xcvii
Relationship to criminal jurisprudence	p civ			
Housing				
Dwellings		p xxvii		
Immigration	p xvii			
Historic - by age	p xx			
by sex	p xix			
by specific nativity	p xxii, xxiv, xxv			
by occupation	p xxii			
by destination	p xxi			
Nativity				R608-615*
General nativity	p xxxiii	pxxxiii		T 4
	R 606-07	R 606-07		
		T 4	T 4	cities

*Cities - Boston, New York, Philadelphia, Baltimore, Cincinnati, Chicago, St. Louis, New Orleans

	United States	States and Territories	Counties	Towns
Specific nativity	p xxxiii R 616-619	R 616-619		
By state of birth	p xxviii R 620-623	p xxix-xxxii R 620-623		p xxxi
By foreign country				
Occupations	R 680	T 6 R 680		

Slavery
  See "Race and condition" above

Apportionment and Density, Geography

| Representative population | R 599 | R 599 | | |

Vital Statistics

Birth rates
| By race and condition | p xxxviii | p xxxviii | | |

Death rates	p xli	p xli		
By age, sex and condition	p xlv			
of centenarians	p xlvi			

| Marriages, marital status | p xxxvi | p xxxvi | | |

Foreign data

Population - essay on population of foreign countries   xlvi-liii
  by age and sex   xlvii
  density   xlix
  life tables and mean age   xlviii
  by cities - Great Britain, Ireland, Prusssia, Netherland,
          Saxony, Sweden, Belgium, and Russia   lii
          Canada (British America) - historic   1
          Mexico - states and territories   li

Disabilities
  Blind - institutions, cities   xxxi, lxxi, R 687
  Great Britain, Ireland, Europe

Deaf and Dumb - institutions, cities in Europe, Canada,
  and Asia   lxv
Publications regarding disabled   R 682

Decennial year	1860	Dubester 38

Census   Eighth Census

Volume   Book 2

Title   Agriculture of the United States in 1860;
                          compiled from the original returns of the
                          Eighth Census

Publication   Washington: Government Printing Office

  Date   1864

Congress   38th Congress, 1st Session

  House/Senate   House Miscellaneous Document, unnumbered

  Serial   1203

Classifications

  Supt. of Documents   I 9.5: Bk 2

  Library of Congress   HA201.1860 B

    card   6-44894

  Dewey   q 317.3 Un308$_r$ v.2

Microforms

  National Archives   Film T825 Reel 7

  Research Publications   Film 1860 Reel 1

Pages   clxxii, 292 pages

Notes   By Joseph C. G. Kennedy, Superintendent of
                          Census

120

1860
Book II - Agriculture   Dubester 38

Contents   Pages

References are to page numbers

	United States	States and Territories	Counties
Social and Economic Characteristics			
Farms			
Containing 3 acres or more	221	221, 193-	193-
Acres of land in farms,			
improved and unimproved	184	184	
Number farms, acres on farms,	222	222	
for 1850			
Slavery	247	247, 223-	223-
For 16 states, District of			
Columbia and territories,			
number of slaveholders,			
number of slaves per slave-			
holder, categories 1 to			
1000 plus			
For 1850	248	248	

Decennial year	1860	Dubester 39

Census   Eighth Census

Volume   Book 3

Title   Manufactures of the United States in 1860;
                      compiled from the original returns of the
                      Eighth Census.

Publication   Under the direction of the Secretary of the
                      Interior. Washington: Government Printing
                      Office

Date   1865

Congress   38th Congress, 1st Session

  House/Senate   House Miscellaneous Document, unnumbered

  Serial   1204

Classifications

  Supt. of Documents I 9.5: Bk 3

  Library of Congress HA201.1860 B2

    card   7-19246

  Dewey   q 317.3 Un308$_r$ v.3

Microforms

  National Archives   Film T825 Reel 7

  Research Publications Film 1850-1860 Reel M-1

Pages   ccxvii, 745 pages

Notes   "Preliminary views" signed: J. M. Edmunds,
                      Commissioner General Land Office and in
                      charge of the Census

Reports and Facsimiles Maxwell Reprint Company, Elmsford, New
                      York. American industry and manufactures
                      in the Nineteenth Century; a basic source
                      collection, volume 6

1860   Dubester 39
Book III Manufactures

This volume on manufactures provides considerable information potentially useful for the study of population. The introduction of over
two hundred pages, provides a great deal of information on the
historical development of individual industries. Manufacturing of
individual products is discussed in great detail. The place of manufacture of items is also quite specific. For each product, the
number of "hands employed, male and female" is stated. There are
numerous unnumbered tables throughout the introductory pages.

Contents	Tables	Pages

    T - Tables I, II and III for each State and Territory

1860
Book III Manufactures

	United States	States and Territories	Counties
Social and Economic Characteristics			
Employment			
Number of hands employed, by sex	p 729	p 729 T 2	T 1,2
Number of hands employed, by sex in manufacture of specific products	p 733-742	T 3	T 1
Number of hands employed in production of specific products, but not all those products listed in Tables I-III.			
Soft or non-durable goods:			
Boots and shoes	lxxiii	lxxiii	
Bookbinding and blank books	cxlv	cxlv	
Carpets	lix	lix	
Cotton goods	xxi	xxi	
Hats and caps	clxii	clxii	
Hemp and manilla cordage	cxviii cxxi	cxviii cxxi	
Hoisery	xlv	xlv	
India rubber goods	lxxxii	lxxxii	
Ladies clothing	lxxxv	lxxxv	
Linen	cxi	cxi	
Men's clothing, shirts, collars, finishing goods	lxv lxvi	lxv lxvi	
Millinary goods and artificial flowers	lxxxviii	lxxxviii	
Musical instruments	cliii	cliii	
Paper	cxxxi	cxxxi	
Printing and lithography	cxxxix cxli cxlii	cxxxix cxli cxlii	
Silk	ciii	ciii	
Straw goods	xciv	xciv	
Wool carding	l	l	
Woolen goods	xxxv	xxxv	
Worsted goods	xxxix	xxxix	
Durable goods			
Agricultural implements	ccxvi ccxvii	ccxvi ccxvii	
Hardware	cxcii	cxcii	
Locomotive Engines	clxxxix	clxxxix	
Nails and spikes	cxcv	cxcv	
Sewing machines	cxc	cxc	
Steel	cxciv	cxciv	

124

1860
Book III Manufactures

	United States	States and Territories	Counties
Products of Mines			
Coal	clxxiii	clxxiii	
	clxxiv	clxxiv	
Iron	clxxvii	clxxvii	
	clxxviii	clxxviii	
	clxxx	clxxx	
	clxxxiii	clxxxiii	
	clxxxiv	clxxxiv	
	clxxxv	clxxxv	
	clxxxvii	clxxxvii	
Salt	cciv	cciv	

<u>Decennial year</u>	1860	Dubester 40

<u>Census</u>   Eighth Census

<u>Volume</u>   Book 4

<u>Title</u>   Statistics of the United States (Including
                         Mortality, Property, &c.,) in 1860; com-
                         piled from the original rturns and being the
                         final exhibit of the Eighth Census, under
                         the direction of the Secretary of Interior

<u>Publication</u>   Washington: Government Printing Office

  Date   1866

<u>Congress</u>   38th Congress, 1st Session

  House/Senate   House Miscellaneous Document, unnumbered

  Serial   1205

<u>Classifications</u>

  Supt. of Documents   I 9.5: Bk 4

  Library of Congress   HA201.1860 B4

    card   6-8716

  Dewey   q 317.3 Un3 1860 v.4

<u>Microforms</u>

  National Archives   Film T825 Reel 7

  Research Publications Film 1860 Reel 1

<u>Pages</u>   lxvi, 584 pages

<u>Notes</u>   By James M. Edmunds, Commissioner of
                         General Land Office in Charge of Census;
                         by Edward Jarvis, M.D., Mortality Statistics

126

1860
Book IV Statistics of the United States   Dubester 40

Contents   Tables   Pages

Observations on the Census, essay on the history
  of censuses from antiquity, for Britain and
  colonies, European countries and the U.S., with
  additional remarks on this volume   iii-xvi

Institutions for the deaf and dumb   xvi-xix

Population and manufactures, hands employed, for
  102 cities of 10,000   xviii-xx

Introduction to mortality statistics   A-TT   xxi-lxvii

Mortality Tables   I-XLVII   3-287

References in lower case Roman numerals and in Arabic numerals are to
page numbers. References in upper case letters and upper case Roman
numerals are to table numbers.

1860
Book IV Statistics of the United States

	United States	Regions for Vital Records	States and Territories	Cities
Demographic Characteristics				
Aggregate population	p xx, E	E,F,G,H	p xx	p xviii 102 cities of 10,000
Colonial	p x			
Historic				
From 1790	p xx	G	p xx	
From 1830		O		
Age		P		
By race and sex		H,I,J,K, L,M		
By sex	I,J,K			
Military age--males 15-50	EE,GG	EE		
Dependent and contributing years - under 20, 20-60, 60-80, over 80		S,T,U,X,Z		
Persons 100 years and over, by year, by age and sex	p 513	p 513	p 513	
Race and condition	HH	E,F	HH	
By age		S,T,U		
By sex		H,I,J,K, L,M		
By sex		E,F		
Free population	p 351	p 340	p 340	
Sex	J	E,H,J		
Ratio by age	p 519			
Social and Economic Characteristics				
Crime	p 512	p 512		
Persons convicted of crime during year				
Persons in prison, June 1				
Disabilities	p xvii			
Deaf and dumb - new institution in District of Columbia				

1860
Book IV Statistics of the United States

Dubester 40--
continued

	United States	Regions for Vital Records	States and Territories	Cities
Education				
See pages 502-504				
Number schools, teachers, pupils	p 505		p 505	
Number by type	p 509		p 510	
School attendance by race, sex, and general nativity	p 507		p 107	
Employment				
Hands employed, by sex in fisheries	p 550		p 550	
in manufactures, in 102 named cities				p xviii
Families				
Free population only				
Number families	p 351		p 351, 340	p 340
Number one person, two person families	p 351			
Average number persons per family	p 351			
Farms	p 339		p 339	
Acres of land in farms, improved and unimproved				
Housing				
Dwellings - New York City and Philadelphia, by wards				p 339
Immigration				
Number immigrants arrived from 1820, by sex	JJ			
Immigrants living, arrived prior to 1850, 1850-1860	p 278			
By age	p 278			
	p 279, 521			
By sex	p 278, 520			

1860
Book IV Statistics of the United States

	United States	Regions for Vital Records	States and Territories	Cities
Income and property				
Income - wages, average monthly wages, with and without board	p 512	p 512		
Real and personal property owned, from 1850	p 294	p 294, 296-	p 296	
Literacy	p 508	p 508		
Persons 20 years and over unable to read and write, by race, sex and by general nativity				
Military				
Historic statistics	p xvi			
Nativity				
See pages 1-lxvi				
General Nativity	II	N	II, MM	NN
Specific Nativity				
By state or region of birth		PP,QQ	OO,LL	
By foreign country	KK,LL		LL	
North-South migration of natives, from 1850	RR,SS,TT			
Paupers	p 512	p 512		
Number paupers supported during year, number as of June 1, by general nativity; cost of support				
Publications and Libraries				
Newspapers and periodicals by type, frequency and circulation	p 321		p 321	
Religion				
Churches, by denomination, accommodations	p 497	p 352	p 352	

1860
Book IV Statistics of the United States

	United States	Regions for Vital Records	States and Territories	Cities
Slavery				
See "Race and condition" above				
Manumission, fugitive slaves, abolition in D.C.	p 337		p 337	
Transportation				
Railroad mileage by location			p 325	
Canals by points connected			p 335	
<u>Apportionment, Density, and Geography</u>				
Density - inhabitants per square mile			p 339	
<u>Vital Statistics</u>				
Deaths				
See pages 1-287 and additional tables XVI-XLVII for added details				
By age	V		V	
by sex			IV	
By sex	I		I	
by age	V		IV	
By cause				
from 1850				
By age	V		VI	
by sex	V		VI	
By sex	II,V,VI		III	
By month	IX, X			
By duration of illness				
By season - month	VII		VIII	
By sex				
Death rate	XI		XI	
By age	R		XI	
By cause	XII, XIV			
from 1850	XIII			
Life tables	p 519			

1860   Dubester 40--
Book IV Statistics of the United States   continued

Foreign data

See Index pages for additional details
Population - Ireland, and nativity   p xxiv
Age - Contributing and dependent age groups - Europe V,W,Y,Z
Deaths - by suicide, England and Sweden   XVIII
Death rates - Europe   Q,X,V
              West Indian British troops 1817-1836   XLIII
Life tables - Europe   XXXVI,
                                                      XXXIX

Decennial year	1860	Dubester 41
Census	Eighth Census	
Volume	Preliminary Report	
Title	Preliminary Report on the Eighth Census, 1860	
Publication	Washington: Government Printing Office	
Date	1862	
Congress	37th Congress, 2nd Session, Volume 9	
House/Senate	House Executive Document 116	
Serial	In Serial 1137, and as separate bound volume	
Classifications		
Supt. of Documents	I 9.2:P91	
Library of Congress	HA201.1860. A2 or A21	
card	6-35773	
Dewey	317.3 Un308p	
Microforms		
National Archives	Film T825 Reel 6	
Research Publications	Film 1860 Reel 1	
Pages	xvi, 294 pages	
Notes	By Joseph C. G. Kennedy, Superintendent	

The Preliminary Report for the Eighth Census was published in May
1862, two years after the enumeration of the population, as a House
Executive Document and before the final volumes. It is one of the
documents in Serial 1137, and does not comprise a separate volume.

Information in the Preliminary Report includes not only data from the
population enumeration, but additional material from a number of
sources. It includes foreign data for comparative purposes as well.

The first 121 pages of the Report consist of a long essay on all
aspects of the included material. The tables, which follow in a section entitled "Appendix", are specifically alluded to in each section
of the essay, making reference to them quite easy.

Contents	Tables	Pages
Index		v-xvi
Preliminary Report		1-121
Appendix	T 1-41	124-294

References are to table numbers except where pages are indicated.

	United States	States & Territories	Counties Cities
Demographic Characteristics			
Aggregate Population	T 1,2	T 1,2,41	T 41
See page 117			counties
See page 2			T 40 cities
Historic from 1790	T 1	T 1	
from 1850			T 40
Race and condition	T 1	T 1	T 41
See pages 5-7			
By sex	T 2	T 2	
Slaves	T 1	T 1	
See pages 9-12			
By sex	T 2	T 2	
Manumitted from 1850	T 4	T 4	
Fugitive from 1850	T 5	T 5	
Owned by Indians - see			
pages 10-11			

1860
Preliminary Report

	United States	States & Territories	Counties Cities
Indians			
By sex	T 2	T 2	
Indian territory by counties	T 3	T 3	T 3
Indians not enumerated in census and retaining their tribal character	T 3	T 3	
Sex	T 2	T 2,41	T 41
See page 9			
Population predictions to 1900			
See page 7			

Social and Economic Characteristics

Disabilities			
Blind			
See pages 41-48			
By condition	p 44	p 44	
Institutions - location and date of founding	p 43	p 43	p 43
Deaf and Dumb			
See pages 32-41			
By condition	T 7	T 7	
Diseases			
See pages 114-117			
As cause of death	T 6	T 6	
Idiotic			
See pages 57-58			
By condition	p 58	p 58	
Insane			
See pages 48-50	p 57	p 57	
Education			
See page 19			

1860
Preliminary Report

	United States	States & Territories	Counties Cities
Employment			
Hands employed, by sex in			
manufacture of			
clothing	T 17	T 17	
cotton goods	T 22	T 22	
woolen goods	T 23	T 23	
boots and shoes	T 25	T 25	
furniture	T 26	T 26	
musical instruments	T 27	T 27	
illuminating gas			
(males only)	T 29	T 29	
soap and candles	T 32	T 32	
products of industry,			
generally	T 33	T 33	
Farms			
See pages 80-101			
Land in farms, acres			
improved and unimproved			
from 1850	T 36	T 36	
Immigration			
See pages 12-19			
Historic from 1820,			
by sex	p 13		
By age and sex	p 15		
By destination, U.S.			
and elsewhere	p 16		
By occupation	p 17		
By birthplace, country			
where born	p 18		
Income and Property			
See pages 79-80			
Value of real and personal property			
Publication and Libraries			
See pages 101-103			
Newspapers and periodicals			
by subject, by frequency,			
and by circulation	T 37	T 37	
Printing statistics	T 15	T 15	

136

1860
Preliminary Report

Dubester 41--
continued

	United States	States & Territories	Counties Cities
Transportation			
See pages 103-106			
For locations, city railways			
Canals points connected	T 39	T 39	
Railroads, including city passenger rail- roads	T 38	T 38	T 38 - 7 major cities

Apportionment, Density and Geography

Apportionment 38th Congress	T 1	T 1	
See page 20			
Gain and loss			
Representative Population		1, p 20	
Density		p 121	

Vital Statistics

Deaths in census year	T 6	T 6	
By age and sex			
By sex and month			
By sex and cause			
By violent deaths, executions, by sex			
Death rates - see pages 22-25			

Foreign Data

Population			
British census 1861			p 112
Irish census			p 113
Scottish census			p 113
Disabilities			
Institutions of blind			p 41-45
Institutions for deaf and dumb			p 33
Institutions for insane			p 49
Immigration and Emigration			
Emigration from Ireland and Britain			p 113
Slavery - world wide			p 9
See also "Race and condition" above			
Vital Statistics			
Death rates in Europe			p 30

1870

Eleventh Census of the United States
Robert P. Porter, Superintendent

MAP
SHOWING IN FIVE DEGREES OF DENSITY THE DISTRIBUTION
UPON THE TERRITORY PART OF THE 100TH MERIDIAN
OF THE
POPULATION OF THE UNITED STATES
(excluding Indians and Alaska)
Compiled from the Returns of Population at the Ninth Census 1870.

Scale

LEGEND

1870

VOLUMES OF THE NINTH DECENNIAL CENSUS

Volume Title	Dubester Number
Book I The Statistics of the Population of the United States	Dubester 45
Book II Vital Statistics	Dubester 49
Book III Industry and Wealth	Dubester 52
Statistical Atlas	Dubester 55
Compendium	Dubester 57

<u>State and territories listed alphabetically in the following order:</u>

Alabama
Arizona Territory
Arkansas
California
Colorado Territory
Connecticut
Dakota Territory
Delaware
District of Columbia
Florida
Georgia
Idaho Territory
Illinois
Indiana
Iowa
Kansas
Kentucky
Louisiana
Maine
Maryland
Massachusetts
Michigan
Minnesota
Mississippi
Missouri
Montana Territory
Nebraska--new state
Nevada--new state
New Hampshire
New Jersey

New Mexico Territory
New York
North Carolina
Ohio
Oregon
Pennsylvania
Rhode Island
South Carolina
Tennessee
Texas
Vermont
Virginia
Washington Territory
West Virginia--new state
Wisconsin

Data for territory of Alaska is provided in some tables in the Compendium. See note on page 22 therein.

1870

THE NINTH DECENNIAL CENSUS

The Ninth Census is the one which is distinguished by its beautiful
maps. Three quarto volumes were published, as well as a statistical
atlas and a compendium. The three volumes and the atlas all have
colored maps, and the compendium is limited to statistical data from
each of the major volumes. The graphic presentation of census data,
begun with the 1870 volumes, continued for the remainder of the
Nineteenth Century.

The atlas, now quite rare, includes 54 color plates graphically
illustrating results of the census. Printed by J. Bien in New York
City, unlike the other volumes it was not a part of the Congressional
Serial set. Maps showing density of population, the distribution of
the foreign born, of literates, and of wealth are found in Volume I.
Age distribution, sex distribution, birth and death rates, and
distribution of those with disabilities are illustrated in the second
volume. The final volume presents the productions of agriculture in
graphic form.

The 1870 Census was of course also distinguished by the fact that
slavery had become a thing of the past with the ending of the Civil
War. The population schedule could thus become a single one for
"inhabitants" rather than one for "free inhabitants" and one for
"slave inhabitants." Two specific inquiries, under a heading of
"Constitutional Relations" were added to the schedule in this regard.
One called for "Male citizens of the U.S. of 21 years and upwards."
The second was an inquiry calling for a determination by the enumerator of "Male citizens of the U.S. of 21 years and upwards whose right
to vote is denied or abridged on other grounds than rebellion or
other crime." The requirement for enumerators in this question probably comes closest to the politicization of the census that has ever
occurred. Results of the effort to determine whether anyone was
being illegally refused the vote do not however appear in any of the
published census volumes.

Three lesser changes were also made in the population schedule.
Sufficient Chinese had entered the country to add a category for
their notation on the inquiry on color. "Indian" was also added as
an alternative. Indians "not taxed" were not to be enumerated, as
were "Indians out of their tribal relations, and exercising the
rights of citizens under State or Territorial laws."

If a child was under one year of age, the month of birth was to be
recorded by the enumerator. Details as to nativity of the population
were also increased, with columns on the schedule for indicating
whether the father and/or the mother were of foreign birth. The

results of these inquiries appear in the tables showing not only nativity of the population, but also parental nativity.

Instructions on completing the inquiry on "Profession, Occupation, or Trade of each person, male or female" were lengthy. "Call no man a 'Commissioner', a 'collector', an 'agent', an 'artist', an 'overseer', a 'professor', a 'treasurer', a contractor', or a 'speculator' without further explanation. . . . The term 'housekeeper' will be reserved for such persons as receive distinct wages or salary for such service. Women keeping house for their own families or for themselves, without any other gainful occupation, will be entered as 'keeping house.'" Grown daughters assisting them will be reported without occupation." (Instructions are cited in Twenty Censuses: Population and Housing Questions, 1790-1980).

The first volume of the 1870 Census thus contains the usual demographic data together with considerable data on nativity and occupation. It also contains reports on schools of all types, churches by denomination, libraries, as well as newspapers and periodicals, all gained from separate inquiries.

The second volume on vital statistics contains data on births and deaths, on the sex ratio, and on ages. Statistics on the disabled are also included in this volume. Maps are used to show the distribution of vital events and of disabled persons.

The volume entitled Wealth and Industry, which is sometimes discovered with a cover title of Industry and Wealth, includes the tables on agriculture, manufactures, mining and fisheries, and provides information on employment in each of these areas. Much of the extensive occupation data, a major section of Volume I, is duplicated in this third volume.

The Compendium was published in 1872, prior to the publication of the three main volumes. It contains data on all subjects included in them. It has smaller pages, but there are nearly 1000 of them.

The effort to publish the final reports of the 1870 Census was made somewhat earlier by the use of the first tabulating equipment to deal with the vast volume of data obtained from the census schedules. Many of the tables in the 1870 volumes include data from 1860 and 1850 adding considerably to their value.

Four new states had been admitted since publication of the 1860 volumes: Wisconsin, Nebraska and Nevada from territorial status, and West Virginia, which had been separated from Virginia. Four new territories had been established: Wyoming, Montana and Idaho, all originally parts of the Louisiana Purchase, and Arizona, from the Mexican cessions and the Gadsden Purchase. In addition, Alaska had been purchased from Russia in 1867 for $7,200,000 in gold. No data was to be included in the 1870 enumeration. Alaska would have to wait until 1880 and 1890 when special attention was given it by the publication of separate volumes on the new territory.

Decennial year	1870	Dubester 45

Census   Ninth Census

Volume   Volume I

Title   The Statistics of the Population of the
                  United States, embracing the tables of race,
                  nationality, sex, selected ages, and occupa-
                  tions. To which are added the statistics
                  of school attendance and illiteracy, of
                  schools, libraries, newspapers and periodi-
                  cals, churches, pauperism and crime, and of
                  areas, families, and dwellings . . .

Publication   Under the direction of the Secretary of the
                  Interior. Washington: Government Printing
                  Office

Date   1872

Congress   42d Congress, 1st Session

  House/Senate   House Miscellaneous Document unnumbered

  Serial   Serial 1473

Classifications

  Supt. of Documents   I 10.5: v. 1

  Library of Congress   HA201.1870. B1

    card   5-19328

  Dewey   q 317.3 Un309 v.1

Microforms

  National Archives   Film T825 Reel

  Research Publications Film 1870 Reel 1

Pages   xlix, 804 pages

Maps   Maps

Notes   By Francis A. Walker, Superintendent of
                  Census

1870   Dubester 45
Volume I - Statistics of the Population

This is the major volume of the 1870 Census. It contains statistics
on all characteristics of the population, including those gained from
the population schedules and others obtained from separate surveys.

Historical notes on areas, political organization, and geographical
divisions, which are found on pages 571 through 592 are the most precise descriptions of state and territorial boundaries which can be
found in any census volume for 1790 through 1890.

Tables which show data for all states and territories and a total for
the United States place territories at the bottom. Tables which provide separate pages for individual states and territories place
territories alphabetically within the list of states.

Occupation tables in this volume correspond to those in Volume III,
   Dubester 53, as follows:

Volume I	Volume III
XXVI	XVII
XXVIIA	XVIII
XXVIII	XIX
XXIX	XX

References are to table numbers.

	United States	States and Territory	Counties	Other*
Demographic Characteristics				
Aggregate population	I, IV,	I, II, IV	III	III
See page xvii	VI, XIX	VI, XIX	XXV(some)	VIII
	XXII	XXII,XXIV	XXIV	XXV
Historic from 1790	I	I, II		
Historic from 1850	IV, XIX	IV, XIX	III	III
Age				
School age, 5 to				
18 years	XXIII	XXIII,XXIV	XXIV,XXV	XXV
Militia age, males				
18 to 45	XXIII	XXIII,XXIV	XXIV,XXV	XXV
Voting age, males				
21 and up	XXIII	XXIII,XXIV	XXIV,XXV	XXV
Population 10 years				
and up	XXVI,	XXVI,		
	XXVIIA,	XXVIA		
	XXVIII	XXX		
	XXIX			
Occupation ages, 10-	XXVIII,	XXVIII,XXIX		
15, 16-59, 60 and up	XXIX	XXX		
Race	I,VI	I, II	III	III
	IX	VI, IX	X	VIII
	XIX	X, XIX		XI, XXI
	XXII	XXII,		
		XXIII		
Historic from 1790	I	I, II		
White, colored, also				
as free colored,				
slave, Chinese,				
Indian				
From 1850	XIX,XXII	XIX, XXII	III	III
Indians - those out				
of and those sus-				
taining tribal				
relations				
See page xvii				
Sex	IX, X	IX, X	XXIV, XXV	XI,XXV
	XIIA, B,	XIIA, XIII		
	XXII, XXIII	XXII, XXIII		
	XXVIIB	XXIV, XXVIIB		
	XXVIII	XXVIII, XXX		

*III--Civil divisions smaller than counties; XXX--Minor civil divisions; VII, XI, XXI--50 principal cities; XXXII--30 major cities

1870
Volume I - Statistics of the Population

	United States	States and Territory	Counties	Other*
Social and Economic Characteristics				
Crime	XIX	XIX		
Number convicted during year				
Number in prison, from 1850				
Education				
Schools				
See page 448	XIIA, B	XXIA, XIII		
From 1850	XIIA, B	XIIA		
School attendance,	IX, XIIA	IX, X	X	XI
pupils		XIIA, XIII		
from 1850	IX, XIIA	IX, XIIA		
Teachers	XIIA	XIIA, XIII		
From 1850	XIIA	XIIA		
Employment				
"See Occupations" below				
Families				
Number families, persons				
Per family	XX	XX		XXI
From 1850	XX	XX		By wards
Housing				
Number dwellings, persons				
per dwelling	XX	XX		XXI
				By wards
Literacy				
Illiterates 10 years and				
up cannot read	IX	IX, X	X	XI
Illiterates 10 to 15,				
15-21, 21 and up,				
cannot write	IX	IX, X	X	XI
Illiterates 20 and up,				
cannot read and write,				
for 1860 and 1850	IX	IX		
Nativity				
General nativity--native	IV,VI,IX	IV,V,VI	III,VII	III,
or foreign born	XIX, XXII	IX, X	X	VIII
	XXIII	XIX, XXII		
		XXIII		XXI
From 1850	IV, XXII	IV, XXII		
From 1860		V		

1870
Volume I - Statistics of the Population

	United States	States and Territory	Counties	Other*
Parental nativity	IV	IV, V	V	
Mother or father or both foreign born				
Specific nativity				
By state of birth, at sea under U.S. flag	VI	IV, V	V	
By foreign county, at sea under foreign flag	VI XXVIII, XXIX	VI XXVIII XXX	VII	VIII
Paupers				
See page 563				
Number persons supported, cost	XIX	XIX		
Occupations				
See pages 557-567 for classifications and comparisons				
Number in gainful and reputable occupations see page 659				
By 4 general classes of occupations agriculture, professional and personal service, trade and transportation, manufactures, mechanical and mining	XXVI,XXVIII	XXVI,XXVIII		
By specific occupation				
Both sexes	XXVIIA XXIX	XXVIIA XXX		XXXII
Females	XXVIIB	XXVIB		
Publications and Libraries				
Newspapers and periodicals	XV, XVI	XV		
See page 481				
By frequency, circulation, subject and type				
Libraries				
See page 472	XIVA, B	XIVA		
By type and number of volumes from 1850				

1870
Volume I - Statistics of the Population

	United States	States and Territory	Counties	Other*
Religion				
See page 501				
Churches, by denomina-	XVIIA,B	XVIIA		
tion, organization, edi-		XVIII		
fices, seats, property				
from 1805	XVIIA	XVIIA		

Apportionment, Density and Geography

	United States	States and Territory	Counties	Other*
Apportionment				
See pages ii-xvi				
Representative				
population	page xvii	page xvii		
Density	XX	XX		
Square miles, persons per				
Square mile, from 1850				
Geography	pages 571-594			
Extensive historical notes on				
area and political organiza-				
tion, acquisition of territory,				
boundaries of states				
Table of parcels				
added				
1780-1868	page 588			

Decennial year	1870	Dubester 49

Census   Tenth Census

Volume   Volume II

Title   The Vital Statistics of the United States,
                    embracing the tables of deaths, births, sex,
                    and age, to which are added the statistics
                    of the blind, the deaf and dumb, the in-
                    sane, and the idiotic

Publication   Under the direction of the Secretary of the
                    Interior. Washington: Government Printing
                    Office

Date   1872

Congress   42d Congress, 1st Session

House/Senate   House Miscellaneous Document unnumbered

Serial   Serial 1474

Classifications

Supt. of Documents I 10.5: v. 2

Library of Congress HA201.1870. B2

card   05-19334; 5-19328

Dewey   q 317.3 Un309 v.2

Microforms

National Archives   Film T825 Reels 8 and 9

Research Publications Film 1870 Reel 1

Pages   xxiii, 679 pages

Maps   Maps

Notes   By Francis A. Walker, Superintendent of
                    Census

1870   Dubester 49
Volume II - Vital Statistics

Contents	Tables	Pages

Age data are in 5 year intervals, single years to age 5
Race data are generally given as white, colored, Chinese and civilized
  Indian.
Specific nativity data are given by state and foreign countries of
  birth.
Texas data are given as East or West of the Colorado River.
States and territories are presented in a single alphabet, but not
  all tables provide data for all territories.

	United States	States and Territories

Demographic Characteristics

	United States	States and Territories
Age		
See pages 549-550 for remarks on age		
Aggregate population by age	RT I	
By sex	XXXII	XXIII
For 1860 and 1850	XXII	
By general nativity - native born	XXIV	XXIV
foreign born	XXV	XXV
Persons 80 years and over by single		
years and by general nativity and	XXXII	
race by age	XXII	
Race		
White	XXVI	XXVI
From 1860 and 1850		
Native white	XXVII	XXVII
Foreign born white	XXVIII	XXVIII
Colored	XXIX	XXIX
From 1860 and 1850		
Chinese	XXX	XXX
Civilized Indian	XXX	XXX

1870
Vital Statistics

Dubester 49--
continued

	United States	States and Territories
Sex		
By race and general nativity	XXI	XXI

Social and Economic Characteristics

Disabilities		
All disabilities by race and sex	X	X
Blind - by age, race and sex	XII	XII
By race, sex and specific nativity	XI	XI
Deaf and dumb, by age, race and sex	XIV	XIV
By race, sex and specific nativity	XIII	XIII
Idiotic, by age, race and sex	XVIII	XVIII
By race, sex and specific nativity	XVII	XVII
Insane, by age, race and sex	XVI	XVI
By race, sex and specific nativity	XV	XV

Vital Statistics

Births		
See pages 515-531 for remarks on construction of tables		
Births during census year, by month, and for 1860 and 1850 census years	XX	XX

Deaths		
Aggregate deaths during census year and for 1860 and 1850 census years	I	I
By age, including rate	II	II
By race	IV	IV
By sex	II	II
By race and sex	IX	
By general nativity	IV	IV
By specific nativity	IV	IV
By sex	III, III	I, II, III
By month	III	III
By cause		
For census year and 1860 and 1850 census years	p xvii	p xvii
By age and sex	V	V
By sex and month	VI	VI
By race and general nativity	VII	VII
By race and specific nativity	VII	VII
By specific occupation	VIII	VIII
By 12 principal causes of death	p xx	p xx
Life tables	RT II, III	

Foreign Data

Births - remarks and tables for England, Wales, France,
   Italy, Norway, Sweden   p 517
Life tables - England and Wales, Prussia   RT IV, V

Decennial year	1870	Dubester 52

Census   Ninth Census

Volume   Volume III

Title   The statistics of wealth and industry of
                     the United States, embracing the tables of
                     wealth, taxation, and public indebtedness;
                     of agriculture; manufactures; mining; and
                     the fisheries. With which are reproduced,
                     from the volume on population, the major
                     tables of occupations

Publication   Under the direction of the Secretary of the
                     Interior. Washington: Government Printing
                     Office

  Date   1872

Congress   42d Congress, 1st Session

  House/Senate   House Miscellaneous Document unnumbered

  Serial   Serial 1475

Classifications

  Supt. of Documents   I 10.5: v. 3

  Library of Congress   HA201.1870B24; HJ243.A45

    card   5-19336; 5-19328

  Dewey   q 317.3 Un309 v.3

Microforms

  National Archives   Film T825   Reel 9

  Research Publications   Film 1870   Reel 2

Pages   v, 843 pages

Maps   Maps

Notes   By Francis A. Walker, Superintendent of
                     Census; occupation tables repeated from
                     Volume I

1870   Dubester 52
Volume III - Statistics of Wealth and Industry

Contents	Tables	Pages
Remarks pertinent to the tables		3
Wealth, taxation and public indebtedness	I-II	3
Agriculture	III-VII	71
Manufactures	VIII-XI	371
Mining	XII-XV	748
Fisheries	XVI	791
Occupations	XVII	795
Errata		
No index		

Occupation tables in this volume correspond to Tables XXVI, XXVIIA, XXVIII and XXIX in Volume I.

	United States	States and Territories	Counties

Demographic Characteristics

No data

Social and Economic Characteristics

	United States	States and Territories	Counties
Employment	VIIIA	VIIIA	
See page 371			
Manufacturing and mechanical industries			
Hands employed, by sex	VIIIA	VIIIA, IXA	IXA
Hands employed, by industry	VIIB	VIIIB	
Males over 16, females over 15			
Youth			
From 1850			
Hands employed, by specific industry	VIIIC	VIIIC, IXB	IXB, XI
by state and county			
38 industry groups	X	X	
also for 1860 and 1850			
Fisheries			
Hands employed	XVI	XVI	
Males over 15, females over 16, youth			

Mining
  See page 748
  Hands employed, men and
    boys   XII   XII

Mining			
See page 748			
Hands employed, men and boys	XII	XII	
By mining industry, by state	XIV	XIV	
By state, by mining industry	XIII	XIII	
By county			XV
Farms			
See page 71			
Number of farms by size	VI	VI	
also for 1860 and 1850		VII	VII
Value of home manufactures on farms	III	III	
Wages paid on farms, including board	III	III, IV	IV
Occupations			
See page 795			
Tables identical to some tables in Volume I			
By crafts, also for 1860	p 802	p 802	
By occupational groups, by sex	XVII	XVII	

| Decennial year | 1870 | Dubester 55 |

Census   Ninth Census

Volume   Atlas

Title   Statistical atlas of the United States based on the results of the Ninth Census, 1870, with contributions from many eminent men of science and several departments of government.

Publication   Compiled under authority of Congress, New York, J. Bien, lithographer

Date   1874

Congress   Not a part of the Congressional Serial Set

Classifications

  Supt. of Documents   I 10.2: At6/1

  Library of Congress   HA201.1870.E

    card   05-19329

  Dewey   f 317.3 Un309A

Microforms

  National Archives   Film T825   Reel 2

  Research Publications Film 1870   Reel 12

Pages   Variously paged, LIV plates

Maps   Maps and diagrams

Notes   This is the first of the statistical atlases, which present data resulting from the Census in graphic form. This large volume, not a part of the Congressional Serial Set as is that for 1890, is now quite rare.

The Statistical Atlas was compiled by Francis A. Walker, Superintendent of the Ninth Census. It is very large, of folio size, and
unlike the other volumes, is not a part of the Congressional Serial
Set. Each of the three parts contains text as well as plates illustrating results of the Ninth Census. Each part is paginated separately. Tables are interspersed among the text.

Contents   Plates

Part I - Physical features of the United States   I-XIV
Part II - Population, Social and Industrial   XV-XXXVIB
  Statistics   XXXVII-LIV
Part III - Vital Statistics

	United States
Demographic Characteristics	
Aggregate population	XVI-XVIII
Pacific area from 1850	XXXVIB
Age	XXXVIII
	XXXIX
Race	XX-XXII
	XXXVIII
Sex	XXXVII-XXXIX
Pacific Area	XXXVIB
Social and Economic Characteristics	
Disabilities	XLVII-L
	LI-LIV
Income and property	XXXIII
Literacy	XXIX
	XXX

156

1870
Statistical Atlas

<u>Decennial year</u>	1870 Dubester 57
<u>Census</u>	Ninth Census
<u>Volume</u>	Compendium
<u>Title</u>	A Compendium of the Ninth Census: June 1, 1870
<u>Publication</u>	Compiled pursuant to a Concurrent Resolution of Congress. Washington: Government Printing Office
Date	1872
<u>Congress</u>	42d Congress, 1st Session
House/Senate	House Miscellaneous Document unnumbered
Serial	Serial 1476
<u>Classifications</u>	
Supt. of Documents	I 10.2: C73
Library of Congress	HA201.1870.C
card	5-19338
Dewey	317.3 Un309C
<u>Microforms</u>	
National Archives	Film T825 Reel 10
Research Publications	Film 1870 Reel 2
<u>Pages</u>	vii, 942 pages
<u>Notes</u>	By Francis A. Walker, Superintendent of Census

1870   Dubester 57
A Compendium of the Ninth Census

The 1870 Compendium was published in November 1872 prior to publication of the three main 1870 volumes. It contains data on population,
agriculture and manufactures as well as wealth, taxation, and indebtedness. Basic data on these subjects were soon to be published in
the three major volumes. The Compendium is of smaller, book size.

Territories, numbering eleven (Alaska, Arizona, Colorado, Dakota,
Idaho, Indian Territory, Montana, New Mexico, Utah, Washington, and
Wyoming) are listed at the bottom of the tables in Tables I-VII. In
other tables and those with data for single states or territories,
they are alphabetically interspersed with the states. Data for all
territories is _not_ given in all tables.

Race data is frequently stated as white or colored, with the latter
including Indians and Chinese.

All tables are numbered in Roman capitals.

Table IX - minor civil divisions - beats, precincts, or surveyed
townships; cities at first indention, towns at second indention.
Tables XIX, XXVII, XLVII, LXVI - fifty largest cities

Contents   Tables   Pages

Annual report of the Superintendent of
   the Census for 1871   1-7

Population, with Race   I-IX   8-373
Nativity and Nationality   X-XX   376-449
School Attendance and Illiteracy   XXI-XXVII   452-483
Schools, Libraries, Newspapers, and Churches   XXVIII-XLII 486-527
Pauperism and Crime   XLIII-XLV   530-538
Areas, Families and Dwellings   XLVI-XLVII   540-543
Sex, and School, Military and Citizenship Ages   XLVIII-LVII 546-592
Occupations   LVIII-LXXI   594-624
The Blind, Deaf and Dumb, Insane and Idiotic   LXXII-LXXIX 626-633
Wealth, Taxation and Public Indebtedness   LXXX-LXXXIII 636-686
Agriculture   LXXXIV-XCV   688-793
Manufactures, Mining and Fisheries   XCVI-CV   796-942

References are to table number.

1870
A Compendium of the Ninth Census

Dubester 57--
continued

	United States	States and Territory	Counties	Other
Demographic Characteristics				
Aggregate population	I, VII, XLIII, XLVIII	I,VII, VIII XLIII XLVIII LVII	VIII LVII	IX XIX, XXVII XLVII
Historic to 1790	I, V	I,V,VIII	VIII	
Age				
School ages, 5 to 18 years	XXI	XXI	LVII	
Militia age, males 15-45	LV	LV	LVII	
Voting age--males 21 and up	LVI	LVI	LVII	
Occupation ages				
Population 10 years and up	LVIII	LVIII		
Population 10-15, 16-50, 60 and up	LIX,LXV	LIX		
Race and condition	II-VII	II,VII,VIII	VIII	IX
White	II,VII, XIII,XXI XXIV, XLII,XLIX	XXI,XXI XXIV,XLIII XLIX	VIII	XVII, XLVII
Colored	III,VII, XIII,XXI XXIV,XLIII L,LI	III, VII, VIII, XXI XXIV,XLIII, L,LII,LIII		
Free colored	IV	IV		
Slave	V	V		
Chinese	VI,VII, XXI,XXIV LIII	VI,VII, XI,XXIV, LIII		XLVII
Japanese	VI,VII	VI,VII		
Civilized Indian See page 19	VI,VII, XXI,XXIV LIV	VI,VII, VIII,XXI XXIV,LIV	VIII	XLVII
From 1790	I-V	I-V,VIII	VIII	
Sex	XXI,XXIV XXVIII, XLVIII LVIII	XXI,XXIV, XXIV, XXVIII, XLVIII,	LVIII	

160

1870
A Compendium of the Ninth Census

	United States	States and Territory	Counties	Other
	LXV LXXII- LXXIX XCVI,XCVII, XCVIII, XCVIX	LVII,LVIII, LXXII- LXXIX XCVI,XCVII, XCVIII,C,CI		

Social and Economic Characteristics

Citizenship
  male citizens | LVI | LVI,LVII | LVII | |

Crime
  See note page 537
  Persons convicted during
    year | XLIII | XLIII | | |
  Number in prison, by race
    and general nativity | | | | |

Disabilities	LXXII	LXXII		
See page 626				
Blind	LXXIII	LXXIII		
Deaf and dumb	LXXIV,LXXV	LXXIV,LXXV		
Idiotic	LXXVIII, LXXIX	LXXVIII LXXIX		
Insane	LXXVI, LXXVII	LXXVI, LXVII		

Education
  See page 486
Schools	XXVII- XXXIII	XXVIII- XXVIV		
School attendance, from 1850	XXI,XXII	XXI-XXIII		XXVII
Pupils	XXVIII- XXXIII	XXVIII, XXXIV		
Teachers	XXVIII- XXXIII	XXVIII- XXXIV		

Employment
  Hands employed
    In manufactures, males
      16 and up, females 15
      and up, children | XCVI,XCVIII XCVIII, | XCVI,XCVII XCVIII,C, | | |

1870
A Compendium of the Ninth Census

	United States	States and Territory	Counties	Other
	XCIX, CII,CIII	CI		
In mining, men and boys above and below ground	CIV	CIV		
In fisheries, males 16 and up, females 15 and up, children	CV	CV		
Families	XLVI	XLVI		XLVII
Number families				
Number persons per family				
From 1850				
Farms				
See page 688	LXXXIV	LXXXIV		
Land in farms, average		XCV		
Size of farm				
From 1850				
Housing	XLVI	XLVI		XLVII
Number dwellings				
Number persons per dwelling				
From 1850				
Literacy				
Illiterates 10 years and up				
Cannot read	XXIV	XXIV		XXVII
Cannot write	XXIV	XXIV		
Illiterates 20 years and up				
cannot read and write	XXV,XXVI	XXV,XXVI		
Nativity				
General nativity - native or foreign born	X,XXIV XLIII, XLVIII XLIX, L,LVI	X,XXIV, XLII,XLIII, LXIX,L-LVI		IX XXVII LXVI, LXVII
From 1850	X	X		
Specific nativity				
By state of birth	XI-XIII	XI-XIII	XVIII	XIX

1870
A Compendium of the Ninth Census

	United States	States and Territory	Counties	Other
By country of birth	XIV	XIV	XVIII	XX
Germany by states and free cities	XV	XV		
British by area	XVI	XVI		
	LX-LXV	LX-LXVI		
Occupations				
See note page 594				
Number engaged in gainful useful occupations	LVIII-LX	LVIII-LX		LXVI, LXVII
Number in each of 4 groups of occupations	LVIII LIX	LVIII LIX		LXVI, LXVII
Specific occupations	LXV			
Paupers				
See note page 530				
Persons supported and cost	XLIII-XLV	XLII-XLV		
For 1860	XLIV	XLIV		
For 1850	XLV	XLV		
Publications and Libraries				
Newspapers	XXXVII-XXXIX	XXXIX		
By type	XXVII			
By frequency	XXVIII			
Libraries				
Number, number volumes, by type of library	XXXV,XXXVI	XXXVI		
From 1850	XXXV			
Religion				
See notes page 514				
Churches- by denomination, organization, edifices, seats, property From 1850	XL,XLI	XLI,XLII		

Apportionment, Density, Geography

	United States	States and Territory	Counties	Other
Apportionment				
"True population" see page 22	II,VII	VII		
Density				
See notes page 542 Density from 1850	XLVI	XLVI		

164

1880

VOLUMES OF THE TENTH DECENNIAL CENSUS

Volume Title		Dubester Number
Volume I	Statistics of the Population of the United States	Dubester 61
Volume II	Report on the manufactures of the United States	Dubester 63
Volume III	Report on the production of agriculture	Dubester 75
Volume IV	Report on the agencies of transportation	Dubester 82
Volume V VI	Report on cotton production--two parts	Dubester 89 Dubester 90
Volume VII	Report on valuation, taxation, and public indebtedness	Dubester 105
Volume VIII	The newspaper and periodical press. Alaska: Its population, industries and resources. The seal islands of Alaska. Ship-building industry in the United States.	Dubester 107
Volume IX	Report on the forests of North America. Portfolio of 16 maps.	Dubester 112
Volume X	Production technology, and uses of petroleum and its products.	Dubester 113
Volume XI XII	Report on mortality and vital statistics	Dubester 117 Dubester 118
Volume XIII	Statistics and technology of the precious metals	Dubester 119
Volume XIV	The United States Mining Laws	Dubester 122
Volume XV	Report on the mining industries of the United States	Dubester 123

Volume Title		Dubester Number
Volume XVI XIX	Report on the water-power of the United States--two parts	Dubester 125 Dubester 134
Volume XVIII XIX	Report on the social statistics of cities, 2 parts.	Dubester 141 Dubester 142
Volume XX	Report on the statistics of wages in manufacturing industries	Dubester 144
Volume XXI	Report on the defective, dependent and delinquent classes of the population	Dubester 145
Volume XXII	Report on power and machinery employed in manufactures	Dubester 146
Compendium	Compendium of the Tenth Census (issued as 2 parts and also with both parts combined in one volume)	Dubester 153
	Apportionment under Tenth Census of the United States	Dubester 155
	The oyster industry	Dubester 156
	The seal-islands of Alaska	Dubester 157
	Statistics of manufactures in the cities of Baltimore, Boston, Brooklyn, Buffalo, Chicago, Cincinatti, Cleveland, Detroit, Jersey City, Louisville, Milwaukee, Newark, New Orleans, New York, Philadelphia, Pittsburgh, Providence, San Francisco, St. Louis, Washington during the cen- sus year.	Dubester 158
	Tabulated statements of the traffic and fiscal operations of the railroads.	Dubester 159

Extra Census Bulletins

	The area of the United States, the several states and territories and their counties.	Dubester 162

1880--continued

Volume Title	Dubester Number
Report on the manufacture of fire-arms and ammunition.	Dubester 164
Statistics of life insurance.	Dubester 165
Cereal production of the United States.	Dubester 166
System of courts of criminal jurisdiction.	Dubester 168

States listed in alphabetical order:

Alabama	Nevada	Territories of:
Arkansas	New Hampshire	
California	New Jersey	Arizona
Colorado--new state	New York	Dakota
Connecticut	North Carolina	District of Columbia
Delaware	Ohio	Idaho
Florida	Oregon	Montana
Georgia	Pennsylvania	New Mexico
Illinois	Rhode Island	Utah
Indiana	South Carolina	Washington
Iowa	Tennessee	Wyoming
Kansas	Texas	
Kentucky	Vermont	States and territories
Louisiana	Virginia	presented in single
Maine	West Virginia	alphabetical order in
Maryland	Wisconsin	some tables, and territories at end of tables in others
Massachusetts		
Michigan		
Minnesota		
Mississippi		Alaska treated separately
Missouri		
Nebraska		

1880

THE TENTH DECENNIAL CENSUS

Twenty-two volumes, a compendium, and a number of separate bulletins and other reports were published as a result of the 1880 Census-- doubtless more volumes and more pages than all previous nine censuses combined.

The act which provided for the 1880 Census called for the appointment by the President of a Superintendent of the Census, the establishment of a census office in the Department of the Interior, and appoint- ments of supervisors and enumerators under the authority of the Superintendent. A large number of special agents were appointed with assignments as to distinct subject matter, resulting in the publica- tion of a number of additional volumes.

The first volume contains the major findings from the population inquiries. New questions were added on the relationship of each per- son to the head of the family or household, one on marital status, two additional questions on "Health" dealing with temporary disability on the day of the census and one on "maimed, crippled, bedridden or otherwise disabled," in addition to the four disability items asked in prior years. There was a question for the first time on unemploy- ment during the census year. The emphasis on interest in national background was exemplified by a question on place of birth of each person's parents, a change from 1870 which simply inquired whether they were of foreign birth. Answers to these questions resulted in numerous tabulations and cross-tabulations by national background.

In addition to Volume I entitled Population, other volumes resulting from the inquiries on the general schedule included one in vital statistics and one on the "defective, dependent and delinquent classes."

The agriculture data resulted in one volume on that subject in addi- tion to two on cotton production. A volume on the forests of North America together with a portfolio of 16 maps, now very rare, provides extensive data on irrigaton systems developed in the West.

In addition to the volume on manufacturers one was published on wages in manufacturing industries. A special effort was made to determine how many essentials could be purchased with wages in individual cities, making this report a valuable one for population study. A third volume on power and machinery employed in manufactures is chiefly interesting for learning about the state of the art.

One volume on the newspaper and periodical press is useful as well as interesting. In addition to listing newspapers in each community, it provides considerable information on communications of the day. The same volume includes two sections on Alaska and one on the ship-building industry.

Contacts in major cities were requested to furnish information on their communities. Although this method resulted in variations in the amounts of data, all of it is useful for learning about over two hundred cities in 1880.

There were additional reports on transportation, on valuation, taxation and public indebtedness, one on petroleum, coke and building stones, and three on metal and mining. Considerable information on individual mining communities appears in the volume on mining laws.

A great deal of the information is compiled in the compendium, which was published in two forms, a single volume and two volumes, each format having nearly 1800 pages.

Data on apportionment was sent to Congress in a House Executive document in 1881, before the main census volumes were published. Another short bulletin was published on the areas of the United States by Henry Gannett, responsible for the excellent maps in 1880.

Colorado was the only new state to join the Union between 1870 and 1880. The territories of Dakota, Idaho, Montana, Washington and Wyoming were to wait for statehood until the next decade, Utah until 1896, and Arizona and New Mexico, 1912. Alaska was of such interest that two sections of an entire volume were published for that far off territory, but its admission as a state was to wait until 1959.

Decennial year	1880	Dubester 61

Census   Tenth Census

Volume   Volume I

Title   Statistics of the population of the United States . . . embracing extended tables of the population of states, counties, and minor civil divisions, with distinction of race, sex, age, nativity, and occupations.

Publication   Department of the Interior, Census Office; Washington: Government Printing Office

Date   1883

Congress   47th Congress, 2d Session, Volume 13 Part 1

House/Senate   House Miscellaneous Document 42, Part 1

Serial   Serial 2129

Classifications

Supt. of Documents   I 11.5: v. 1

Library of Congress   HA201.1880.B 1 v. 1

card   7-18862

Dewey   q 317.3 Un310 v. 1

Microforms

National Archives   Film T825 Reels 10 and 11

Research Publications   Film 1880 Reel 1

Pages   lxxxix, 961 pages

Maps   Maps and charts

Notes   By Francis A. Walker, Superintendent

1880
Volume I - Population

The introduction to this volume is a general discussion of the move-
ments of population from 1790 to 1880 by Frances A. Walker and Henry
Gannett. It includes maps for each decade "showing in five degrees
of density" the distribution of population as well as the extent of
the movement westward, and the current name and boundary of each
territory for each census. It describes population developments, the
extent of the frontier, settled and vacant areas, density of population, and centers of population, and comments on sex and race distribution, foreign born, and the influence of physical features of the
land on the population. The appendix cites the census district for
each supervisor and shows his name.

Volume I has two sets of tables, both numbered in Roman numerals.
The first set of 46 tables is in the introductory section, the pages
of which are also numbered in Roman. The second set is in the main
body of the volume, and pages are numbered in Arabic. Where material
is referred to in the table guide, tables in the introductory section
are referred to by page, and those in the main part are referred to
by Roman numerals.

Because of the inevitable confusion, it is suggested that anyone
searching for very specific information (such as the number of
foreign born from the German Empire in the population of Monroe
County, Illinois) use the extensive index pages, where both the
entries "foreign-born" and "Illinois" would lead one to page 504,
where one would find that 2529 of the 3187 of the foreign born in
Monroe County were from the German Empire, of a total population of
10,495.

Contents	Tables	Pages
Introduction - Includes 46 tables numbered in Roman numerals, referred to on the following pages by page number only		1
Progress of the Nation 1790-1880		xi
Elements of the Population		xxxiv
Influence of the physical features on the distribution of the population		xlii
Appendix - Supervisors' districts		lxxix
General Population tables		
I Population by states and territories	I a-kk	1-45
II Population by states and territories, all censuses 1790-1880	II	47-86
III Population of civil divisions less than counties	III	87-375

1880
Volume I - Population

Dubester 61--
continued

	Tables	Pages
Population by race, sex and nativity	IV-XIX	378-545
Population by ages, specific and select	XX-XXIII	548-666
Areas, dwellings and families	XXIV-XXV	668-671
Foreign parentage	XXVI-XXVII	674-692
Alaska population	XXVIII	693-699
Occupations	XXIX-XXXVI	703-909
Miscellaneous statistics		
Newspapers and periodicals	M I-IV	912-915
Public schools	M V-VIII	916-918
Illiteracy	M VIII	919-925
Defective, dependent and delinquent	M IX-XI	926-929
Index - extensive index, cities tables and page number by state and territory, city, subject		931-961

Upper case Roman numerals - Population tables
Lower case Roman numerals - Introductory section page numbers
Some tables include territories in alphabetical listing of states

Tables for "Other" (areas) smaller than states
II, III - minor civil divisions and unincorporated places
VI, IX, XII, XIII - cities and towns of 4,000
XXV - 100 largest cities
XV, XVI, XXXV - 50 largest cities

	United States	States and Territory	Counties	Other
Demographic Characteristics				
Aggregate population	I a	I a	II	III
	I b	I b	III	
	M VIII	M VIII		XXXV
				XXV
Historic from 1790	I c	I c	II	II
from 1870			III	III
Alaska--including divisions, by race		XXVIII	XXVIII	

1880
Volume I - Population

	United States	States and Territory	Counties	Other
Age				
Single years by race, sex and general nativity	XX	XXI		
School age 5-17 by sex	XXII	XXII	XXIII	XXIII
By race and general nativity (white)	XXII	XXII		
Natural militia males 18-44	XXII	XXII	XXII	XXII
By race and general nativity (white)	XXII	XXII		
Voting age males 21 and up	XXII	XXII	XXIII	XXIII
By race and general nativity (white)	XXII	XXII		
Race				
Notes pages xxxvi	I a	I a		XXV
From 1860	IV	IV V	V	
From 1870				VI
By sex and general nativity				
White	XVIII	XVIII		
Colored, Chinese, Japanese, civilized Indian	XIX	XIX		
Sex				
Notes pages xxxiv	I a XVII M VIII	I a XVII M VIII		XXXV
By race, white	XVIII	XVIII		
Colored, Chinese, Japanese, Civilized Indian	XIX	XIX		
By general nativity	XVIII	XVIII		
Colored, Chinese, Japanese, Civilized Indian	XIX	XIX		

Social and Economic Characteristics

	United States	States and Territory	Counties	Other
Crime and imprisonment				
Prisoners by race	M XI	M XI		
By sex				
By general nativity				

1880   Dubester 61--
Volume I - Population   continued

	United States	States and Territory	Counties	Other
Disabilities	M IX	M IX		
Blind, deaf mutes, idiotic and insane				
By race				
By sex				
By general nativity				
Education and Schools				
Public school pupils	M VII	M VII		
By race and sex				
Average daily attendance by race				
Public school teachers	M VI	M VI		
By race and sex				
Policies, total months paid				
Public schools	M V	M V		
By level				
Number for colored children				
Buildings and seats				
Finances				
Families	XXIV	XXIV	XXV	
Number families				
Persons to a family from 1850	XXIV	XXIV		
Housing	XIV	XXIV	XXV	
Number dwellings				
Persons to a dwelling from 1850	XXIV	XXIV		
Immigration and Migration				
Notes pages 457-479				
By foreign country, decades from 1821 to 1850, page 459-464				
Migration - see nativity pages 472-476				
Literacy				
Persons 10 years and over	M VIII	M VIII		
Unable to read, number and %				

1880
Volume I - Population

	United States	States and Territory	Counties	Other
Persons unable to write by age groups 10 and over, 10-14, 15-20, 21 and over	M VIII	M VIII		
By race, sex and general nativity (white)				
Nativity and foreign parentage notes on place of birth, tables on pages xxxix-xli, 457-479; and foreign parentage 674-679				
General nativity	I a	I a VIII	VIII	p 471 50 cities
From 1860	VII	VII		
From 1870		VIII	VIII	IX
By sex	XVII	XVII		
By race - white	XVIII	XVIII		
colored	XIX	XIX		
By nativity of parents	XXVI	XXVI		
Specific nativity				
By state	X	X	XIV	XV
By race - Native white	XI	XI		
Native colored	XII	XII		
By foreign country	XIII	XIII p 465-469	XIV	p 469 total 50 cities
Of parents	XXVI	XXVI XXVII		XVI,XXXV p 675 NY
Occupations				
Notes pages 703-711				
Number in occupations, % population	p 705			
Occupational groups-four	XXIX	XXIX	XXXV	
Agriculture, professional and personal, trade and transportation, and manufacturing, mechanical, mining	XXX	XXX		

1880
Volume I - Population

	United States	States and Territory	Counties	Other
By sex	XXIX	XXIX		
By age and sex	XXX	XXX		
By nativity, specific foreign countries	XXX	XXX		
Specific occupations				
20 occupations	XXXI	XXXI		
265 occupations	XXXII			
By nativity, specific foreign countries				
265 occupations	XXIII	XXIII		
A--All occupied persons				
B--Males				
C--Females				
Approximately 75 occupations		XXXIV		XXXVI 50 cities
By age group and sex				
By nativity				
Paupers	M X	M X		
Aggregate number				
Inmates of almshouses				
Outdoor paupers				
Publications and Libraries				
Newspapers and publications				
By frequency, circulation	M I	M I		
By type, characteristic	M II	M II		
By language	M III	M III		
Religions, by denomination	M IV	M IV		
Religion and churches	M IV	M IV		
Religious newspapers, by denominations				

Apportionment, Density, Geography

	United States	States and Territory	Counties	Other
Density	p xxvii I d	p xxvii I d		
		XXVIII	XXVIII	

1880
Volume I - Population

	United States	States and Territory	Counties	Other
From 1790	I d	I d		
From 1850	XXIV	XXIV		
Settled and vacant areas	p xxi			
Urban areas and cities	p xxvii			
Center of population	p xxxi			
By latitude and longitude	p LXVII			
Population as related to topographical and geographical features	I e p XLII	I e		
By race--colored	I f	I f		
By nativity--foreign population	I g	I g		
By elevation	I h,i,j,k	I h,i,j,k		
By temperature mean annual	I l,m,n,o	I l,m,n,o		
mean July	I p,q,r,s	I p,q,r,s		
mean January	I t,u,v,w	I t,u,v,w		
maximum	I x,y,z,aa	I x,y,z,aa		
minimum	I bb,cc, dd,ee	I bb,cc, dd,ee		
By annual rainfall Spring and summer rainfall	I ii,jj,kk	I ii,jj,kk		

<u>Decennial year</u>	1880	Dubester 63
		separates 64-74
<u>Census</u>	Tenth Census	
<u>Volume</u>	Volume II	

<u>Title</u> Report on the manufactures of the United States . . . embracing general statistics and monographs on power used in manu- factures; the factory system; interchange- able mechanism; hardware, cutlery, etc.; iron and steel, silk manufacture, cotton manufacture; woolen manufacture; chemical products and salt; glass manufacture.

<u>Publication</u> Department of the Interior, Census Office; Washington: Government Printing Office

Date 1883

<u>Congress</u> 47th Congress, 2d Session, Volume 13 Part 2

House/Senate House Miscellaneous Document 42, Part 2

Serial Serial 2130

<u>Classifications</u>

Supt. of Documents I 11.5: v. 2

Library of Congress HA201.1880.B 1 v. 2   HD9514.S95 1881a (iron and steel)
TP857.U6 (glass)

card 7-18862

Dewey q 317.3 Un310 v. 2

<u>Microforms</u>

National Archives Film T825 Reels 12 and 13

Research Publications Film 1880 Reel M-1

<u>Pages</u> xlix, 1198 pages

<u>Maps</u> Maps and illustrations

<u>Notes</u> By Herman Hollerith (power); Carroll D. Wright (factory system); Charles H. Fitch (interchangeable mechanisms, hardware); James Swank (iron and steel); William Wychoff (silk); Edward Atkinson (cotton); George William Bond (wood); Wm. L. Rowland (chemicals and salt); Jos. D. Weeks (glass)

178

Contents	Tables	Pages numbered at bottom

Most tables show men above 16 employed, women above 15 employed, and
  children and youth employed, as well as average number of hands
  employed.

	United States	States and Territory	Counties	Other

Demographic Characteristics

Aggregate population	p xvi	p xvi		p xxiii 100 cities

	United States	States and Territory	Counties	Other
Social and Economic Characteristics				
Employment				
In manufactures				
Hands employed				
Males 16 and over				
Females 15 and over				
Children and youth		IVA	IVA	p xxiii 100 cities
From 1850	I	I		VI
Males under 16, females under 15, by sex and age		p xxxv		p xxxv
Rank of manufactures by number of hands employed				p xxiv
By industry	II	IVB	V	VI
By state	III,VII	III,VII		
Cotton industry, by sex and age males under 16, females under 15; youth and children	p 543 p 955	p 543 p 955		
Manufacture of agricultural implements	p 690	p 690		
Iron and steel, from 1870	p 737 p 750	p 750-761	p 761-768	
Woolen industry	p 964	p 967		
Chemical products and salt	p 994 p 1000 p 1014	p 1014 p 1020		
Glass industry	p 1043			
Manufacturing, mechanical and mining industries - hands employed, by sex and age groups, by general nativity		p xxx	p xxx	p xxxiii 50 cities
By specific nativity		p xxxvii		p xxxviii
Farms				
Rank in number of farms v. number of manufacturing establishments		p xii		

1880
Volume II Manufactures

	United States	States and Territory	Counties	Other
Housing				
Housing provided for workers, plates of elevations and floor plans	p 604			
Income				
By specific establishments, by sex, wage rates for factories, from 1840		p 578		
Iron and steel industry wages	p 847			
Occupations				
By general and specific nativity	p xxxvi			
By specific establishments, factories	p 578			

Foreign Data

Housing--provided for workers in England, France, Belgium and Germany		p 604
Income--iron and steel industry wages in Britain		p 877

Decennial year   1880   Dubester 75
                                                separates 76-81

Census   Tenth Census

Volume   Volume III

Title   Report on the production of agriculture . . .
                        embracing general statistics and monographs
                        on cereal production; flour-milling;
                        culture and curing of tobacco; manufacture
                        and movement of tobacco; and meat production

Publication   Department of the Interior, Census Office;
                        Washington: Government Printing Office

  Date   1883

Congress   47th Congress, 2d Session, Volume 13 Part 3

  House/Senate   House Miscellaneous Document 42, Part 3

  Serial   Serial 2131

Classifications

  Supt. of Documents   I 11.5: v. 3

  Library of Congress   HA201.1880.B 1 v. 3   HD9034.B8 (cereal)

    card   7-18862

  Dewey   q 317.3 Un 310 v. 3

Microforms

  National Archives   Film T825 Reel 13

  Research Publications Film 1880 Reel A-1

Pages   xxxii, 1149 pages

Maps   Maps and illustrations

Notes   By William H. Brewer (cereal); Knight
                        Neftel (flour-milling); J. B. Killebrew
                        (tobacco culture); J. R. Dodge (tobacco
                        manufacture, distribution); Clarence W.
                        Gordon (cattle, sheep and swine)

This is primarily a volume on agriculture and the production of farms. However in its essays, it provides considerable information on the lives and habits of farmers and ranchers. Anyone studying rural population during the period of this Census would do well to peruse this volume.

The writers and compilers of the volume have made use of sources other than the census schedules for the extensive essays, sources which historians would look upon favorably as primary materials.

For example, one citation is from the "narrative of a sheepman of San Saba County, Texas, listing his "investments including in addition to the cost of sheep the expenditures for cooking utensils and quilts." This example is found in the chapter on production of meat, Texas, page 27.

References in upper case Roman numerals are to table numbers. References in lower case Roman numerals following a "p" are page numbers.

	United States	States and Territory	Other
Social and Economic Characteristics			
Farms			
Number of farms	I,II	I,II	V,VII
	VI	V,VI,VII	
From 1850	I		
From 1860	p xiv	II	
Land in farms	I,VI	I,II,VI	VII
		VII	
Improved and unimproved	I,VI	VI,VII	VII
From 1850	I		
From 1860	p xiv	II	
Average size of farm--			
number acres	I	I	
From 1860	p xiv	II,III	
By specific size of farm	III	III	
Tenure of farmers--owned,			
fixed rental, shares	p xiv	V	V
By specific size	IV	IV	
Value of farms	I,VI	VI,VII	VII
From 1850	I		
Percentage improved and			
unimproved	II	II	
From 1860	II	II	

1880
Volume III - Agriculture

Foreign Data

Grain consumption per capita, production estimates   p 382
    European countries, Canada

| Decennial year | 1880 | Dubester 82 |
| | | separates 83-87 |

Census

Tenth Census

Volume

Volume IV

Title

Report on the agencies of transportation in the United States, including the statistics of railroads, steam navigation, canals, telegraphs, and telephones

Publication

Department of the Interior, Census Office; Washington: Government Printing Office

Date

1883

Congress

47th Congress, 2d Session, Volume 13 Part 4

House/Senate

House Miscellaneous Document 42, Part 4

Serial

Serial 2132

Classifications

Supt. of Documents

I 11.5: v. 4

Library of Congress

HA201.1880.B 1 v. 4

card

7-18862

Dewey

q 317.3 Un310 v. 4

Microforms

National Archives

Film T825   Reels 13 and 14

Research Publications

Film 1880   Reel T-1

Pages

869 pages

Notes

By Armin E. Shuman, expert (railroads and telegraphs and telephones); T. C. Purdy, special agent (steam navigation and canals)

1880   Dubester 82
Volume IV - Transportation

_____

This volume contains considerable information on the names of railroads, the condition of steam vessels, the construction of canals,
points connected, telegraph messages and telephone lines. There are
a number of maps.

References are to page numbers except where a T precedes a Roman
numeral to indicate a table number.

	United States	States and Territory	Other
Social and Economic Characteristics			
Employment			
Railroad employees	p 20		
By region	T VI	T VI	
Steamship crews	p 691	p 691	
Telegraph employees	p 773, 775		
Income			
Railroad	p 20		
Transportation			
Railroad passengers, passenger miles	p 11, 19		
By railroad	T IV		
Railroad accidents--killed, injured	p 13		
By regions	p 14		
Steamship passengers	p 702		

1880
Volume IV - Transportation

Apportionment, Density and Geography

Geography
  Population density compared
    to miles of railroads
    completed, from 1840   p 317

Vital Statistics

Deaths from railroad accidents   T VII
  By region and by railroad
Deaths from construction of
  steamboats from 1807   p 662

Foreign Data

  Postal telegraphs--European
    countries   p 805

187

Decennial year	1880	Dubester 89 and 98 separates 90-97 separates 99-104

Census   Tenth Census

Volume   Volumes V and VI

Title   Report on cotton production in the United
                  States; also embracing agriculture and
                  physico-geographical descriptions of the
                  several cotton states and of California,
                  Parts 1 and 2.

Publication   Department of the Interior, Census Office;
                  Washington: Government Printing Office

  Date   1884

Congress   47th Congress, 2d Session, Volume 13,
                  Parts 5 and 6

  House/Senate   House Miscellaneous Document 42, Parts 5
                  and 6

  Serial   Serial 2133 and 2134

Classifications

  Supt. of Documents   I 11.5: v. 5 and v. 6

  Library of Congress   HA201.1880.B 1 v. 5 and 6

    card   7-18862; HD9071-7

  Dewey   q 317.3 Un310 v. 5 and 6

Microforms

  National Archives   Film T825 Reels 14 (Part 1) and 15 (Part 2)

  Research Publications   Film 1880 Reels A-1 and A-2

Pages   Part 1 - v, 924 pages; Part 2 - 848 pages

Notes   By Eugene Woldemar Hilgard, special agent
                  in charge.
                  Part I inclues Louisiana, Mississippi,
                  Tennessee and Kentucky, Missouri, Arkansas,
                  Texas and Indian Territory. Part 2 includes
                  Alabama, Florida, Georgia, South Carolina,
                  North Carolina, New Mexico, Utah and Arizona

---

This is a two volume set which provides considerable detail on cotton agriculture. Following a general discussion and statistical tables on the entire cotton raising area, cotton farming in each state is discussed in detail.

In addition to data on each area, with population by sex and race, there is data on the amount of land tilled, a list of other crops, and reproduction of answers to a schedule of some 56 questions for individual areas. Names of correspondents for each area are published. One section of the questions deals with "Labor and system of farming."

Note that page numbers are those at the bottom of each page, as each state section is paginated separately at the top of the page.

Information on each state is presented as follows:

	Pages numbered at bottom
Contents	
Contents for each state	
Tabulated results of the enumeration	Tables I and II
Part I - Physico-geographical and agricultural features	Table III
Part II - Agricultural occupations of the counties	
Part III - Cultural and economic details--including names of correspondents and summaries of answers to schedule of questions	

Part I

1880   Dubester 89 and 98
Volumes V and VI - Cotton Production   continued

Part II

	United States	States and Territory	Geo-graphical Regions	Counties
Demographic Characteristics				
Aggregate population of agricultural regions	Cotton states Table II page 5	Table II, page 5 Table I each state		
Race White and colored	Table II	Table I III	Table I III	Table I
Sex		Table I		
Social and Economic Characteristics				
Employment Farming practices, labor		Schedule	Schedule	
Farms Size of farms		Schedule	Schedule	
Housing Home ownership of laborers		Schedule	Schedule	
Income Manner of payment, wages, system of credits		Schedule	Schedule	

Schedule--answers to questions on the "Schedule" of 56 inquiries,
         found in Part III for each state

<u>Decennial year</u>	1880	Dubester 105

<u>Census</u>   Tenth Census

<u>Volume</u>   Volume VII

<u>Title</u>   Report on valuation, taxation and public indebtedness in the United States

<u>Publication</u>   Department of the Interior, Census Office; Washington: Government Printing Office

Date   1884

<u>Congress</u>   47th Congress, 2d Session, Volume 13 Part 7

House/Senate   House Miscellaneous Document 42, Part 7

Serial   Serial 2135

<u>Classifications</u>

Supt. of Documents   I 11.5: v. 7

Library of Congress   HA201.1880.B 1 v. 7

card   7-18862

Dewey   q 317.3 Un310 v. 7

<u>Microforms</u>

National Archives   Film T825 Reels 15 and 16

Research Publications   Film 1880 Reel 4

<u>Pages</u>   x, 909 pages

<u>Maps</u>   Maps and charts

<u>Notes</u>   Compiled under the direction of Robert P. Porter, special agent

1880   Dubester 105
Volume VII - Valuation, taxation and
public indebtedness

Most of the tables in this volume in the 1980s would be included in
the Census of Governments, rather than a Census of Population. Only
those tables which reflect population data are included in the table
guide below.

There is considerable historical data on foreign debt, by country.
As examples, there is discussion of English capital debt paid off for
negro emancipation in 1834, in regard to the Irish famine of 1846-
1847, on U.S. loans from foreign countries, and on borrowings by the
Continental Congress. There is also extensive data on state and
local community capital projects throughout the volume.

Intro - Introductory tables
Val   - Valuation statistics tables
PI   - Public indebtedness tables

1880
Volume VII - Valuation, taxation and
public indebtedness

Dubester 105--
continued

	United States	States and Territory	Counties	Cities of 7500
Demographic Characteristics				
Aggregate population	p 13	p 8, 13		p 215-235
From 1870	p 13	p 8, 13		
Of regions	p 24			
from 1860, 1870	vi, vii	vi, vii		
Social and Economic Characteristics				
Farms - number of farms	Int T X			
Income and property				
See pages 1-21				
Value of real and personal estate, per capita, rank of states	Int T X,XI, XII, XIII XII, XIII XIV, XV, XIX	Int T XI-XV XIX XIX	Val TIII	Val TIII
By region	Val T II	Val T II		
For 1870	Int T IV, V	Int T IV, V		
For 1860	II, III	II, III		
For 1850	I	I		

<u>Decennial year</u>	1880	Dubester 107
		separates 108-111

<u>Census</u>   Tenth Census

<u>Volume</u>   Volume VIII

<u>Title</u>   The newspaper and periodical press. Alaska:
                      its population, industries, and resources.
                      The seal islands of Alaska. Ship building
                      industry in the United States.

<u>Publication</u>   Department of the Interior, Census Office;
                      Washington: Government Printing Office

 <u>Date</u>   1884

<u>Congress</u>   47th Congress, 2d Session, Volume 13 Part 8

  <u>House/Senate</u>   House Miscellaneous Document 42, Part 8

  <u>Serial</u>   Serial 2136

<u>Classifications</u>

  <u>Supt. of Documents</u> I 11.5: v. 8

  <u>Library of Congress</u> HA201.1880.B 1 v. 8   PN4855.N6 (newspapers)

   <u>card</u>   7-18862

  <u>Dewey</u>   q 317.3 Un 310 v. 8

<u>Microforms</u>

  <u>National Archives</u>   Film T825 Reel 16

  <u>Research Publications</u> Film 1880 Reels 4 (newspapers); 1 (Alaska);
                      A-1 (seal islands); and M-1 (ship building)

<u>Pages</u>   iv, 436, 188, 188, and 276 pages

<u>Maps</u>   Maps and illustrations

<u>Notes</u>   By S. N. D. North (newspapers); Ivan
                      Petroff (Alaska); Henry W. Elliott (Alaska
                      seal islands); Henry Hall (ship building)

<u>Reprints and facsimiles</u> Maxwell Reprint Company, Elmsford, New York.
                      American industry and manufactures in the
                      19th Century, v. 9

1880
Volume VIII - Newspapers, Alaska and Shipbuilding   Dubester 107

This volume consists of four parts on three very different subjects. The four parts are paginated separately.

Contents

	United States	States and Territory	Counties and Cities
The Newspaper and Periodical Press			
Demographic Characteristics			
Aggregate population of towns with one or more daily reports			
Social and Economic Characteristics			
Language--see below			
Newspapers			
By title			
1775 and name of publisher		p 27	p 27

	United States	States and Territory	Counties and Cities
1810		p 38	p 38
1820 NY newspapers		p 46,NY	p 46-NYC
1835-1880 in existence			
50 years		p 61	p 61
Number of daily newspapers			
From 1776		p 47	
From 1880			p 66
Morning and evening		p 107	
Circulation as related to			
population	XII	XII	p 77
By major cities, by title			p 98
Newspapers and periodicals	I	I	
By frequency, AM, PM, and			
by subject		XIII	XIII
Number counties with			
newspapers	II,III	II,III	
Circulation			
From 1850	XI	XI	
Language of publication	XIV	XIV	
Published in German	VIII	VIII	
Other foreign languages	IX	IX	
Religious papers by denomination			
nation	p 120		
	X	X	
Catalog of newspapers and			
periodicals by place			
of publisher		p 199-	
name frequency, character		355	
and date of establishment			

Foreign data

Population and newspapers and other periodicals, with
   circulation all continents, 49 countries   p 74
Number papers and periodicals published by frequency
   Britain, and daily papers in England by town.   p 134

1880   Dubester 107--
Volume VIII - Newspapers, Alaska and Shipbuilding   continued

---

	Territory	Divisions	Settlements

Population, Industries are
  Resources of Alaska and
  Territory Divisions
  Settlements

The Seal Islands of Alaska

Demographic Characteristics

Aggregate population

	Territory	Divisions	Settlements
6 regions or divisions	p 33		
map facing p. 1			
Arctic		p 4	4
Yukon		p 11	11
Kuskokoim		p 16	16
Aleution		p 23	23
Kodiak		p 28	28
South Eastern		p 31	31

Population from earlier reports			
1818-1868	33-41		33-41
Age	36		36
Race, ethnic division	33,177	4,11,16,23 28,31,37	4,11,16, 23,28, 31,33
Sex	33-41		33-41

Social and Economic Characteristics

	Territory	Divisions	Settlements
Education	41		
Employment--Extensive dis- cussion of seal hunting	SI		
Housing--1843 period	37		37
Illustrations of Seal Island hunts	SI21		
Language--Glossary of Russian and technical words	SI173		
Religion--Russian church membership	38,42		
Slavery in 1861	38		38

Note--numbers refer to population
  of Alaska pages, SI number to
  Seal Islands pages

Shipbuilding Industry

Very complete presentation of shipbuilding, drawings of various types of vessels for different purposes, statistics of fishing industry, as well as overall statistics of boats. The section on canal boats deals with individual canals, dock locations, and other useful data regarding the transportation of population.

	United States	States Territories
Social and Economic Characteristics		
Employment		
In fishing industry--fishermen and shoremen	SB 2	SB 2
In construction of vessels-- Number of hands employed in construction of new vessels, and repair of vessels, by type of vessel and location of use	SB 260	SB 260

Note--SB refers to section on shipbuilding

Decennial year	1880	Dubester 112

Census   Tenth Census

Volume   Volume IX

Title   Report on the Forests of North America
                          (exclusive of Mexico)

Publication   Department of the Interior, Census Office;
                          Washington: Government Printing Office

  Date   1884

Congress   47th Congress, 2d Session, Volume 13 Part 9

  House/Senate   House Miscellaneous Document 42, Part 9

  Serial   Serial 2137 and 2138 (plates)

Classifications

  Supt. of Documents   I 11.5: v. 9

  Library of Congress   HA201.1880.B 1 v. 9

    card   7-18862; 7-19235

  Dewey   q 317.3 Un 310 v. 9

Microforms

  National Archives   Film T825 Reels 16 and 17

  Research Publications   Film 1880 Reel A-3

Pages   ix, 612 pages; portfolio of 16 maps

Maps   Maps

Notes   By Charles S. Sargent, special agent
                          Serial 2138 is portfolio of 16 very large
                          folded maps

1880   Dubester 112
Volume IX - Forests of North America

Contents   Pages

References are to page numbers.

	United States	States and Territory

Social and Economic Characteristics

	United States	States and Territory
Employment		
Lumbering industry	486	486
Average number of hands employed, and maximum number at any one time of year		
By sex, males above 16, females above 15, children and youth		
Saw mills	488	488
Average number of hands employed		
Maximum number at any one time of year		
Housing		
Wood used as fuel for domestic purposes	489	
Income		
Lumbering industry		
Wages paid during the year	486	486

Note - There is a very rare set of plates to accompany this volume.
        Sixteen very large folded maps are bound as a separate Serial
        Set piece.

200

Decennial year	1880	Dubester 113
		separates 114
		115

Census   Tenth Census

Volume   Volume X

Title   Report on the production technology, and
                         uses of petroleum and its products. The
                         manufacture of coke. Building stones of
                         the United States, and statistics of the
                         quarry industry for 1880.

Publication   Department of the Interior, Census Office;
                         Washington: Government Printing Office

  Date   1884

Congress   47th Congress, 2d Session, Volume 13 Part 10

  House/Senate   House Miscellaneous Document 42, Part 10

  Serial   Serial 2139

Classifications

  Supt. of Documents   I 11.5: v. 10

  Library of Congress   HA201.1880.B 1 v. 10

    card   7-18862;

  Dewey   q 317.3 Un310 v. 10

Microforms

  National Archives   Film T825   Reel 17

  Research Publications Film 1880 Reels M-2 (petroleum, coke) and
                         MI-1 (building stones)

Pages   vii, 319; v, 114; ix, 480

Maps   Maps and illustrations

Notes   By S. F. Peckham (petroleum) special agent
                         Joseph D. Weeks (coke) special agent

1880   Dubester 113
Volume X - Petroleum, Coke and Building Stones

This volume deals primarily with technology. It does, however, contain some information on employment and wages, and considerable information on the stone used in the construction of buildings in cities.

There are colored illustrations of granite, marbles, sandstone and
other stones from individual quarries.

Contents   Pages

	United States	States and Territory	Other
Social and Economic Characteristics			
Employment			
Petroleum industry			
Labor in the production of petroleum	143		
By area - number employed	187		
Coke industry			
Employees	3, 8		
By sex and age	13, 14	13, 14	
Unemployed	16	16	
Building stone industry			
Laborers employed, for quarrying and for dressing, males over and under 16	46	46	
By type of rock	50	50	
Housing			
Stone buildings			100
Stone pavements, sidewalks, curbs, location of quarries			
Stone construction in cities			280-363

202

1880
Volume X - Petroleum, Coke and Building Stones

Dubester 113--
continued

	United States	States and Territory	Other
Income and property			
Income - wages in petroleum industry	187		
wages, methods of payment in coke industry	3, 8		

Foreign Data

Historical data on the petroleum industries of Russia, Galicia, Canada, Japan, Peru and Italy — 14-18

Decennial year	1880	Dubester 117

Census   Tenth Census

Volume   Volume XI Part 1

Title   Report on mortality and vital statistics of
                        the United States. Part 1. Statistics of
                        deaths by states, principal cities.

Publication   Department of the Interior, Census Office;
                        Washington: Government Printing Office

  Date   1885

Congress   47th Congress, 2d Session, Volume 13 Part 11

  House/Senate   House Miscellaneous Document 42, Part 11

  Serial   Serial 2140

Classifications

  Supt. of Documents   I 11.5: v. 11

  Library of Congress   HA201.1880.B 1 v. 11

    card   7-18862;

  Dewey   q 317.3 Un310 v. 11

Microforms

  National Archives   Film T825 Reels 17 and 18

  Research Publications Film 1880 Reel VS-1

Pages   lxiii, 767 pages

Notes   By John S. Billings, Surgeon, U.S. Army

204

Contents	Tables	Pages

	United States	States and Territory	Grand Groups	Cities
Demographic Characteristics				
Aggregate population	I, II	I, II	p xiv	p 3
From 1860	I	I		
By race	II	II		
Indians on reservations				
by sex	p 12			
Vital Statistics				
Deaths	I	I		VIII
Total deaths	I	I		
From 1860	I	I		
Death rate	p 5, 11	p 11, I		p 3,5
By age				
Under one year - rate	p 1	p 1		
By race		p 2		
Under 3 months, 1 month,			p 9	
by sex, by rural-urban				
Age groups	p 6, 7			
By sex	III, IV, VII	III, IV		
By race	II	II, V	V	
Under one year		p 2		
By sex	II	II		
By age	IV	IV		

1880
Volume XI Mortality and Vital Statistics, Part I

	United States	States and Territory	Grand Groups	Cities
Indians on reservations	p 12, X	p 15		
Rate		VI	VI	
By sex	I-IV	I-IV		p 3,
Rate	p 5, 11 II	p 11, II	I	VIII p 5
By cause	VII	VII	VII	VIII
By race	p 13, 16			
By sex				p 5, VIII
By race and sex	p 12, 14 XI		XI	
Rate	p 14			
Indians on a reservation, by age and sex	p 12, X			
Chinese	IX			
Irish and German parentage	p 16, XII		XII	
By month	p 17-25			p 22
As related to births	p 11	p 11		

Foreign Data

Europe - death rate, under one year		p 1
total deaths		p 4
by age		p 7
Germany - by city, death rate by age		p 8

Decennial year	1880	Dubester 118

Census   Tenth Census

Volume   Volume XII Part 2

Title   Report on mortality and vital statistics of
                                the United States. Part 2. Statistics of
                                deaths by locality, cause, etc. Portfolio
                                of 36 plates and 38 diagrams

Publication   Department of the Interior, Census Office;
                                Washington: Government Printing Office

   Date   1886

Congress   47th Congress, 2d Session, Volume 13 Part 12

   House/Senate   House Miscellaneous Document 42, Part 12

   Serial   Serial 2141 and 2142 (plates and diagrams)

Classifications

   Supt. of Documents   I 11.5: v. 12

   Library of Congress   HA201.1880.B 1 v. 12

      card   7-18862;

   Dewey   q 317.3 Un310 v. 12

Microforms

   National Archives   Film T825 Reel 18

   Research Publications   Film 1880 Reel VS-1

Pages   clviii, 803 pages; portfolio of 36 plates
                                and 38 diagrams

Maps   Maps. 2141; charts 2142

Notes   By John S. Billings, Surgeon, U.S. Army
                                Serial 2142 is portfolio of charts and
                                diagrams

This volume relates deaths to locality, specifically to the Grand
Groups, a term for regions. It also provides extensive data on specific diseases. There are many maps and diagrams illustrating the
statistical data.

An extensive table of contents, as well as a precise index obviate
the need for detailed tables. The introductory section of 158 pages
contains numerous comments and tables.

	United States	States and Territory	Grand Groups Counties	Cities
Demographic Characteristics				
Aggregate population		XIII	Counties of 10,000 XIII Grand Groups LXII	Cities IIIB
By age and sex	LXIII	LXIII		
By race and sex	LIV		LIV	
Vital Statistics				
Births				
By race and sex	LI	XIII LI	XIII Grand Groups LI	XIII
Birth rate	LIV,LV	LIV,LV	LIV,LV	

1880
Volume XII Mortality and Vital Statistics, Part II

Deaths	XIII	XIII	XIII	XIIIB
				XXII
By age				
Under one year, under 5,				
all ages	XIII	XIII	XIII	XIIIB
				XXII
By race	XIII	XIII	XIII	XIIIB
By sex	XIII,XV	XIII	XIII,XV	XIIIB
Infant deaths	LI	LI		
Rural-urban by sex				
By month, Massachusetts, N.J.			LII, LIII	
By cause	XIII	XIII	XIII	XIIIB
	XVIII	XVIII	XVIII	
From 1850	XIX			
By age				
By Irish and German				
parentage	XX		XX	
By race			XIV	
By age, race and sex	XXI		XXI	
By Irish and German				
parentage				XXII
By month				
By age and sex	XIV		XIV	XXII
Rate	XVI,XVII	XVII	XVII	
By sex, urban-rural				
Rate	XV		XV	
By specific causes-				
detailed data	XXXIII		XXXV	XXIII,
				XXXII
				XXXIV
From cancer	XXXV		XXXV	
	XXXIX		XXXIX	
	XLII			
	XLVI		XLII-XLVI	
By marital status	XL			
By nativity	XXXVIII	XXXVIII		
By occupation	XLI			
Life tables by age and sex	LVII	LVII		
By race and general				
nativity	LVI			
White	LVIII	LVIII		
Native	LIX	LIX		
Foreign born	LX	LX		
Colored	LXI	LXI		
For certain states and				
cities	LXIV			

| Decennial year | 1880 | Dubester 119
separates 120
121 |

Census   Tenth Census

Volume   Volume XIII

Title   Statistics and technology of the precious
                          metals

Publication   Department of the Interior, Census Office;
                          Washington: Government Printing Office

  Date   1885

Congress   47th Congress, 2d Session, Volume 13 Part 13

  House/Senate   House Miscellaneous Document 42, Part 13

  Serial   Serial 2143

Classifications

  Supt. of Documents   I 11.5: v. 13

  Library of Congress   HA201.1880.B 1 v. 13 TN173.U5
                                               TN413.A5K5 (statistics)
                                               HG457.W6 (gold and
                                                           silver)

    card   7-18862;

  Dewey   q 317.3 Un310 v. 13; q 338.2 K585 Un310t

Microforms

  National Archives   Film T825 Reel 19

  Research Publications   Film 1880 Reel M-2

Pages   xiv, 514 pages

Notes   Prepared under the direction of Clarence
                          King; By S. F. Emmons and G. F. Becker
                          (precious metals); Clarence King
                          (statistics); Albert Williams, Jr. (gold
                          and silver)

1880   Dubester 119
Volume XIII Precious Metals

This volume is primarily about the technology of the mining of precious metals. Very specific data is included about mine production
by named locations. There are some descriptions of mining towns.
Employment, length of shift and age data is somewhat incidental, but
very precise. Accident data is represented in great detail. The
volume also includes a 22 page directory of mines, by name of claim
and by state. Names of the geologists in charge of the collection of
data are listed.

	United States	States and Territory
Social and Economic Characteristics		
Employment		
Deep mines - number employees, staff foremen, miners, surface men	XXXVIII (p 156)	XXXVIII
Wages per shift - miners and foremen	XL (p 157)	
Comstock mines, Nevada - employment by classification, wages		XLI (p 158)
Amalgamating mills - classifications, hours and wages per shift, Ontario Mill, Summit County, Utah		CXIV (p 278)
Homestake Mining Co, Dakota		p 279
Leadville, Colorado		p 294
Utah mines, Summit County		p 440
Directory of mines, by name of claim		p 511
Vital Statistics		
Deaths		
Deep mines and all mines, fatal and non-fatal accidents, by cause	XLIX-LIX	XLIX-LIX
Percentage, proportion for number mines, number employees	p 173-177	p 173-177
Placer mines - fatal and nonfatal accidents	p 264	

<u>Decennial year</u>	1880	Dubester 122

<u>Census</u>   Tenth Census

<u>Volume</u>   Volume XIV

<u>Title</u>   The United States mining laws and regulations thereunder, and State and territorial mining laws, to which are appended local mining rules and regulations.

<u>Publication</u>   Department of the Interior, Census Office; Washington: Government Printing Office

Date   1885

<u>Congress</u>   47th Congress, 2d Session, Volume 13 Part 14

House/Senate   House Miscellaneous Document 42, Part 14

Serial   Serial 2144

<u>Classifications</u>

Supt. of Documents   I 11.5: v. 14

Library of Congress HA201.1880.B 1 v. 14 KF1819.U5

  card   7-18862;

Dewey   q 317.3 Un310 v. 14 or q 622.007 Un310m

<u>Microforms</u>

National Archives   Film T825 Reel 19

Research Publications Film 1880 Reel M-1

<u>Pages</u>   vii, 705 pages;

<u>Notes</u>   Compiled under the direction of Clarence King, special agent

---

This volume is exactly what the title implies, a compilation of mining laws. It consists of three parts:

   U.S. mining laws and regulations
   Mining laws of the following states and territories:
     Arizona
     California
     Colorado
     Dakota
     Idaho
     Montana
     Nevada
     New Mexico
     Oregon
     Utah
     Washington
     Wyoming
  Local mining laws and regulations for areas in all of the above
    except Wyoming

Although there is no information in this volume which could strictly be called population data, there is, in the section on local laws and regulations, much material which might be useful in the study of population. For example, for each mining area shown, there are minutes of meetings, together with names of officers and recorders and some names of those in attendance. There is reference to employment or non-employment of Mexican citizens and other foreign nationals, reference to mine locations, to water and claim rights, and to the age at which one might stake a claim. For example, in the Ward Mining District of Boulder County, Colorado, sixteen years was sufficient age to stake a claim.

Decennial year	1880	Dubester 123

Census   Tenth Census

Volume   Volume XV

Title   Report on the mining industries of the
                          United States exclusive of precious
                          metals), with special investigation into
                          the iron resources of the Republic and into
                          the cretaceous coals of the Northwest.

Publication   Department of the Interior, Census Office;
                          Washington: Government Printing Office

  Date   1886

Congress   47th Congress, 2d Session, Volume 13 Part 15

  House/Senate   House Miscellaneous Document 42, Part 15

  Serial   Serial 2145

Classifications

  Supt. of Documents   I 11.5: v. 15

  Library of Congress   HA201.1880.B 1 v. 15 or TN23.Pg80

    card   7-18862

  Dewey   q 317.3 Un310 v. 15 or q 622.09 Un310m

Microforms

  National Archives   Film T825 Reels 19 and 20

  Research Publications   Film 1880 Reel MI-1

Pages   xxxviii, 1025 pages

Maps   Maps and illustrations

Notes   By Raphael Pumpelly

This volume, like its companion Volume XIII on Precious Metals, deals primarily with the geological and geographical aspects of the mining industries of the less precious minerals: iron ore, anthracite and bituminous coal, copper, lead and zinc.

Incidental to the major purpose of the volume is some employment data. For most minerals, statistics are provided for hands employed, age of miners as below or above sixteen years, work above or below ground, and classification of mining employees as miners, laborers and administrative staff. Wage data is in most instances limited to total wages paid.

There is an extensive directory of mines and metallurgical establishments by state on pages 857-986.

References are to page numbers.

	United States	States and Territory	Counties
Social and Economic Characteristics			
Employment			
Hands employed in mines	1, p xxviii	14,15,16	
Age - men and boys under 16, proportion by type of mine	p xxxv		
By types of mines			
Iron ore	15,16	14,15,16	14
Anthracite coal		27,28	27
Bituminous coal	30,34	29-34,41	29
Copper	49,50 64,66	49,50,64	
Lead and zinc	51,52 59	51,52 53,54	
Base metals	66		
Minor metals	75		

Note: Most tables show above and below ground work, as men or boys, with classifications as miners, laborers or administrative staff

	United States	States and Territory	Counties
Income and property			
Annual earnings			
Iron miners	17	17	
Bituminous coal miners	35	35,43,44	
Lead miners	53,54	53,54	
Copper miners	64		
Smelting workers	66,67		

Decennial year	1880 Dubester 125
Census	Tenth Census
Volume	Volume XVI
Title	Report on the water-power of the United States. Part I
Publication	Department of the Interior, Census Office; Washington: Government Printing Office
Date	1885
Congress	47th Congress, 2d Session, Volume 13 Part 16
House/Senate	House Miscellaneous Document 42, Part 16
Serial	Serial 2146

Classifications

Supt. of Documents	I 11.5: v. 16
Library of Congress	HA201.1880.B 1 v. 16
card	7-18862
Dewey	q 317.3 Un310 v. or q 338.3 Un310w pt. 1

Microforms

National Archives	Film T825 Reel 20
Research Publications	Film 1880 Reel M-2
Pages	xxxix, 874 pages
Maps	Maps and illustrations
Notes	By Prof. W. P. Trowbridge, Chief Special Agent; George F. Swaim (New England, Middle, and Southern Atlantic; Dwight Porter (Long Island Sound, Hudson River, Lake George, New York State Canals); James L. Greenleaf (Lakes Huron and Erie)

216

In this volume there is no population information of a specific nature
such as that included in the tables for other volumes. However, there
is considerable information useful for the study of populated areas.
Examples include products manufactured at mills at specific stream
locations, names of mills and owners of water rights, locations of
roads and railroads.

Information is presented on the regions of the United States by
geographical areas in the following order:
  Eastern New England
  Tributary to Long Island Sound
  Hudson River Basin and Lake George outlet
  Tributary to Lake Ontario and New York State canals
  Drainage basins of Lakes Huron and Erie, and Niagara Falls and
    River
  Middle Atlantic watershed
  South Atlantic watershed
  Eastern Gulf Slope

Maps of many cities, sketches of dams, elevations and other illustrated material provide valuable historical data.

Decennial year   1880   Dubester 134
                                                separates 135-139

Census   Tenth Census

Volume   Volume XVII

Title   Reports on the water-power of the United
                        States. Part II

Publication   Department of the Interior, Census Office;
                        Washington: Government Printing Office

  Date   1887

Congress   47th Congress, 2d Session, Volume 13 Part 17

  House/Senate   House Miscellaneous Document 42, Part 17

  Serial   Serial 2147

Classifications

  Supt. of Documents   I 11.5: v. 17

  Library of Congress   HA201.1880.B 1 v. 17

    card   7-18862

  Dewey   q 317.3 Un 310 v. 17; q 338.3 Un310w pt. 2

Microforms

  National Archives   Film T825 Reel 21

  Research Publications Film 1880 Reel M-3

Pages   xiv, 788 pages

Maps   Maps and illustrations

Notes   By Prof. W. P. Trowbridge, Chief special
                        agent; James L. Greenleaf (Northwest,
                        Mississippi River); Dwight Porter
                        (Mississippi River, Ohio River, and Ohio
                        State Canals; Walter G. Elliott (cities)

218

1880
Volume XVII - Water Power Part II   Dubester 134

This volume, includes much the same type information as that found in
Part I. Like that volume, it should not be discounted for the study
of populated area.

Included in this volume are the following areas:

    The Northwest
    The Mississippi River and tributaries
    The Ohio River and Ohio State Canals

The most valuable section of the volume for the study of population
is the final one, entitled "The Water Supply of Certain Cities and
Towns of the United States". This section consists of 272 pages, and
provides extensive discussions of the methods of providing water to
large numbers of cities, even very small cities. There are approxi-
mately one hundred illustrations of places, pumping stations, water
works, together with endless detail on expenditures of water companies.

A final section, beginning on page 689 (bottom of the page number)
includes the following information on each city for which data was
found:

    Population
    Data of first introduction of water
    Daily water consumption
    Number of water takers

Other information, such as whether the water company was privately or
municipally owned is included.

An index to cities is included on page 779.

                                                              Cities

---

Demographic Characteristics

Aggregate population   p 689

Social and Economic Characteristics

Housing   p 689
    Daily water consumption
    Number of water takers (residence and commercial)
    Date of introduction of water to the city

Decennial year	1880	Dubester 141

Census   Tenth Census

Volume   Volume XVIII

Title   Report on the social statistics of cities.
                      Part 1. The New England and the Middle
                      States.

Publication   Department of the Interior, Census Office;
                      Washington: Government Printing Office

  Date   1886

Congress   47th Congress, 2d Session, Volume 13 Part 18

  House/Senate   House Miscellaneous Document 42, Part 18

  Serial   Serial 2148

Classifications

  Supt. of Documents I 11.5: v. 18

  Library of Congress HA201.1880.B 1 v. 18

    card   7-18862

  Dewey   q 317.3 Un310 v. 18

Microforms

  National Archives   Film T825 Reel 21

  Research Publications Film 1880 Reel 2

Pages   vii, 915 pages

Maps   Maps and illustrations

Notes   Compiled by George E. Waring, Jr., special
                      agent. Note the specific cities on the
                      following pages.

TABLE OF CONTENTS.

_____

These volumes are the result of a monumental effort by the Census
Office to obtain current and historical information on each of 222
cities. Since information was obtained through the "volunteer aid of
city officials and public spirited citizens" there is an uneven
quality and quantity of data provided for the many individual cities.

Thirty-two categories of information were requested on each city.
The accompanying charts give the categories of data requested, and
the order in which it is presented.

Caution should be taken to consider both lists in searching for an
individual city, as the "Western States" group includes states which
would no longer be considered the "West", but would more likely be
called the "Midwest." There are separate listings of cities for each
volume.

At the beginning of the section for each city, the population since
1790 is shown, and the current population by sex, race and general
nativity.

Maps of most cities are included.

The plan for the description of the cities follows. Not all
correspondents provided information in each category.

    Population
    History
    Location - including railroad communication, tributary country,
       typography, climate
    Streets
    Waterworks
    Gas
    Public buildings
    Public parks and pleasure grounds
    Places of amusement
    Drainage
    Cemeteries
    Markets
    Sanitary authority
    Infectious diseases
    Municipal cleansing
    Police
    Fire
    Commerce and navigation
    Manufactures
    Public schools
    Map of the sewer system

1880
Volumes XVIII and XIX - The Social Statistics
of Cities

	Cities
Demographic Characteristics	
Aggregate population	x
Historic from 1790	x
Race	x
Sex	x
Social and Economic Characteristics	
Disabilities and health	
Health - infectious diseases	x
Education	x
Employment	x
Manufactures	
Nativity	x
Transportation	x
Apportionment, Density and Geography	
Geography - tributary country, typography, climate	x

<u>Decennial year</u>	1880	Dubester 142
		separate 143

<u>Census</u>   Tenth Census

<u>Volume</u>   Volume XIX

<u>Title</u>   Report on the social statistics of cities.
                  Part 2. The Southern and the Western
                  States.

<u>Publication</u>   Department of the Interior, Census Office;
                  Washington: Government Printing Office

Date   1887

<u>Congress</u>   47th Congress, 2d Session, Volume 13 Part 19

  House/Senate   House Miscellaneous Document 42, Part 19

  Serial   Serial 2149

<u>Classifications</u>

  Supt. of Documents   I 11.5: v. 19

  Library of Congress   HA201.1880.B 1 v. 19

    card   7-18862

  Dewey   q 317.3 Un310 v. 19

<u>Microforms</u>

  National Archives   Film T825 Reel 22

  Research Publications   Film 1880 Reel 2

<u>Pages</u>   vi, 843 pages

<u>Maps</u>   Maps and illustrations

<u>Notes</u>   Compiled by George E. Waring, Jr., special
                  agent. Note the specific cities.

TABLE OF CONTENTS.

SOUTHERN STATES.

WESTERN STATES.

v

VI

TABLE OF CONTENTS.

<u>Decennial year</u>	1880	Dubester 144

<u>Census</u>   Tenth Census

<u>Volume</u>   Volume XX

<u>Title</u>   Report on the statistics of wages in manu-
                           facturing industries; with supplementary
                           reports on the average retail prices of
                           necessities of life, and on trade societies,
                           and strikes and lockouts.

<u>Publication</u>   Department of the Interior, Census Office;
                           Washington: Government Printing Office

  Date   1886

<u>Congress</u>   47th Congress, 2d Session, Volume 13 Part 20

  House/Senate   House Miscellaneous Document 42, Part 20

  Serial   Serial 2150

<u>Classifications</u>

  Supt. of Documents   I 11.5: v. 20

  Library of Congress   HA201.1880.B 1 v. 20

     card   7-18862

  Dewey   q 317.3 Un310 v. 20

<u>Microforms</u>

  National Archives   Film T825 Reels 22 and 23

  Research Publications   Film 1880 Reel 4

<u>Pages</u>   xxxiv, 571; vii, 117; v, 21; v, 29 pages

<u>Notes</u>   By Joseph D. Weeks, special agent.

1880   Dubester 144
Volume XX - Wages, Prices, Trade Societies, Strikes
and Lockouts

Information in this volume was developed from the answers to schedules
sent by the Census Office to manufacturing and retail establishments
and trade unions throughout the country. Much of the data identifies
respondents not only by location but by name of company and trade
union as well. It includes data which today would be part of the
economic rather than the population census.

Each of the four parts has an introductory essay and is paginated
separately.

Contents   Pages

1880   Dubester 144--
Volume XX - Wages, Prices, Trade Societies, Strikes continued
and Lockouts

	United States	States and Territory	Local Areas

M - Manufactures section
N - Necessities of life section
T - Trade societies section
S - Strikes and lockouts section
References are to page numbers

Social and Economic Characteristics

	United States	States and Territory	Local Areas
Employment and unemployment			
Manufactures section - names and localities of individual manufactures			M pages
Hours of labor per day, by state		Mxxx	
By year, from 1830	Mxxviii		
By industry, from 1830	Mxxxii	Mxxxii	M
Trade societies			
Ten major societies, by name	T 413		
Local unattached societies and branches, by industry and state	T 419	T 14-19	
Strikes and lockouts	S 5	S 5	
By industry	S 9 12,14	S 5,14	
By classification of employee	S 22		
By cause	S 18	S 18	
By result	S 26		
By days and work lost, by industry	S 27		
Income and property			
Methods of payment for labor-- cash v. company store, by industry	M xxii	M xxii	
Interval of payment, by industry	M xxiv M xxvi	M xxiv	
Cost of necessities of life			N pages
By name of store and location			
Wages, by various classifications			M pages
Occupations			
See "Employment" above			
Classifications in various manufacturing establishments			M pages

1880   Dubester 144--
Volume XX - Wages, Prices, Trade Societies, Strikes <u>continued</u>
and Lockouts

<u>Foreign Data</u>

Employment - Rates of pay and hours of
    work for employees
    of gas works in Great Britain and
    Ireland   M 75
        Strikes in Great Britain   S 1, 6

Decennial year	1880	Dubester 145

Census   Tenth Census

Volume   Volume XXI

Title   Report on the defective, dependent, and
                    delinquent classes of the population of the
                    United States.

Publication   Department of the Interior, Census Office;
                    Washington: Government Printing Office

  Date   1888

Congress   47th Congress, 2d Session, Volume 13 Part 21

  House/Senate   House Miscellaneous Document 42, Part 21

  Serial   Serial 2151

Classifications

  Supt. of Documents   I 11.5: v. 21

  Library of Congress HA201.1880.B 1 v. 21

    card   7-18862

  Dewey   q 317.3 Un310 v. 21

Microforms

  National Archives   Film T825 Reel 23

  Research Publications Film 1880 Reel 1

Pages   iv, 581 pages

Notes   By Frederick Howard Wines, special agent.

1880   Dubester 145
Volume XXI - Defective, Dependent and Delinquent Classes

_____

This volume includes information on the four groups of disabled
persons: the blind, deaf and dumb, idiotic and insane, as well as
prisoners and homeless children and paupers. In the case of institutionalized persons, the names of the institutions are given.

	United States	States and Territory	Counties	Other
Crime and Punishment				
Prisoners	p xi, p xxiv p xxlvii	p xxi CXIV	Counties with cities of	Cities of 50,000
	p xxlvii CXIV,CXXXI	CXXXI	CXVI	p xxiii
From 1850	p xx, p xxi CXV	CXV		
Ratio to number paupers	p xix			
By type of offense	p xlvii			
By race, sex and general nativity	CXXIV, CXXV	CXXIV, CXXV		CXXV
By type of prison	p xl CXVII CXVIII CXIX CXXVII CXXXIII	CXVII CXVIII CXIX CXXVI CXXXIII		

1880
Volume XXI - Defective, Dependent
and Delinquent Classes

	United States	States and Territory	Counties	Other
By state of residence	CXXII	CXXII		
By length of sentence	CXXVII	CXXVII		
	CXXVIII	CXXVIII		
	CXXIX	CXXIX		
By time already served	CXXIII	CXXIII		
By fine paid	CXXX	CXXX		
By age				
Single years, by race, sex, general nativity	CXX,CXXIV	CXXIV		
Age groups, by race, sex, general nativity	CXXI	CXXI		
Juveniles, by race, sex, general nativity	CXXXII	CXXXII		CXXXII
By race	p xi,xxi	p xxi	CXVI	p xxiii
	CXIV	CXIV		
By sex	p xi,xxi	p xxi	CXVI	p xxiii
	CXIV	CXIV		
By general nativity	p xi,xxi	p xxi	CXVI	p xxiii
	CXIV	CXIV		
Foreign born by country and offense	p xlix CXXVI			
Police Statistics				cities of 5000

Note: Names of institutions shown on
CXVIII, CXIX, CXXII, CXXIII   CXXXVI

Disabilities				
All physical disabilities, blind, deaf and dumb, idiotic, insane				
By race, sex, and general nativity	p xi,xii	p xii		Cities of 50,000 p xxiii
By age single years	p xxv,xxix			
From 1850	p VII,p xix			
By residence after release from institution	p xxxvi			
With more than one disability	p xxxvii LXXXIII, CIV	LXXXIII, CIV		

1880
Volume XXI - Defective, Dependent
and Delinquent Classes

	United States States	States and Territory	Counties	Other
Blind				
From 1830	LXV	LXV		
By age	LXIV, LXX- LXXV LXXVII LXXIX LXXXII	LXXII LXXIV LXXVII LXXIX LXXXII		
By race	LXIV	LXIV		
By sex	LXIV	LXIV		
By general nativity	LXIV	LXIV		
By race, sex, and nativity		LXVI	LXVI	Cities of 50,000
By institution or at home	LXVIII LXXVI	LXVIII LXXVI LXIX		
By degree of blindness	LXXVI	LXXVI		
By special institutions	LXXXI	LXXXI		
Note--Specific institutions named in	LXIX, LXXXI			
Deaf and dumb	LXXXIV			Cities of 50,000 LXXXV
In 1830				
By age	LXXXVIII LXXXVIII XC,XCII, XCIII,XCIII XCV,XCVI XCVII,VIII	XC,XCI		
By race	LXXXIV	LXXXIV		
By sex	LXXXIV	LXXXIV		LXXXV
By general nativity	LXXXIV	LXXXIV		LXXXXV
By institution or at home	LXXXVI	LXXXVI LXXXVII		
By special institution	LXXXIX CIII	CIII		
By cause	XCIX,C	XCIX,C		
In institutions	CI	CI		
By sex, race and general nativity	CII	CII		

1880
Volume XXI - Defective, Dependent
and Delinquent Classes

	United States	States and Territory	Counties	Other
Note--Specific institutions named in	LXXXVII, CI,CII			
Idiots	XXXIII	XXXIII		XXXVI Cities of 50,000
From 1850, by race sex and general nativity	XXIV	XXXIV		XXXVI
By age	XL-L	XLII XLIII		
By race	XXXIII	XXXIII XXXIV		XXXVI
By sex	XXXIII	XXXIII XXXIV		XXXVI
By general nativity	XXXIII	XXXIII XXXIV		XXXVI
By institution or at home	XXXVII	XXXVII		
By specific institution				XXXVIII XXXIX LIV
By cause or type	LI,LIII, LIX	LI,LIII, LIX		
By race	LII	LII		
By size of head???	LV	LV		
By ability to use hands	LVI	LVI		
By ability to use feet	LVII	LVII		
By ability to speak	LVIII	LVIII		
By ????? to other idiots	LX	LX		
By marital status	LXI	LXI		
By educational ????	LXII	LXII		
With other physical disabilities	LXIII	LXIII		
Note--Specific institutions named in	XXXIX			
Insane	I	I		III Cities of 50,000 IV
		III		
From 1850 by race, sex, and general nativity	II	II		

1880
Volume XXI - Defective, Dependent
and Delinquent Classes

	United States	States and Territory	Counties	Other
By age	VII IX,XIII XXIII,XXIV	VIII		
By race	I	I,III		III
By sex	I	I,II		III
By general nativity	I	I,III		III
By institution or at home	V	V		
In seclusion, under restraints	XIX,XX XXVIII	XIX,XX XXVIII,XXIX,		XXVIII, XXIX
By specific institution	XXIX			VI,XXI
Expenditures of 92 institutions				XXX
Admissions				XXX
Treated				XXXI
By number of attacks	XIV,XXV	XIV,XXV		XXV
By type	XV,XVI XXVI	XV,XVI XXVI		XXVI
By relationship to others insane	XVII	XVII		
By marital status	XVIII XXVII	XVIII XXVII		XXVII
With physical disabilities	XXII	XXII		
Expenditures of 92 asylums	XXX			XXX

Note--Specific institutions
named in VI,XXV,XXVII,XXVIII,XXIX,XXX

Families
  See homeless children under
  paupers
  Paupers and homeless children
  In almshouses

	United States	States and Territory	Counties	Other
By age, race and sex				
Single years by general nativity	CX			
Age groups	CXII	CXII		
By race, sex and general nativity	CVI	CVI		
From 1850	CVIII	CVIII		

1880
Volume XXI - Defective, Dependent
and Delinquent Classes

	United States	States and Territory	Counties	Other
By time spent in almshouse	CIX	CIX		
By physical condition	CXIII	CXIII		
By ratio to prisoners	p xix			
By whether relatives in same institution	CXIII	CXIII		
Outdoor paupers				
By age, by race, sex and general nativity	CXI			
By race, sex and general nativity	CVII	CVII		
Homeless children (in almshoues, outdoor and in other institutions)				
By race, sex and general nativity	CV	CV		

Decennial year   1880   Dubester 146
                separates 147-152

Census   Tenth Census

Volume   Volume XXII

Title   Report on power and machinery employed in manufactures.

Publication   Department of the Interior, Census Office; Washington: Government Printing Office

Date   1888

Congress   47th Congress, 2d Session, Volume 13 Part 22

House/Senate House Miscellaneous Document 42, Part 22

Serial   Serial 2152

Classifications

Supt. of Documents I 11.5: v. 22

Library of Congress HA201.1880.B 1 v. 22

card   7-18862

Dewey   q 317.3 Un310 v. 22

Microforms

National Archives Film T825 Reel 24

Research Publications Film 1880 Reel M-3

Maps   Illustrations

Notes   By Prof. W. P. Trowbridge (power and machinery), chief special agent; Herman Hollerith (iron and steel); F. R. Hutton (tools and machinery, pumps); Charles H. Fitch (boilers and marine engines); Henry Hall (ice industry)

1880   Dubester 146
Volume XXII - Power and Machinery in Manufactures;
The Ice Industry

This volume has seven parts, each with separate pagination. A great
deal of the volume deals with the state of the art of various mechanical devices. There are numerous drawings of machinery, and some
illustrations of men at work. There is also considerable information
on steamships, characterized as ocean and inland passenger ships,
ferries, etc., with notations as to home ports and routes plied.

The final section on the ice industry is useful for determining the
size and development of cities. Amount of ice sold for consumption
in twenty large cities, methods of cutting and delivery, and where
stored may be useful for the study of the history of individual
cities.

	United States	States and Territory	Cities
Social and Economic Characteristics			
Employment and unemployment			
Iron and steel works - hands employed, by 5 types of works, from 1870	p 9	p 9	
Ice companies - hands employed, number and names of companies, first date of delivery of ice, etc.	p 1-43		20 cities
Housing			
Ice sold to families, also to breweries, butter dealers, butchers, etc.			20 cities p 38
Transportation			
Steamships, ports, routes. See tables on steam vessels		p 6, 7	p 5, 7

Decennial year	1880	Dubester 153

Census   Tenth Census

Volume   Compendium

Title   Compendium of the Tenth Census (June 1,
                          1880)

Publication   Department of the Interior, Census Office;
                          Washington: Government Printing Office

Date   1883, two volumes; issued also as single
                          volume 1883; as two volumes 1885-1888

Congress   47th Congress, 1st Session, Volume 24 Part 1

House/Senate   House Miscellaneous Document 64, Parts 1
                          and 2

Serial   Serial 2059 (Part 1) and 2060 (Part 2)

Classifications

Supt. of Documents   I 11.2: C73

Library of Congress   HA201.1880.D (2 volumes) HA201.1880.C
                          (one volume)

card   6-36733

Dewey   q 317.3 Un310c pts. 1 and 2

Microforms

National Archives   Film T825 Reels 24 and 25

Research Publications   Film 1880 Reel 3

Pages   Part 1 - lxxvi, 923, xxxix pages
                          Part 2 - lx, 925-1771 pages
                          Single volume lxxvi, 1769 pages

Notes   Issued as one and as two volumes with same
                          pagination.

The 1880 Compendium was published as a single volume and as two
volumes. The same pagination was used in both cases. The first
volume included pages 1 through 923 and the second volume pages 925
through 1771.

Contents	Tables	Page
Table of contents		iii
Introduction--including census Acts, reports of the Superintendent of the Census, notes and special reports, expenditures, correspondence, documents relating to South Carolina Census		lxxvi
Population	I-XLIX	1-648
Agriculture	XLIII-XLIX	649-923

In two volume set, page 923 is end of first volume, second volume
begins with page 925

	United States	States and Territory	Counties	Cities
Demographic Characteristics				
Aggregate population	p xlii	p xvxlii		minor civil divisions
	I	I	XVIII	XIX cities of 4000
		XVIII	XIXI	XXVI 100 cities
				CIX 50 cities
				XXXII XXXIII-
Historic from 1790	II,III	II,III		
Historic from 1860		XVIII	XVIII	
Urban population, number of cities	V	V		
Alaska, divisions, settlement by race		CX	CX	

1880
Compendium

	United States	States and Territory	Counties	Cities
Age	XLIIA	XLIIA		
Single years 1-80				
By race and sex				
Native white males	XLIIB	XLIIB		
Native white females	XLIIC	XLIIC		
Foreign born white males	XLIID	XLIID		
Foreign born white females	XLIIE	XLIIE		
Colored males	XLIIF	XLIIF		
Colored females	XLIIG	XLIIG		
10 years and over by sex	CI	CI		
School age 5-17 by sex		XLI	XLI	
21 and over, male	XL	XL		
Natural militia 18-44	XXXIX	XXXIX	XLI	
Males		XLI		
By race and general				
nativity (white)	XXXIX	XXXIX		
Voting age 24 and males	XL	XLI	XLI	
By race and general				
nativity (white)		XLI		
Race	I	I	XXIII	
White-colored	XXI	XXI		
Chinese, Japanese,				
Colored, Indians	XXII	XXII		
White	XXXV	XXXV		
Colored	XXXVI	XXXVI		
Chinese, Japanese	XXXVII	XXXVII		
Civilized Indians	XXXVIII	XXXVIII		
Historic to 1860		XXIII	XXIII	
Historic to 1870				XXXIV cities of 4000 CIX 100 cities
Sex	I	I		
By age	XLII	XLII		

Social and Economic Characteristics

	United States	States and Territory	Counties	Cities
Crime and prisoners				
Prisoners by race, sex and				
general nativity	CXLIII	CXLIII		CLIII-CLVI

1880
Compendium

	United States	States and Territory	Counties	Other
By type of institution	CLII	CLII		CLIII-CLVI

Note--Specific institution found in CLIII, CLIV, CLV

Disabilities
  See notes pages 1659-1670

	United States	States and Territory	Counties	Other
All graphs--blind, deaf, idiots and insane	CXLIV			
By race, sex and general nativity	CXLVI			
Blind	CXL	CXL		
By institution	CL	CL		CL
Deaf-mutes	CXLI	CXLI		
By institution	CLI	CLI		CLI
Idiots	CXXXIX	CXXXIX		
By institution	CXLVII-CXLIX	CXLVII-CXLIX		CXLVII-CXLVIII
Insane	CXXXVIII	CXXXVIII		
By institution	CXLV CXLVI	CXLV CXLVI		CXLVI

Education and Schools
  See notes pages 1635-1638

	United States	States and Territory	Counties	Other
Pupils by race and sex, average daily attendance	CXXXVI	CXXXVI		
Teachers by race and sex, average salaries	CXXXVI	CXXXVI		
Public schools--buildings seats, segregation, finances	CXXXV	CXXXV		

Employment

	United States	States and Territory	Counties	Other
Fisheries	CVI			
Manufactures				
Heads employed--males	L	L		20 cities
Above 16, females above 15, children and youth				LIII
From 1850	L	L		
By Industry	LI,LIV	LI,LII, LIV	LII	LIII
Railroads	LXXXV			
Telegraph	XCVII			

	United States	States and Territory	Counties	Other
Families				
Number and persons to a family	CVIIIC	CVIIIC		100 cities
From 1850				CIX
Note--Specific insitutions found in CL, CLI, CXLVII, CXLVII, CXLVII				
Housing				
Number dwellings, persons to a dwelling	CVIIIB	CVIIIB		100 cities
From 1850				CIX
Institutional Population				
See crime and prisoners and disabilities above				
Language	CXXXIII	CXXXIII		
Number of newspapers by language				
Literacy and illiteracy				
Persons unable to read	CXXXVII	CXXXVII		
Unable to write by sex and age groups 10 and up, 10-14, 15-20, 21 and up				
Also 1860 and 1870				
Nativity				
General nativity (native or foreign born)	I	I,XXV	XXV	Places of 4000 XXVI
From 1860	XX	XX,XXV	XXV	
From 1870				XXVI
By age and sex (whites only)	XLIIB-E			
By sex and race	XXXIV-XXXVIII	XXXIV-XXXVIII		
Specific				50 cities
Natives by state of birth, by race	XXVII	XXVI, XXXI	XXXI	XXXII

1880
Compendium

	United States	States and Territory	Counties	Other
By race	XXVIII XXIX	XXVIII- XXIX		
Foreign born by country	XXX	XXX- XXXI	XXXI	XXXIII
By occupational group	CII	CII		CV
By specific occupation	CIII			
By nativity of parents				
See notes pages 1406-7	CVII	CVII		
Newspapers and Publications				
Number, periods of issue circulation, classification			CXXXI- CXXXIV	CXXX- CXXXIV
Language, religious papers by denomination				
Occupation				
See pages 1343-1355				
Population 10 and over shown by sex				
Total occupied by sex and by occupational group	CI	CI		50 cities
(4 groups)	CI	CI		CI
Age group (10-15, 16-59, 60+)	CII	CII		CV
Specific nativity	CII	CII		CV
By specific occupation		CIV		
By age groups and sex	CIII			
By specific nativity	CIII			
US-265 occupations, states 100				
Change in number occupied 1870	p 1345			
Paupers	CXLII			
See pages 1666-1667				
In institutions, outside,				
By issue, sex and general nativity				
Property records				
Assessed value of real and personal property	CXXIV	CXXIV		

1880
Compendium

	United States	States and Territory	Counties	Other
Geography, Density, and Apportionment				
Density	IV,CVIII	VI,CVIII		
From 1790	IV	IV		
Urban population	V			
Geographical distribution by	VI			
drainage basins, elevation, topography	XVII			
Temperature, rainfall, latitude and longitude				
Vital Statistics				
See notes pages 1705-1725				
Deaths by sex and age (-1,-5, total)	CLVII			
By cause	CLVIII	CLVIII		

Decennial year	1880	Dubester 155

Census   Tenth Census

Volume   General Reports

Title   Apportionment under Tenth Census of the United States. Tabular statements exhibiting the total population of each State and Territory; the apportionment of members of Congress from 293 to 325; moiety question, &c; together with remarks of Hon. S. S. Cox, chairman.

Publication   Department of the Interior, Census Office; Washington: Government Printing Office

Date   January 7, 1881

Congress   46th Congress, 3rd Session, Volume 18

House/Senate   House Executive Document 65

Serial   In Serial 1968

Classifications

Supt. of Documents   I 11.2: Ap 6

Library of Congress JK 1341.A3

card   9-25937

Dewey   q 317.3 Un310a

Microforms

Research Publications Listed in catalog as on Film 1880 Reel 4, but not actually on film

Pages   24 pages

Notes   With remarks on Hon. S. S. Cox, Chairman

1880   Dubester 155
Apportionment under Tenth Census of the United States

This is a document transmitting to the House of Representatives the
population count of states and territories resulting from the 1880
Census. It includes a statement by the Chairman of the House
Committee on the Census proposing a bill for reapportionment and
other material describing the methods and problems of apportioning
House seats.

	United States	States and Territory
Demographic Characteristics		
Aggregate population	p 1, 6	p 1, 6
Apportionment, Density, Geography		
Apportionment		
Bill proposing apportionment of 301		
House seats	p 4	p 4
Effect on state allocations of seats		
between 293 and 325 in number	p 5	p 5
Tables showing allocations for each	Table A	
state with 293 to 325 seats	p 6	p 6
Letter on mathematical problems such		Table B
as moiety in distribution of seats		p 19

<u>Decennial year</u>	1880	Dubester 156

<u>Census</u> Tenth Census

<u>Volume</u> General Reports

<u>Title</u> The history and present condition of the fishery industries. The oyster industry.

<u>Publication</u> Department of the Interior, Census Office; Washington: Government Printing Office

Date 1881

<u>Congress</u> Not a Congressional publication

<u>Classifications</u>

Supt. of Documents I 11.2: Oy8; also FC 1.6: Sec. X, Monograph B

Library of Congress SH365.A314

Dewey q 639 In40

<u>Microforms</u>

National Archives Film T825 Reel 25

Research Publications Film 1880 Reel A-3

<u>Pages</u> 251 pages

<u>Maps</u> Illustrations

<u>Notes</u> By Ernest Ingersoll. This publication and the one on the Seal Islands of Alaska were originally intended to have been incorporated in a separate final volume of the Tenth Census. Instead, they are considered as a general publication. They may also be found as reports of the Fish Commission.

The Oyster Industry, which was published both as a Census report and a report of the Fisheries Commission provides a thorough study of the industry. It includes the names of vessels of the oyster fleet, tonnage, the size of crews and the amount of their wages.

There are useful commentaries for the study of population such as the following, part of a discussion of the oyster industry of Prince Edward Island (page 7):

> "One half of the fishermen are heads of families, the other half being made up of boys and young unmarried men and the vagabond element . . . with a full crop, fishermen expect to pay for their winter's supply of provisions, chiefly flour."

<u>Decennial year</u>	1880	Dubester 157

<u>Census</u>   Tenth Census

<u>Volume</u>   General Reports

<u>Title</u>   The history and present condition of the fishery industries: The Seal Islands of Alaska.

<u>Publication</u>   Department of the Interior, Census Office; Washington: Government Printing Office

Date   1881

<u>Congress</u>   Not a Congressional publication

<u>Classifications</u>

  Supt. of Documents   I 11.2: Al 1; I 11.5a Al 1; also FC 1.6: Sec IX, monograph A

  Library of Congress   SH361.E38

  Dewey   q 639.E158s

<u>Microforms</u>

  Research Publications Film 1880 Reel A-3

<u>Pages</u>   176 pages

<u>Maps</u>   Illustrations

<u>Notes</u>   By Henry W. Elliott. This publication and the one on the oyster industry were originally intended to have been incorporated in a separate final volume of the Tenth Census. Instead they are considered as a general publication. They may also be found as a report of the Fish Commission. This report on the Seal Islands is also incorporated in Volume VIII, and information on its contents is included with that volume.

Decennial year	1880	Dubester 158

Census   Tenth Census

Volume   General Reports

Title   Statistics of the manufactures of the
                  cities of Baltimore, Boston, Brooklyn,
                  Buffalo, Chicago, Cincinnati, Cleveland,
                  Detroit, Jersey City, Louisville,
                  Milwaukee, Newark, New Orleans, New York,
                  Philadelphia, Pittsburgh, Providence, San
                  Francisco, St. Louis, and Washington,
                  during the census year, June 1, 1879-May
                  31, 1880.

Publication   Department of the Interior, Census Office;
                  Washington: Government Printing Office

   Date   1882

Congress   Not a Congressional publication

Classifications

   Supt. of Documents   I 11.2:M31

   Library of Congress   HC 101.A4.1882

   Card   7-18842

   Dewey   q 317.3 Un310m

Microforms

   Research Publications Film 1880 Reel M-1

Pages   32 pages

1880   Dubester 158
Statistics of the manufactures of the cities of Baltimore

Organized by city and industry, this volume presents data on manufactures in twenty principal cities:

Baltimore	Milwaukee
Boston	Newark
Brooklyn	New Orleans
Buffalo	New York
Chicago	Philadelphia
Cincinnati	Pittsburgh
Cleveland	Providence
Detroit	San Francisco
Jersey City	St. Louis
Louisville	Washington

The major value for population study is in the employment data.

---

                                                    20 Principal
                                                    Cities

Social and Economic Characteristics

Employment
  By city by industry
  Greatest number of hands employed at any
    one time during the year   x
  Average number of hands employed   x
    Males above 16 years
    Females above 15 years
    Children and youth

Decennial year   1880   Dubester 159

Census   Tenth Census

Volume   General Reports

Title   Tabulated statements of the traffic and
                        fiscal operations of the railroads in the
                        United States. Group no. 1, embracing
                        Maine, New Hampshire, Vermont,
                        Massachusetts, Rhode Island and Connecticut

Publication   Department of the Interior, Census Office;
                        Washington: Government Printing Office

  Date   1881

Congress   Not a Congressional publication

Classifications

  Supt. of Documents   I 11.6: R 13

  Library of Congress   HE2711.A2.1881

  Dewey   317.3 Un310t

Microforms

  Research Publications Film 1880 Reel T-1

Pages   46 pages

Notes   By Robert P. Porter

1880   Dubester 159
Extra Census Bulletin - Tabulated Statements of the
Traffic and Fiscal Operations of the Railroads Group I

This bulletin is limited to railroads of the New England area.
Specific railroads are named, and their total mileage shown.

	States and Territories

Social and Economic Characteristics

Employment
  Railroad employees - 11 categories   p 43

Income
  Total payroll
  Salaries of general officers and clerks   p 27

Transportation
  Railroads by name and number of miles of track
  Earnings from passengers - local passengers and
    through passengers   p 14
  Passengers - number carried one mile during year   p 29
  Passenger trains - average number of cars in
    passenger trains   p 32
  Average rate of fare per mile - local fare,
    through fare, and season ticket   p 42

Vital Statistics
  Deaths and injuries   p 46
    Passengers, employees and others, from causes
      beyond their control and from own negligence

Decennial year	1880	Dubester 160

Census
Tenth Census

Volume
Bulletins

Title
Census Bulletins 1-303

Publication
Department of the Interior, Census Office;
Washington: Government Printing Office

Date
1880-1882

Congress
Not a Congressional publication

Classifications

Supt. of Documents
I 11.3:1-303

Library of Congress
HA201.1880.A1

Dewey
q 317.3 Un310b

Pages
various paging

Notes
This is a bound volume of the preliminary
bulletins which were later incorporated in
the final volumes of the Tenth Census.
Sets of these bulletins at the Library of
Congress and the Census Bureau Library were
incomplete as of April 1982.

<u>Decennial year</u>	1880	Dubester 161
<u>Census</u>	Tenth Census	
<u>Volume</u>	Bulletins	
<u>Title</u>	Forestry Bulletins 1-25	
<u>Publication</u>	Department of the Interior, Census Office; Washington: Government Printing Office	
Date	1881-1883	
<u>Congress</u>	Not a Congressional publication	

<u>Classifications</u>

Supt. of Documents	I 11.7:1-25
Library of Congress	SD11.A467
Dewey	q 317.3 Un310f
<u>Pages</u>	Various paging
<u>Notes</u>	This is a bound volume of the forestry bulletins which were incorporated in the final volume, Volume IX, the Forests of North America, Dubester 112.

Decennial year	1880	Dubester 162

Census   Tenth Census

Volume   Extra Census Bulletin

Title   The areas of the United States, the several
                        states and territories and their counties

Publication   Department of the Interior, Census Office;
                        Washington: Government Printing Office

  Date   1881

Congress   Not a Congressional publication

Classifications

  Supt. of Documents   I 11.6: Ar3

  Dewey   317.3 Un310ar

Microforms

  Research Publications Film 1880 Reel 4

Pages   20 pages

Maps   one map

Notes   By Henry Gannett

258

1880   Dubester 162
Extra Census Bulletin

Contents   Pages

	United States	States and Territory	Counties
Apportionment, Density, Geography			
Geography			
Area in square miles	p 4		p 11
Gross areas, boundaries	p 5		
Coast waters - bays, gulfs, sounds etc.			
Rivers and smaller streams			
Lakes and ponds			
Total water surface			
Total land surface			

Decennial year   1880   Dubester 163

Census   Tenth Census

Volume   Extra Census Bulletin

Title   Report on the cotton production of the
                        State of Louisiana, with a discussion of
                        the general agricultural features of the
                        State

Publication   Department of the Interior, Census Office;
                        Washington: Government Printing Office

Date   1881

Congress   Not a Congressional publication

Classifications

  Supt. of Documents   see I 11.5: v.5

  Library of Congress   HD9077.L8.A3.1880

  Dewey   q 317.3 Un310co

Microforms

  Research Publications Film 1880 Reel A-3

Pages   iv, 99 pages

Maps   Illustrations

Notes   By Eugene W. Hilgard. Included in the
                        final volume, Report on Cotton Production
                        in the United States, see Dubester 89.

Decennial year	1880	Dubester 164

Census   Tenth Census

Volume   Extra Census Bulletin

Title   Report on the manufacture of firearms and
                            ammunition

Publication   Department of the Interior, Census Office;
                            Washington: Government Printing Office

Date   1882

Congress   Not a Congressional publication

Classifications

  Supt. of Documents   I 11.6: F61

  Library of Congress   UF533.A5.1882

    card   8-29485

  Dewey   317.3 Un310fr

Pages   vi, 37 pages

Notes   By Charles H. Fitch. No copy located at
                            the Library of Congress, April 1982

Decennial year   1880   Dubester 165

Census   Tenth Census

Volume   Extra Census Bulletin

Title   Statistics of life insurance

Publication   Department of the Interior, Census Office;
                        Washington: Government Printing Office

  Date   1882

Congress   Not a Congressional publication

Classifications

  Supt. of Documents   I 11.6: L62

  Dewey   317.3 Un310in

Pages   73 pages

Notes   No population information

Decennial year   1880   Dubester 166

Census   Tenth Census

Volume   Extra Census Bulletin

Title   Tables showing the cereal production of the
                               United States . . . by counties as returned
                               at the Census of 1880

Publication   Department of the Interior, Census Office;
                               Washington: Government Printing Office

  Date   1881

Congress   Not a Congressional publication

Classifications

  Supt. of Documents   I 11.6: C33

  Library of Congress   HD9034.A3.1880

  Dewey   317.3 Un310ce

Microforms

  Research Publications   Film 1880   Reel A-3

Pages   36 pages

Notes   No copy located at the Library of Congress,
                               Spring 1982

Decennial year	1880	Dubester 167

Census   Tenth Census

Volume   Extra Census Bulletin

Title   Tables showing the cotton production of the
                  United States . . . by counties as returned
                  at the Census of 1880

Publication   Department of the Interior, Census Office;
                  Washington: Government Printing Office

  Date   1881

Congress   Not a Congressional publication

Classifications

  Supt. of Documents   I 11.6: C82

  Library of Congress   HD201.1880.A2

  Dewey   317.3 Un310co

Microforms

  Research Publications   Film 1880   Reel A-3

Pages   5 pages

Notes   No population information; acres and bales
                  only.

<u>Decennial year</u>	1880	Dubester 168
<u>Census</u>	Tenth Census	
<u>Volume</u>	Extra Census Bulletin	
<u>Title</u>	Tables, with annotations showing the system of courts of criminal jurisdiction in the United States. A preliminary study in criminal jurisprudence.	
<u>Publication</u>	Department of the Interior, Census Office; Washington: Government Printing Office	
<u>Congress</u>	Not a Congressional publication	
<u>Classifications</u>		
Supt. of Documents	I 11.6: J87	
card	27-16547	
Dewey	317.3 Un310ju	
<u>Pages</u>	38 pages	
<u>Notes</u>	By Fred J. Wines. Dubester notes that this item was housed in the Library of Congress Law Library. No copy could be located there in Spring 1982.	

Eleventh Census of the United States
Robert P. Porter, Superintendent

MAP
SHOWING SIX DEGREES OF DENSITY THE DISTRIBUTION
OF THE POPULATION OF THE
UNITED STATES
at the Eleventh Census
1890.
COMPILED BY
HENRY GANNETT, GEOGRAPHER.

Scale

LEGEND

I
II
III
IV
V
VI

A. Hoen & Co. Lith. Baltimore.

1890

VOLUMES OF THE ELEVENTH DECENNIAL CENSUS

Volume	Title	Dubester Number
I	Report on population of the United States. 2 parts.	Dubester 177 Dubester 178
II	Report on the insane, feeble-minded, deaf and dumb, and blind.	Dubester 179
III	Report on crime, pauperism and benevolence, 2 parts.	Dubester 180 Dubester 181
IV	Report on vital and social statistics. 4 parts	Dubester 184 Dubester 185 Dubester 186 Dubester 187
V	Reports on the statistics of agriculture	Dubester 188
VI	Report on manufacturing industries, 3 parts.	Dubester 193 Dubester 194 Dubester 195
VII	Report on mineral industries	Dubester 199
VIII	Report on population and resources of Alaska	Dubester 200
IX	Report on statistics of churches	Dubester 201
X	Report on Indians taxed and not taxed	Dubester 202
XI	Report on insurance business, 2 parts.	Dubester 204 Dubester 205
XII	Report on real estate mortgages	Dubester 206
XIII	Report on farms and homes	Dubester 207
XIV	Report on transportation systems, 2 parts	Dubester 209 Dubester 210
XV	Report on wealth, debt, and taxation, 2 parts	Dubester 216 Dubester 217

1890--Continued

Volume Title		Dubester Number
Atlas	Statistical Atlas of the United States	Dubester 220
Abstract	Abstract of the Eleventh Census	Dubester 221
Abstract	Abstract of the Eleventh Census, 2nd edition, revised and enlarged	Dubester 222
Compendium	Compendium of the Eleventh Census, 3 parts.	Dubester 224 Dubester 225 Dubester 226
	Report on Education	Dubester 229
	Report on the social statistics of cities	Dubester 320
	Special report on the occupations of the population	Dubester 231
	Vital statistics of Boston and Philadelphia	Dubester 232
	Vital statistics of New York City and Brooklyn	Dubester 233
	Vital statistics of the District of Columbia and Baltimore	Dubester 234
	Apportionment of members of the House of Representatives	Dubester 235

Bulletins

	Population of the United States by minor civil divisions	Dubester 238
	Population by color, sex, and general nativity, with school, militia and voting ages.	Dubester 239
	Manufactures in cities	Dubester 240

Extra Census Bulletins

	The five civilized tribes in Indian Territory: The Cherokee, Chickasaw, Choctaw, Creek and Seminole Nations	Dubester 242

1890--Continued

Volume Title	Dubester Number
Indians, Eastern band of Cherokees of North Carolina	Dubester 243
Indians, The Six Nations of New York. Cayugas, Mohawks, Oneidas, Onondagas, Senecas, Tuscaroras	Dubester 244
Moqui Pueblo Indians of Arizona and Pueblo Indians of New Mexico	Dubester 245

States and territories listed in alphabetical order:

Alabama
Arizona Territory
Arkansas
California
Colorado
Connecticut
Delaware
Florida
Georgia
Idaho
Illinois
Indiana
Iowa
Kansas
Kentucky
Louisiana
Maine
Maryland
Massachusetts
Michigan
Minnesota
Mississippi
Missouri
Montana--new state

Nebraska
Nevada
New Hampshire
New Jersey
New Mexico Territory
New York
North Carolina
North Dakota--new state
Ohio
Oklahoma Territory
Oregon
Pennsylvania
Rhode Island
South Carolina
South Dakota--new state
Tennessee
Texas
Utah Territory
Vermont
Virginia
Washington--new state
West Virginia
Wisconsin
Wyoming--new state

Alaska treated separately

1890

THE ELEVENTH DECENNIAL CENSUS

The Eleventh Census was the last to be entirely administered and published by the Interior Department. It was 1897 before the last of the final volumes were published. After the 1900 enumeration, the Census Office was transferred to the new Commerce Department to become the Bureau of the Census, the title and location which it retains today.

Publications of the Eleventh Census numbered fourteen volumes (several of which have two or more parts), a three volume compendium, an abstract, a number of census bulletins, and a statistical atlas. Like the preceding census, the main volumes were bound in a black cloth departmental edition and in calfskin as documents in the Congressional Serial Set. Because of the order of publication of the individual reports, there is a confusing array of book and volume numbers under the various classification systems. The last parts published were the two books of Volume I--Population.

This is the first census in which a separate questionnaire was used for each household, a practice which continues today. In addition to the inquiries which had been made in 1880, a number of new ones were added: mother of how many children, and how many were living; whether a veteran of the Civil War or a widow of a veteran; number of years in the U.S. and naturalization status; months unemployed, ability to speak English, and if not, language or dialect spoken; whether suffering from acute or chronic disease, whether crippled, maimed or deformed; and whether a prisoner, convict, homeless child or pauper. There were special schedules used for the disabled, for institutionalized persons, for Indians, including those living in tribes and those living on reservations, and on farms and homes.

Volume I, with its two parts, includes most of the basic data from the usual demographic and social and economic inquiries: age, race, sex, nativity, housing, education, literacy, occupations and citizenship. It also includes some of the data from the special schedules. Much of the same data is also found in the Compendium volume and in shorter form in the Abstract.

There are three parts to the volume on manufactures, classified by state and industry. Considerable information on classifications and numbers of employees in the manufacture of specific products, and on average wages and annual earnings are included. In addition to the main volume on agriculture, there is one on farms and homes which provides extensive detail on the tenure of farms, and another on real estate mortgages which includes maps of each state showing, to the county level, the relationship of farm mortgages to the value of farm acreage. Similar tables, but no maps, are provided for home ownership and encumbrances in urban areas.

As in 1880, there was considerable interest in the institutionalized population, or more properly in the causes of institutionalization. Findings from the separate schedules resulted in a volume entitled Crime, Pauperism and Benevolence. This volume corresponds in subject to the 1880 volume entitled Defective, Dependent and Delinquent Classes of the Population.

There are four parts to the volume on Vital Statistics, all of which, except for a very few pages on births, are devoted to death statistics. In addition, there are three bound bulletins comparing deaths in Baltimore to those in the District of Columbia, in Boston to Philadelphia, and in New York City to Brooklyn.

A separate illustrated volume was published on Alaska, with extensive essays on the population and culture. Indians were also the subject of a complete volume, filled with black and white as well as colored illustrations. The Indian population of each state and territory is counted and discussed in separate chapters. Information from surveys of the Indian population back to the time of Thomas Jefferson are incorporated in this volume. In addition, four extra census bulletins on Indians of various areas, also illustrated, were published as part of the Eleventh Census.

Transportation by land and by water was the subject of another two part volume. Although most of the material is devoted to finances of transportation companies, there is considerable detail as to the names and locations of railroads and city street railways, as well as the number of passengers and employees. Likewise, the second part, on water transportation, provides information on individual ports and passage through them.

For the 1890 reports, the Census Office sent inquiries to each religious organization concerning the number of members or communicants and church edifices and accommodations as well as finances, a practice which would surely be considered unconstitutional today. However, the information did result in a useful volume for historical purposes, with many details for each state and many smaller areas by denomination.

The single volume on social statistics for 1890 is not so valuable or interesting as the two volume set for 1880, and does not provide details and maps for individual cities as did the latter. Most of the information consists of tables on municipal governmental services rather than text for each city as in 1880.

There are bound special reports on occupations and education, most of the data in which are incorporated in the main volumes of the 1890

Census. Dubester includes several copies of bound preliminary bulletins, found in the Library of Congress, in his listing, most of the data from which was eventually consolidated in the final volumes.

Two versions of an Abstract were published, the first a House document of some 250 pages, printed in 1894. A revised edition with 50 more pages was published in 1896. The abstracts contain data, in more limited form, from most, if not all, of the subjects of the Eleventh Census.

The Statistical Atlas, unlike the one published with the 1870 Census, is part of the Congressional Serial Set. It is a large folio volume with 63 colored plates, many black and white diagrams, and a number of pages of text. Information is included on most of the subjects of the 1890 Census, together with historical maps showing the spread of population, and the changing ranks of states and large cities. Considerable space is devoted to nativity, to disabilities, to occupations and to agriculture.

New states since 1880 were Idaho, Montana, North and South Dakota, Washington and Wyoming. The territories remaining were Utah, to become a state in 1900, Oklahoma in 1910, and New Mexico and Arizona both admitted in 1912. Hawaii would not be organized as a territory until 1900, and Alaska, 1912, both to await statehood for nearly another half century.

Decennial year   1890   Dubester 177

Census   Eleventh Census

Volume   Volume I, Part I

Title   Report on population of the United States,
                               Part I

Publication   Department of the Interior, Census Office;
                               Washington: Government Printing Office

  Date   1895

Congress   52d Congress, 1st Session, Volume 50, Part 8

  House/Senate   House Miscellaneous Document 340, Part 18

  Serial   Serial 3018

Classifications

  Supt. of Documents   I 12.5: Bk. 15

  Library of Congress   HA201.1890 B. 1 v. 1. pt. 1

    card   7-24047

  Dewey   q 317.3 Un311 v. 1, pt. 1

Microforms

  National Archives   Film T825 Reels 25 and 26

  Research Publications   Film 1890 Reel 1

Pages   ccxiii, 968 pages

Maps   Maps

1890   Dubester 177
Volume I Part I - Population

This is the main population volume for 1890. It provides population
data for the United States, for states, territories, counties, minor
civil divisions, cities, towns, villages and boroughs.

Data is provided on sex, race and general nativity, as well as state
or territory or foreign country of brith, as well as foreign paren-
tage. The volume also includes tables on marital status, on age for
school population, males of militia and voting age. There are tables
on housing and on families. An appendix provides information on
Indian Territory, Indian reservations and on Alaska.

References are to table numbers

Tables without letter designation 1-95
Tables with letter designation A 1-8

1890
Volume I Part I - Population

	United States	States and Territory	Counties	Other
Demographic Characteristics				
Aggregate population	1,9	1,4,9	4,5	Minor civil divns.- 5
See pages xi-xvii and cci				Cities of 25,000-6
Notes reformation of counties, Table 4				Cities, towns, of 1000-8
Notes on minor civil divisions, page 49				
From 1790	1	1,4	4,4	
increase from 1790	2	2		7
From 1880				8
Alaska		A 2	A 2	Villages of 300 - A 3
See page cci				
Temporary and permanent white population	A 88			
Temporary white summer population	A 7	A 7		
Indian Territory and reservations	A	A 1	A 1	
Age				
See pages clxxvi-clxxvii				
School ages 5-20, 5-17, 18-20	63-65	79	79	Cities of 25,000 72-74
By race, general nativity (white)				
By parental nativity	63-65			72-74
By sex	66-71			73-74
Military age - males 18-44	75	75,79	76,79	76
By race, general nativity and parental nativity	75	75		76
Voting age - males 21 and up, by race, general nativity	77	77,79	79	78
By parental nativity	77	77		78
Alaska, by sex and race		A 4	A 4	
Race				
See pages xciii-ciii				
See pages cc for Indian population				
White	9,20	9,20	21,22	places of 2500-19

1890
Volume I Part I - Population

	United States	States and Territory	Counties	Other
Colored	20	22	22	23
Negro descent - negro, mulatto, quadroon, octaroon	10	10,21		19
Chinese, Japanese, civilized Indian		21		19
From 1850, white and negro	13	13		
From 1860, Chinese, Japanese, civilized Indians	14	14		
From 1870,				
white and negro		15	15	
Chinese		16	16	
Japanese		17	17	
Civilized Indian		18	18	
By sex	20,21	20,21	22	23
Alaska		A 2 - A 4	A 2,	A 3
By sex		A 2 - A 6	A 2,	A 3
			A 3	
			A 5-7	
			A 6	
			A 7	
Sex				
See pages lxxi-lxxviii	9	9,79	22,79	places of 25,000-19
				cities of 25,000-80
From 1850	11	11		
By race	20,21	20,21	22	

Social and Economic Characteristics

Citizenship
  Alaska - white males by age

		A 6	A 6	

Employment
  Alaska - white males, temporary
    summer employees, by industry

		A 7	A 7	

Families
  See pages clxxxviii-cc
  Families and persons per
    family

	87	87,88	88	cities 25,000 by wards 89

	United States	States and Territory	Counties	Other
From 1850	87	87		
By number of persons per family 1-21 persons plus	92	92		93-95
Housing				
See pages clxxxviii-cc				
Dwellings, persons per dwelling	86	86,88	88	89
From 1850	86	86		
By persons per dwelling	90	90		cities of 25,000-91 cities of 100,000 by wards 94 - cities of 100,000 by wards - 94
Number families per dwelling				
Average number families per dwelling				
Language				
Alaska - linguistic stock, by sex		A 5	A 5	
Marital status				
See pages clxxix-clxxxviii				
By sex	81,82	81,83		cities of 25,000-84 cities of 100,000- 85
By age, race and general nativity	82	83		
Alaska		A 2, A 4		A 3
Nativity				
See pages lxxix-xciii				
For natives by state and territory, ciii-cxxxii				
For foreign by country of birth cxxxiv-cliii				
On foreign parentage cliv-clxxiv				

	United States	States and Territory	Counties	Other
General nativity	9	9,15	15	places of 2500-19,23
From 1850	12	12		
By parental nativity	35-49	35-49		50-62
By foreign country	37-49	37-49		52-62
Native white by parental nativity	9, 20	9, 20	22,22	23
Specific nativity				
Natives by state of birth	24-27, 29	24-27, 29		cities of 25,000-29
Foreign by country of birth	32	32	33	34

Apportionment, Density, Geography

Apportionment
  See pages ccvii-ccxiv
  Citation of acts since
    1789   ccx
  1890 and proposed for
    1891   ccix   ccix

Density   3   3
  See pages xxiv-xxxv -
    density
  From 1790
  See pages xxviii-xxxiii -
    vacant and settled areas
  See pages xxxvi-xxxvii -
    center of population

Geography
  See pages xxxvii-lxiv -
    geographical distribution
  Maps of states and terri-
    tories for each decennial
    census, 1790-1890 begin-
    ning facing page xix

Decennial year	1890	Dubester 178

Census   Eleventh Census

Volume   Volume I, Part II

Title   Report on population of the United States,
                          Part II

Publication   Department of the Interior, Census Office;
                          Washington: Government Printing Office

  Date   1897

Congress   52d Congress, 1st Session, Volume 50, Part 8

  House/Senate   House Miscellaneous Document 340, Part 18

  Serial   Serial 3019

Classifications

  Supt. of Documents   I 12.5: Bk. 16

  Library of Congress   HA201.1890 B. 1 v. 1. pt. 2

    card   7-24047

  Dewey   q 317.3 Un311 v. 1, pt. 2

Microforms

  National Archives   Film T825   Reel 26

  Research Publications   Film 1890   Reel 1

Pages   clxxv, 824 pages

This volume provides extensive data on age, school attendance, illiteracy, inability to speak English, citizenship of foreign born adult males, nativity, occupations, and veterans.

In the 824 pages of the body of the volume, and in the 175 introductory pages, there are numerous tables within each subject. Information is usually divided into tables by age, sex, color, and general nativity. In most instances, data on nativity is provided for whites only. In the case of native whites, data is usually provided for parental nativity.

Table guides for the report on Education, also bound separately as Dubester 229, are included with that volume.

Contents	Tables	Pages

The order of tables showing nativity and parental nativity is as follows:
    native white of native parentage,
    native white of foreign parentage
    foreign white
    colored (Negro, Chinese, Japanese, civilized Indians)

Data is provided for the United States as a whole, for states and territories, and for 124 cities of 25,000.

Much of the data in the major tables is shown in somewhat different form than that in the introductory essays, identified by Roman numeral page numbers.

References are to table numbers.

1890
Volume I Part II - Population

	United States	States and Territory	Cities
Demographic Characteristics			
Aggregate population	1	2	8
Age			
By five year intervals	1,3	2,3	8
See pages xv-xxvii for essay and tables, and for 1880 data			
Under 1 year and 1-4 years	1		8
By race and sex	1,4-7	2,4-7	8
By sex	1,3	2,3	8
By nativity			
By sex, by general nativity and parental nativity	1,4-6	2,4-6	8
Social and Economic Characteristics			
Citizenship			
See pages lxvi-lxxiv for essay and tables			
Citzenship of males of 21 years and over who were foreign born shown as aliens or naturalized citizens; for aliens, ability to speak English	71	71	72
Aliens by country of birth	73	73	74
By years in United States	75	75	76
Education			
The data on education in this section are compiled both from population schedules and from reports from schools. The tables in the final section, The Report on Education, are not included here.			
See Dubester 229 for separately published identical report, for table guide.			
See pages xxvii-xxx and 1-46.			
Persons attending school during the census year	9,24	9	
By age	10,18,24	10,18	25
Under 5, 5-9, 10-14, 15-19, 20 and over			

1890
Volume I Part II - Population

	United States	States and Territory	Cities
By race	9	9	
By age and sex	11-17	11-17	26-29
	19-23	19-23	
By sex	10-24	10-23	25-30
By general and parental nativity	9,12-15	9,12-15	26-28
	19-21,24	19-21	
By months in school	18-23		30
Teachers, by race and sex	7	7	
Institutional population			
See pages clxxiv-clxxv			
Inmates of soldiers homes-male	131	131	
By age	132		
By race	131	131	
By general and parental nativity	131	131	
By language-ability to speak English	133		
By literacy	133		
By marital status	133		
By health condition	133		
Note--Names of specific homes shown in 131			
Language			
Inability to speak English, aged 10 and up	59-67	59-67	68-70
See pages lx-lxv			
By age	61-67	61-67	70
By race	59-60	59-60	68-69
	62-67	62-67	
By sex	60-67	60-67	69-70
By general and parental nativity	59-60	59-60	68-69
Inmates of soldiers homes	133		
Literacy			
Illiterate persons - can read but not write or could neither read nor write	31-48	31-47	49-58
See pages xxx-lx for essay and tables and comparisons with 1880			
By age - age groups	40-48	40-47	54-58

1890
Volume I Part II - Population

	United States	States and Territory	Cities
By race	31,34-49 41-48	31,34-49 41-47	55-58
By sex	32-48	32-47	49-58
By general and parental nativity	31,34-37 42-45	31,34-37 42-45	51-52 55-57
Can read butnot write/can neither read nor write	32-39 48	32-39	49-53
Military			
See pages clxxii-clxxiv			
Veterans, soldiers and widows	123-128	123-126	129-30
United States veterans and widows	123,125,127 129	123,125	129
Confederate veterans and widows	124,126,128 130	124,126	130
Nativity			
Note - nativity is not a separate section in this volume, but nearly every major subject has tables dealing with nativity and parental nativity			
Aggregate population	1	2	8
By age	4-6	4-6	8
Race - data on nativity limited to whites			
Sex	1	2	
Citizenship	71,73,75	71,73,75	72,74, 76
Education	9,12-15 24	9,12-15 19-21	26-28
Foreign born adult males	71	71	72
Language - inability to speak English	59-60 63-66	59-60 63-66	68-69
Literacy - illiterates, by sex by age	31,34-37 42-45 48	31,34-37 42-45	50-52 55-57

1890
Volume I Part II - Population

	United States	States and Territory	Cities
Occupations			
Aggregate population gainfully employed			117
By age	77,83-89	77,83,116	118
By race	81,82,85-89 92-96	81	118
By sex	77-79,81-82 85,90-96	77,79,81 90	117
Males	99-100 101-115 119-120	99,101, 108,110 114,116	
By citizenship - foreign born adult males	114,115	114	
By employment - number unemployed	101,102-107 121,122	101,116	118
By language - persons gainfully employed who cannot speak English	99,100	99,116	118
By literacy	90,91	90,116	118
By marital status	90,91	90,116	118
By nativity and parental nativity	80,82,85-87 92-94 98,100 103-105 108,110-113	80,81 108 110	118
By specific occupations	78,79,82,84 85,89,91-96 98,100, 102-107,109 111-113,115 121,122	116	118

<u>Decennial year</u>	1890	Dubester 179

<u>Census</u>   Eleventh Census

<u>Volume</u>   Volume II

<u>Title</u>   Report on the insane, feeble-minded, deaf
                 and dumb, and blind in the United States

<u>Publication</u>   Department of the Interior, Census Office;
                 Washington: Government Printing Office

Date   1895

<u>Congress</u>   52d Congress, 1st Session, Volume 50,
                 Part 16

   House/Senate   House Miscellaneous Document 340, Part 26

   Serial   Serial 3031

<u>Classifications</u>

   Supt. of Documents   I 12.5: Bk. 8

   Library of Congress   HA201.1890 B. 1 v. 2 or HV 1553 b B5

      card   7-24047

   Dewey   q 317.3 Un311 v. 2

<u>Pages</u>   xi, 755 pages

<u>Maps</u>   Maps and charts

<u>Notes</u>   By John S. Billings, Expert Special Agent

1890   Dubester 179
Volume II - The Insane, Feeble-Minded, Deaf and Dumb
and Insane

This volume contains nearly one hundred tables of demographic and
other data on the four categories of disabilities named in the title.
For each disability, there are tables to show race, sex, nativity and
parental nativity, birthplace of mother, and age as well as age of
incidence of the disability. Most tables contain several variables.

The analysis section provides extensive text on each disability, comparative figures for European countries, and additional tables,
charts and diagrams.

	United States	States and Territory	Counties	Cities of 50,000
Disabilities				
Blind	222	22-224	224	225
See pages 127-153				
By race, sex, nativity and parental nativity				
From 1850, ratio to population	223	223		
Age				
From 5-20 years	231	231		
Of incidence	232-233			
Race	222,226	222		
Sex	222,226			
Institutionalized	229-230			
Named institutions	230			230
Literacy				
Ability to read and/ or write	237-238			
Nativity and general nativity	222	222		
Birthplace of mothers	226-230			
Occupations	239-242			
Marital status	236			
Cause	234-235			
Congenital	236			
Other relatives blind	243-244			
Blind in one eye only	245-247	125		246

1890   Dubester 179--
Volume II - The Insane, Feeble-Minded, Deaf and Dumb
and Insane

	United States	States and Territory	Counties	Cities of 50,000
Deaf				
Deaf but not dumb	187,207	187,207		192
Deaf and dumb	188	188,190	190	191
Age	193-194	193-194		
	196-199	196-199		
	202	202		
	207-208	207		
Age of occurrence	194,204	194		
	204-206	204-206		
Race	187-188	187-188	190	191-
		190		192
Ratio to population, from 1850	189	189		
Sex	187-188	187-188	190	191-
				192
Ratio to population, from 1850	189	189		
Institutionalized, in schools for deaf	200-201			
	203-205			
Named institutions	200			200
Literacy	213-215			
Nativity	187-189	187-189	190	191-
	196-200	196-200		192
Ratio to population, from 1850	189			
Birthplace of mothers	198-201			
Occupations	216-219			
Deaf and dumb				
Marital status	212			
Cause	209-211			
Congenital	193,195	193,195		
	197	197		
Noncongenital	194,195	195		
	198	198		
Other relatives deaf	220-221			
Feeble-minded	171	171	173	174
See pages 69-90				
Ratio to population	172	172-173		
Age	177-180			
Aged 5-20	179	179		
At incidence	182			

1890   Dubester 179--
Volume II - The Insane, Feeble-Minded, Deaf and Dumb
and Insane

	United States	States and Territory	Counties	Cities of 50,000
Race	171	171	173	174
Sex	171	171	173	174
Institutionalized	175-176,178			175-176
Institutions by name				
Institutions for insane	176			
Literacy	186			
Nativity and parental nativity	171	171	173	174
By birthplace of mother	177-179	179		
Marital status	181			
By cause	180	180		
Congenital or non-congenital	181			
Other relatives feeble-minded or insane	183			
Other relatives blind or deaf	184			
Insane	150	150,152	152	153
See pages 7-68				
Ratio to population, from 1850	151	151		
Age	155,163			
At incidence	157,165			151
Race	150	150	152	153
Ratio to population, from 1850	151	151		
Sex	150	150	152	153
Ratio to population, from 1850	151	151		
Institutionalized	154		154	
By named institution				
By type of insanity	160,163 165			
Military				
Civil War veterans	167			
Nativity and parental nativity	150	150	152	153
Ratio to population, from 1850	151	151		

288

1890   Dubester 179--
Volume II - The Insane, Feeble-Minded, Deaf and Dumb
and Insane

	United States	States and Territory	Counties	Cities of 50,000
By birthplace of mother	155,157-8 169			
Deaths				
Feebleminded and insane	170			
Insane				
Marital status	166			
Type of insanity	159-164			
Urban-rural residence	164			
With other disability	168			
Other relatives insane	167			

Foreign Data

See analysis pages for each disability for comparative data for
European nations.

Decennial year	1890	Dubester 181

Census   Eleventh Census

Volume   Volume III, Part I

Title   Report on the crime, pauperism, and benevolence in the United States. Part I Analysis

Publication   Department of the Interior, Census Office; Washington: Government Printing Office

Date   1896

Congress   52d Congress, 1st Session, Volume 50, Part 14

     House/Senate   House Miscellaneous Document 340, Part 24

     Serial   Serial 3028

Classifications

     Supt. of Documents   I 12.5: Bk. 4

     Library of Congress   HA201.1890 B. 1 v. 3, pt. 1; HV 1553 b B5

     card   7-24047

     Dewey   q 317.3 Un311 v. 3 pt. 1

Microforms

     National Archives   Film T825 Reel 27

     Research Publications   Film 1890 Reel 2

Pages   vii, 411 pages

Notes   By Frederick H. Wines, Expert Special Agent

1890   Dubester 181
Volume III   Part I - Crime, Pauperism and Benevolence

Special schedules were developed and used in the 1890 Census for persons resident in institutions. Separate schedules were used for prisons, for juvenile reformatories, for almshouses, and for benevolent institutions. These include hospitals for children, for the aged, and the general population. Schedules also contain inquiries on institutionalized persons in each family. This is the first of two volumes presenting the data developed from these schedules. The Census also found, in addition to those institutionalized persons, 24,220 "outside paupers." Statistics on these persons are not included in this volume.

Data on age, race, sex, citzenship, disabilities, education, employment, family, language, literacy, marital status, veteran status, nativity and parental nativity, and occupations in and out of the institution, were crosstabulated and presented in some 336 tables in this volume. Tables apparently were given numbers by the Census Office, but they do not appear in the published volumes. The following guide indicates whether the subject was crosstabulated for each of the categories of institutionalized persons. Anyone searching for the information would, however, need to look at the volume itself to find the correct table. Most data are on a national basis. Only a few tables provide information by state.

Contents

1890
Volume III Part I - Crime, Pauperism
and Benevolence

	Prisoners	Juveniles in Reformatories	Paupers in almshouses	Inmates in Benevolent Institutions
Demographic Characteristics				
Age				
Of institutionalized persons, proportion of population	x	x	x	x
Race	x	x	x	x
Sex	x	x	x	x
Social and Economic Characteristics				
Citizenship			x	x
Crime				
By offense	x	x		
By sentence	x			
By duration of imprisonment	x			
By type institution	x			
Recidivists	x			
Possible penalties for specific crimes, for each state	x			
Disabilities				
Health	x	x	x	x
Able-bodied persons			x	x
Alcohol use	x	x		
Education				
School attendance for children				x
Persons having had trade school	x	x		
Employment	x	x		
Whether employed when arrested	x	x		

1890
Volume III Part I - Crime, Pauperism
and Benevolence

	Prisoners	Juveniles in Reformatories	Paupers in almshouses	Inmates in Benevolent Institutions
Family				
Mothers of children			x	x
Abandoned, surrendered and orphaned children, foundlings			x	x
Children born in institution			x	x
Whether relatives in institutions			x	x
Institutionalized persons	x	x	x	x
Language				
Ability to speak English	x	x	x	x
Literacy	x	x	x	x
Military				
Veteran soldiers, sailors or marines	x	x	x	x
Nativity	x	x	x	x
Foreign born, length of residence in the United States, by specific country				
Parental nativity, by specific country				
Occupations				
In free life	x		x	x
In prison	x	x		
Vital Statistics				
Births in institution			x	x
Marital status	x	x	x	x

Decennial year	1890	Dubester 182

Census   Eleventh Census

Volume   Volume III, Part II

Title   Report on crime, pauperism, and benevolence.
                        Part II. General tables.

Publication   Department of the Interior, Census Office;
                        Washington: Government Printing Office

  Date   1895

Congress   52d Congress, 1st Session, Volume 50,
                        Part 14

  House/Senate   House Miscellaneous Document 340, Part 24

  Serial   Serial 3029

Classifications

  Supt. of Documents   I 12.5: Bk. 5

  Library of Congress   HA201.1890 B. 1 v. 3, pt. 2

    card   7-24047

  Dewey   q 317.3 Un311 v. 3 pt. 2

Microforms

  National Archives   Film T825 Reels 27 and 28

  Research Publications Film 1890 Reel 2

Pages   xi, 1035 pages

Notes   By Frederick H. Wines, Expert Special Agent

1890   Dubester 182
Volume III Crime, Pauperism and Benevolence
Part II - General Tables

This volume provides demographic and social characteristics in great
detail on prisoners, juveniles offenders, paupers and inmates of benevolent institutions. The institutions are by name. Frequently there
are three tables for a single subject, in which case the first is the
count for both sexes, next for male, third for female.

	United States	States and Territory	Counties	Other

Social and Economic Characteristics

Prisoners				
Tables 1-131				
Where no data is provided for states, it is usually provided by regions				
Aggregate	1	1		
Proportion of population	4	4		
Age	162-79	71-3		
Race	1	1		
Sex	2-3	2-3		
Citizenship				
Naturalization status of foreign born	58-59			
Disabilities and health	38-40 96-97,100	38-40		41-43
Education	84-87			
Employment status	91-92			
Language				
Ability to speak English	60			
Literacy	82			
Military prisoners	102			
Nativity	1	1		
Parental nativity	1,54-7	1,54-57		
Occupations	88-90			
In prison	93-95			
Marital status	80			
By type institution	5	5 6-11	12-14 15-17	18-23 18-23
Counties with no prisoners			57	
Workhouses	24-26	24-26		27-29

1890
Volume III Crime, Pauperism and Benevolence
Part II - General Tables

	United States	States and Territory	Counties	Other
Leased prisoners	30-32	30-32	33-35	
Military and naval prisons	36	36		
By offense	44-46,48	47-48		
More than one charge	49-53	49-53		
Disabilities and health	101			
Ability to speak English	61			
Literacy	83			
Marital status	81			
By federal conviction	104			
By repetition of imprisonment	103			
By sentence	105-130			
Juvenile Offenders Tables 132-197 Tables without data for states usually have data by regions				
Aggregate	132,136-8	132,136-8		
Proportion of population, from 1880	135			
Age	154-157	154-156		
Race	163-165	163-165		
Sex	133-134	133-134		
Disabilities and health	178-179 183-184	178-179 183-184		
Education in trades	176			
Language Ability to speak English	152-153			
Literacy	174			
Nativity	132			
Parental nativity	148-151			
Occupations	180-182			
Marital status	172			
By offense	139-143			
By age	160,166			
By literacy	175			
By marital status	173			
By sentence	189-197	189-191		

1890
Volume III Crime, Pauperism and Benevolence
Part II - General Tables

Dubester 182--
continued

	United States	States and Territory	Counties	Other
Institutionalized population				
Almshouse Paupers Tables 198-266				
Tables without data for states usually have date for regions				
Aggregate	198	198	202	
Proportion of population, from 1850	201	201		
Counties without almshouses			697-9	
Age	211-219	211-219		
Race	198	198	202	
Sex 199-200	199-200	199-200	203-204	
Disabilities and health	225, 252-254 264-266	252-254 264-266		
Education in almshouse	241-242			
Income-support	234-236			
Homeless children	243-245			
Nativity				
Foreign born	227			
Nativity of parents	205-208	208		
Language				
Ability to speak English	210			
Literacy	221			
Occupations	228-230			
Marital status	220			
By cause	231-233			
By relations in almshouse	237-239			
Births				
Children ever born to women in almshouse	226			
Born in almshouse	249-251			
Illigitimate	246-248			
Parental status, foundings	255-263			
Counties and towns without almshouses			697-8	698-9

1890   Dubester 182--
Volume III Crime, Pauperism and Benevolence   continued
Part II - General Tables

	United States	States and Territory	Counties	Other
Inmates of benevolent institutions Tables 267-335 Tables without data for states usually have data by regions				
Aggregate	267 276-281	267 276-281 282	282	
Age	289-291	289-291		
Children	270-272	270-272		
Adults	273-275	273-275		
Race	267	267,282	282	
Sex	268-269	268-269	282	
Children	271-272	271-272		
Adults	274-275	274-275		
Citizenship	287			
Foreign born by naturalization status				
Disabilities and health	297,312-314			
Education of children	315-317			
Income - support	306-308			
Language				
Ability to speak English	288			
Literacy	293			
Nativity	267	267	282	
Foreign born	297			
Nativity of parents	283-285	282,286	282	
Occupations	300-302			
Marital status	292			
By cause	303-305			
By relations in institutions	309-311			
Births				
Children ever born to women in institution	298			
Children born in institution	324-326			
Illigitimage children	321-323			
Parental status, foundlings	327-335			

| Decennial year | 1890 | Dubester 184 |

Census   Eleventh Census

Volume   Volume IV, Part I

Title   Report on vital and social statistics in
                          the United States. Part I. Analysis and
                          rate tables.

Publication   Department of the Interior, Census Office;
                          Washington: Government Printing Office

  Date   1896

Congress   52d Congress, 1st Session, Volume 50,
                          Part 18

  House/Senate   House Miscellaneous Document 340, Part 28

  Serial   Serial 3033

Classifications

  Supt. of Documents   I 12.5: Bk. 20

  Library of Congress   HA201.1890 B. 1 v. IV, pt. 1

    card   7-24047

  Dewey   q 317.3 Un311 v. 4 pt. 1

Microforms

  National Archives   Film T825 Reel 28

  Research Publications   Film 1890 Reel 3

Pages   xvii, 1059 pages

Maps   Maps

Notes   By John S. Billings, M.D., Deputy Surgeon-
                          General, United States Army (Retired),
                          Expert Special Agent. See page 2 for notes
                          on all four parts of this volume on vital
                          and social statistics.

Part I   Analysis of the general returns: Tables of
    ratios and death rates for the census year, with
    maps and diagrams, and an appendix describing the
    various areas for which data are presented in the
    report   Dubester 184

Part II   Analysis of the registration returns for
    the census year of the 28 cities having a popula-
    tion of 100,000 and upward; a description of the
    general characteristics of the wards in these
    cities, with the death rates therein, and general
    and rate tables relating to such cities, with maps
    and diagrams   Dubester 185

Part III   General tables of deaths for the census
    year   Dubester 186

Part IV   General tables of deaths for the census
    year, and also the general tables of deaths in the
    6 year registration area   Dubester 187

This report on vital statistics encompasses four parts, each over a
thousand pages. In spite of its broad title, it is almost completely
devoted to statistics of deaths and their analysis.

Only a few pages in part I are required for the tables on birth and
birth rates, and in part II for comparable tables for the 28 large
cities. Ten pages are required in Part I for tables on the expec-
tation of life and ages of the living population. The remaining four
thousand pages are devoted to death statistics. These are shown by
cause and by month of occurrence. There are crosstabulations by age
and sex, by race, by general nativity and parental nativity, by
birthplace of mother, by occupation and by marital status.

<u>Decennial year</u>	1890	Dubester 185

<u>Census</u>   Eleventh Census

<u>Volume</u>   Volume IV, Part II

<u>Title</u>   Report on vital statistics in the United
                             States. Part II. Cities of 100,000 popu-
                             lation and upward.

<u>Publication</u>   Department of the Interior, Census Office;
                             Washington: Government Printing Office

  Date   1896

<u>Congress</u>   52d Congress, 1st Session, Volume 50,
                             Part 18

  House/Senate   House Miscellaneous Document 340, Part 28

  Serial   Serial 3034

<u>Classifications</u>

  Supt. of Documents   I 12.5: Bk. 21

  Library of Congress   HA201.1890 B. 1 v. 4, pt. 2

    card   7-24047

  Dewey   q 317.3 Un311 v. 4 pt. 2

<u>Microforms</u>

  National Archives   Film T825 Reel 29

  Research Publications   Film 1890 Reel 3

<u>Pages</u>   ix, 1181 pages

<u>Maps</u>   Maps

<u>Notes</u>   By John S. Billings, M.D., Deputy Surgeon-
                             General, United States Army (Retired),
                             Expert Special Agent. See notes for Part
                             I, Dubester 184.

Decennial year	1890	Dubester 186

Census

Eleventh Census

Volume

Volume IV, Part III

Title

Report on vital social statistics in the United States. Part III. Statistics of deaths.

Publication

Department of the Interior, Census Office; Washington: Government Printing Office

Date

1894

Congress

52d Congress, 1st Session, Volume 50, Part 18

House/Senate

House Miscellaneous Document 340, Part 28

Serial

Serial 3035

Classifications

Supt. of Documents

I 12.5: Bk. 22

Library of Congress

HA201.1890 B. 1 v. 4, pt. 3

card

7-24047

Dewey

q 317.3 Un311 v. 4 pt. 3

Microforms

National Archives

Film T825 Reels 29 and 30

Research Publications

Film 1890 Reel 4

Pages

v, 1051 pages

Notes

By John S. Billings, M.D., Deputy Surgeon-General, United States Army (Retired), Expert Special Agent. See notes for Part I, Dubester 184.

<u>Decennial year</u>	1890	Dubester 187

<u>Census</u>   Eleventh Census

<u>Volume</u>   Volume IV, Part IV

<u>Title</u>   Report on vital social statistics in the
                        United States. Part IV. Statistics of
                        deaths.

<u>Publication</u>   Department of the Interior, Census Office;
                        Washington: Government Printing Office

  Date   1895

<u>Congress</u>   52d Congress, 1st Session, Volume 340,
                        Part 18

  House/Senate   House Miscellaneous Document 340, Part 28

  Serial   Serial 3036

<u>Classifications</u>

  Supt. of Documents   I 12.5: Bk. 23

  Library of Congress   HA201.1890 B. 1 v. 4, pt. 4

    card   7-24047

  Dewey   q 317.3 Un311 v. 4 pt. 4

<u>Microforms</u>

  National Archives   Film T825 Reel 30

  Research Publications Film 1890 Reel 4

<u>Pages</u>   v, 1033 pages

<u>Notes</u>   By John S. Billings, M.D., Deputy Surgeon-
                        General, United States Army (Retired),
                        Expert Special Agent. See notes for Part
                        I, Dubester 184.

Decennial year   1890   Dubester 188
                                                separates 189-191

Census   Eleventh Census

Volume   Volume V

Title   Report on the statistics of agriculture in
                        the United States, agriculture by irriga-
                        tion in the western part of the United
                        States, and statistics of fisheries in the
                        United States.

Publication   Department of the Interior, Census Office;
                        Washington: Government Printing Office

 Date   1895

Congress   52d Congress, 1st Session, Volume 50,
                        Part 10

  House/Senate   House Miscellaneous Document 340, Part 20

  Serial   Serial 3021

Classifications

  Supt. of Documents   I 12.5: Bk. 1 and I 12.2: Ag8

  Library of Congress   HA201.1890 B. 1 v. V

    card   7-24047

  Dewey   q 317.3 Un311 v. 5

Microforms

  National Archives   Film T825 Reel 31

  Research Publications Film 1890 Reel A-1

Pages   Statistics vii, 606 pages; irrigation viii,
                        283 pages (TC 823.6. N5) fisheries v. 37
                        pages

Notes   3 reports bound in one volume

1890
Volume V Agriculture

This volume includes three separate reports on agriculture, irrigation and on fisheries. Each is separately paginated and carries
introductory pages. In the case of the first two reports there are
extensive essays and numerous tables. There are also a considerable
number of maps showing production by county and per capita, production of various grains, and other agricultural data. Maps of irrigated areas for the Western States are also included.

Table numbers shown for the first report on agriculture are denoted
by A and table numbers for fishery reports are indicated by F. No
tables are shown for irrigated farm reports; however, this section
should be consulted when seeking information on irrigated farms as
there are a number of unnumbered tables.

References are to tables except where page number is indicated.

A - Agriculture tables
F - Fishery tables

	United States	States and Territory	Counties
Social and Economic Characteristics			
Employment			
Alligator hunters	F p 37	F p 37	
Bird hunters	F p 37	F p 37	
Carp culturalists	F p 37	F p 37	
Fisheries industry			
Fishermen and shoremen	F 1,3	F 1	
For 1880	F 1	F 1	
By industry	F 2,4	F 4	
Farms			
Acres in farms			
Improved and unimproved	A 1,2	A 1,6	A 5,6
From 1850	A 2	A 2	
Average size of farms	A 2	A 2,5	A 5
From 1850	A 2	A 2,5	A 5
Number of farms	A 1,2	A 1,2,5,6	A 5,6
From 1850	A 2	A 2	

1890
Volume V Agriculture

	United States	States and Territory	Counties
Tenure			
Farms cultivated by owner, rented, or on shares	A 3,4	A 3,5	A 5
By size of farm	A 4	A 4,5	A 5

Decennial year	1890	Dubester 193

Census   Eleventh Census

Volume   Volume VI, Part I

Title   Report on manufacturing industries in the
                    United States. Part I. Totals for states
                    and industries.

Publication   Department of the Interior, Census Office;
                    Washington: Government Printing Office

Date   1895

Congress   52d Congress, 1st Session, Volume 50,
                    Part 12

  House/Senate   House Miscellaneous Document 340, Part 22

  Serial   Serial 3024

Classifications

  Supt. of Documents   I 12.5: Bk. 11

  Library of Congress   HA201.1890 B. 1 v. 6, pt. 1

    card   7-24047

  Dewey   q 317.3 Un311 v. 6 pt. 1

Microforms

  National Archives   Film T825   Reel 31 and 32

  Research Publications Film 1890   Reel M-1

Pages   v, 1002 pages

1890   Dubester 193
Volume VI Manufactures Part I - States and Industries

In the Eleventh Census, special agents were assigned to visit each
"productive industry". The results of their tabulations are
published in the three volumes on Manufactures. There are 369
classes of industries on which reports were made.

A copy of the schedule used to determine labor and wages is found on
page 13. In addition to questions of classification of employees and
wages, there are questions on "months in operation" and "number of
hours in the ordinary day of labor."

Employees are divided by sex and age as follows:

Males above the age of 16, females above 16 years, and children

1890
Volume VI Manufactures Part I -
States and Industries

	United States	States and Territory	Counties
Social and Economic Characteristics			
Employment			
See pages 13-28			
Average number manufacturing employees	p 4	p 5-8	
From 1850	p 4	p 5-8	
By age and sex*	p 1	T 1,3	T 6
By industry	T 2,4,5	T 5,6	
By age and sex*			
States with large or small numbers of female employees		p 15-17	
Income and property			
Average annual earnings per employee	p 20	p 22	
By industry	p 21, 23-27		
Total wages	T 1	T 1	T 6
By industry	T 2	T 6	T 6
Average weekly earnings by age and sex	T 8	T 8	

Tables 3-6 classify employees as
    officers, firm members and
      clerks
    operatives, skilled and
      unskilled
    pieceworkers

Table 8 provides detailed information on selected industries and
    classifies the above categories more precisely

Age and sex is presented as
    Males above 16 years
    Females above 15 yars
    Children

Decennial year	1890	Dubester 194

Census   Eleventh Census

Volume   Volume VI, Part II

Title   Report on manufacturing industries in the
                          United States. Part II. Statistics of
                          cities.

Publication   Department of the Interior, Census Office;
                          Washington: Government Printing Office

  Date   1895

Congress   52d Congress, 1st Session, Volume 50,
                          Part 12

  House/Senate   House Miscellaneous Document 340, Part 22

  Serial   Serial 3025

Classifications

  Supt. of Documents   I 12.5: Bk. 12

  Library of Congress   HA201.1890 B. 1 v. 6, pt. 2

    card   7-24047

  Dewey   q 317.3 Un311 v. 6 pt. 2

Microforms

  National Archives   Film T825 Reel 32

  Research Publications   Film 1890 Reel M-1

Pages   xvii, 827 pages

1890   Dubester 194
Volume VI Manufactures Part II - Cities

This volume, like Part 1 of Manufactures includes reports from all
establishments in the mechanical and manufacturing industries.
Establishments with products of $500.00 or more are included. This
volume presents the data by city and a shorter table comparing 100
cities covered in 1880 with their manufactures in 1890.

For each of the 165 cities that have a population of 20,000 or more,
each manufacturing industry is listed in alphabetical order. The
same three classifications of employees is used as in Part 1. Males
above 16, females above 15, and children.

Manufactures are also arranged by product with cities in alphabetical
order.

                                                             Cities

---

Social and Economic Characteristics

Employment   All tables

Income and property
  Wages   All tables

Decennial year	1890	Dubester 195
		separates 196-198

Census   Eleventh Census

Volume   Volume VI, Part III

Title   Report on manufacturing industries in the
                          United States. Part III. Selected
                          industries.

Publication   Department of the Interior, Census Office;
                          Washington: Government Printing Office

  Date   1895

Congress   52d Congress, 1st Session, Volume 50,
                          Part 12

  House/Senate   House Miscellaneous Document 340, Part 22

  Serial   Serial 3026

Classifications

  Supt. of Documents   I 12.5: Bk. 13

  Library of Congress   HA201.1890 B. 1 v. 6, pt. 3

    card   7-24047

  Dewey   q 317.3 Un311 v. 6 pt. 3

Microforms

  National Archives   Film T825 Reels 32 and 33

  Research Publications   Film 1890 Reel M-1

Pages   vii, 725 pages

1890   Dubester 195
Volume VI Manufactures Part III -
Selected Industries

Contents   Pages

	United States	States and Territories

Social and Economic Characteristics

	United States	States and Territories
Employment	Throughout volume	Throughout volume
Income and property Wages	Throughout volume	Throughout volume

Tables similar in format to Part I

Decennial year	1890	Dubester 199

Census   Eleventh Census

Volume   Volume VII

Title   Report on mineral industries in the United States.

Publication   Department of the Interior, Census Office; Washington: Government Printing Office

Date   1892

Congress   52d Congress, 1st Session, Volume 50, Part 1

House/Senate   House Miscellaneous Document 340, Part 1

Serial   Serial 3008

Classifications

Supt. of Documents   I 12.5: Bk. 14

Library of Congress   HA201.1890 B. 1 v. 7

card   7-24047

Dewey   q 317.3 Un311 v. 7

Microforms

National Archives   Film T825 Reel 33

Research Publications Film 1890 Reel M I-1

Pages   xvi, 858 pages

Maps   Maps and illustrations

Notes   Under direction of David T. Day, Special Agent. This volume is mainly concerned with statistics and finances of mining industries, and is organized by metal. There are only occasional references to employees, average number employed, and average number of working days. Therefore there is no table guide to this volume.

Decennial year	1890	Dubester 200

Census   Eleventh Census

Volume   Volume VIII

Title   Report on population and resources of Alaska

Publication   Department of the Interior, Census Office;
                        Washington: Government Printing Office

  Date   1893

Congress   52d Congress, 1st Session, Volume 50,
                        Part 9

  House/Senate   House Miscellaneous Document 340, Part 7

  Serial   Serial 3020

Classifications

  Supt. of Documents   I 12.5: Bk. 2

  Library of Congress   HA201.1890 B. 1 v. 8

    card   7-24047

  Dewey   q 317.3 Un311 v. 8

Microforms

  National Archives   Film T825 Reel 33

  Research Publications Film 1890 Reel 5

Pages   xi, 282 pages

Maps   Maps and illustrations

This volume is particularly valuable for the study of Alaska. It is filled with reproductions of paintings and photographs of the people, their homes and individual settlements. It includes discussions of manners and customs, methods of building houses, descriptions of ceremonies, and other types of information about the population. Data are presented in great detail for even the tiniest settlements. The index is extensive.

Tables begin a new set of numbers with each chapter, and are therefore referred to by page number rather than table number in the guide below.

Contents   Pages

1850
Volume VIII - Population and Resources of Alaska

	Territory	Districts	Villages
Demographic Characteristics			
Aggregate population	3	3, 163	3, 163
From 1860, Russian census	p x	p x	
Age	p 178	174-175	
By race and sex			
Race	3	3-7	3-7
By sex			
By linguistic stock		58-59	58-59
By permanent or temporary			
residence, whites	179	179	
Sex	3	3-7	3-7
Tourist ship passengers	250		
Social and Economic Characteristics			
Education	186-193	186-193	186-193
Employment			
See pages 199-261, chapters			
on fur trade, fisheries, mines			
and commerce			
Families	162, 173-176	162-165	163-165
Housing	162	162-165	163-165
Language	153, 158-159	196	
	196-198		
Literacy	193-195	193	
By age, race and sex			
Nativity			
General nativity	3	3-7	
Specific, by country of			
birth, race and citizen-			
ship	197-198		

1890
Volume VIII - Population and Resources of Alaska

	Territory	Districts	Villages
Occupations			
See pages 199-261			
Temporary summer white residents by sex and by citizenship	179	179	
Religion	181-186		
Transportation			
Tourist ship passengers 1884-1890	250		

Apportionment, Density and Geography

Geography
   See pages 9-18 and chapters
   on individual districts 181

Vital Statistics

Births			
Children ever born to women		171,176	
Marital status			
By race		177-178	

Foreign Data

Chinese residents
   Items supplied for workers 222

318

Decennial year	1890	Dubester 201

Census   Eleventh Census

Volume   Volume IX

Title   Report on statistics of churches in the
                       United States at the Eleventh Census: 1890

Publication   Department of the Interior, Census Office;
                       Washington: Government Printing Office

Date   1894

Congress   52d Congress, 1st Session, Volume 50,
                       Part 7

House/Senate   House Miscellaneous Document 340, Part 17

Serial   Serial 3017

Classifications

Supt. of Documents   I 12.5: Bk. 3

Library of Congress   HA201.1890 v. 9

card   7-24047

Dewey   q 317.3 Un311 v. 9

Microforms

National Archives   Film T825 Reel 34

Research Publications Film 1890 Reel 1

Pages   xxviii, 812 pages

Maps   Maps and charts

Notes   By Henry K. Carroll, Special Agent

1890   Dubester 201
Volume IX - Statistics of Churches

Every church or denomination having members or communicants was requested by the Census Office to furnish information on its organization, church edifices, halls, and its seating capacity. In addition, the value of church property, the number of communicants or members, and ministers were also of great interest. The Census reported 143 denominations in addition to various independent congregations for a total of 165,177 church organizations with 142,521 edifices. This volume provides extensive data/resulting from these inquiries. Only those data dealing with population are noted in the following tables.

Contents   Pages

    Organizations and members by states and territories by counties, by subgroups and conferences.

References are to tables except where page numbers are indicated.

	United States	States and Territory	Counties	Cities of 25,000

Social and Economic Characteristics

Occupations				
Ministers - by denomination	T 9, 10			

1890
Volume IX - Statistics of Churches

Dubester 201--
continued

	United States	States and Territory	Counties	Cities of 25,000
Religion				
Church organizations	T 1,8 9,10	T 1,8 p 52-87	p 52-87	p 91-115
by denomination	T 1,9, 10	T 1		
In cities				p xvii
Members or communicants by denomination	T 7	T 7		
By race				
Black communicants	p xxvi	p xxvi		
By denomination	T 11			
By state		T 11		
Denominations		p 117-812	p 117-812	p 117-812
By state, county, and by subgroup or conference				

321

Decennial year	1890	Dubester 202

Census   Eleventh Census

Volume   Volume X

Title   Report on Indians taxed and not taxed in
                        the United States (except Alaska)

Publication   Department of the Interior, Census Office;
                        Washington: Government Printing Office

  Date   1894

Congress   52d Congress, 1st Session, Volume 50,
                        Part 6

  House/Senate   House Miscellaneous Document 340, Part 15

  Serial   Serial 3016

Classifications

  Supt. of Documents   I 12.5: Bk. 7

  Library of Congress   HA201.1890 B. 1 v. 10
                        E98.C3 U5; E77.U52r

    card   7-24047

  Dewey   q 317.3 Un311 v. 10

Microforms

  National Archives   Film T825 Reel 34

  Research Publications Film 1890 Reel 5

Pages   vii, 683 pages

Maps   Maps and illustrations

Reprints and facsimiles AMS Press, New York 1973 (E98.T24053)

322

This is the most comprehensive of all census volumes on Indians. It
includes not only detailed data from 1890, but also reports of
earlier counts of the Indian population, back to the Thomas Jefferson
Report of 1782.

In addition to the statistical data gathered, there is an essay on
the "conditions" of Indians in each state and territory. Territories
are shown in alphabetical order with states.

A somewhat standard format is used for each state and territory, as
follows:

    Total Indian population
    Indians in prison, not otherwise enumerated
    Reservation Indians not taxed, and not counted in the general
        census
    Indians off reservations, self-supporting and taxed, and counted
        in the general census
    Population on reservations, by sex, by agencies or reservations

Information as to social and economic characteristics of the various
states includes in many cases the subjects listed below. Information
is more fully presented in states with the largest Indian populations.
In addition, there are essays on individual groups such as Pueblos,
with statements in these specific areas:

    education   language
    employment   literacy
    families   occupations
    housing   religion

The volumes are handsomely illustrated with lithographs of color
paintings, photographs of Indians, Indian villages and houses. There
are many maps, including some from very early dates.

Contents   Pages

References are to page numbers

In case of pages only first page is shown; several tables run four
    pages.

	United States	States and Territories	Tribes	Reservation, Location
Demographic Characteristics				
Aggregate population - Reports				
1782 Jefferson	3		3	
1822 Morse	5	5	5	
1832 Drake	12		12	
1850 Schoolcraft	15	15	15	
1850 Census	16	16	16	
1860 Census	17	17		
1867 Taylor		18	18	
1870 Census	21	21		
1880 Census		23	23	
1890 Census	24, 81	24, 81		
Principal population table		98	98	98
Data for each state, beginning		132-634		
Indian groups which had become extinct		35	35	
Principal tribes by name			36	
Indian agencies				92
By age				
Aged Indians, over 80 years, by name and tribe	94		94	94
School age				
By race	all			
Non-Indians counted in Indian census	81	81		
By sex	24, 26 27, 81	23, 26 27, 81 98	98	98

1890
Volume X-Indians

	United States	States and Territories	Tribes	Reservation, Location
By general nativity		23		
By residence				
Off or on reservation, by				
sex	25	25		
Indian census	25, 27	25, 27		
General census	26, 28	26		
From 1860	28	28		
Ration Indians	69, 70	69, 70		70

Social and Economic Characteristics

	United States	States and Territories	Tribes	Reservation, Location
Citizenship				
Methods of Indians obtaining citizenship	663			
Crime	77, 93 95	101	101	101
Indian judges	77			77
Education	85			85
School houses		100	100	100
Employment				
Indian judges	77			77
Apprentices	93	100	100	100
Families		112	112	112
Farms				
Crops raised by Indians and by the government		113	113	113
Stock owned by Indians and by the government		115	115	115
Housing	93	100	100	100
Income		114	114	114
Trade houses - establishment date				63 locations

1890
Volume X-Indians

	United States	States and Territories	Tribes	Reservation, Location
U.S. appropriations	75, 77			
Trust funds	78			
Income from Indian lands	92			
Sources of income		100	100	100
Payments of U.S. to Indians from 1776	641			By reservation
Language				
Linguistic groups, stock	37			37
map	36			
Indians who can use English	93, 99	99	99	99
Literacy	93, 99	99	99	99
Military				
Indian wars from 1789 by date, U.S. Soldiers				
Employed	637			
Killed and wounded	638			
Occupations	1	100	100	100
Religion		100	100	100
Expenditures of religious' societies for Indian schools and missions	88			
Number missionaries	93			
Number churches, communicants, buildings	93			

Apportionment, Density, Geography

	United States	States and Territories	Tribes	Reservation, Location
Geography				
Areas of reservations - acres tillage, irrigable for grazing		91, 111	111	111
Areas of Indian Agencies		92		

	United States	States and Territories	Tribes	Reservation, Location
Vital Statistics				
Note - tables run four pages				
Births	93	93, 100	100	100
Children under one year	99	99	99	99
Deaths	93	101	101	101
Number killed by Indians,				
and by whites	93	101	101	101
Suicides	93	101	101	101
Whites killed by Indians	93	101	101	101
Marriages and divorces	93			
Polygamy	93	101	101	101
Marital status		101	101	101
Foreign Data				
Census of Indians of Canada, 1890	669			

Decennial year	1890	Dubester 204

Census

Eleventh Census

Volume

Volume XI

Title

Report on insurance business in the United States, Part 1. Fire, marine and inland insurance

Publication

Department of the Interior, Census Office; Washington: Government Printing Office

Date

1894

Congress

52d Congress, 1st Session, Volume 50, Part 5

House/Senate

House Miscellaneous Document 340, Part 14

Serial

Serial 3014

Classifications

Supt. of Documents

I 12.5: Bk. 9

Library of Congress

HA201.1890 B. 1 v. 11

card

7-24047

Dewey

q 317.3 Un311 v. 11 pt. 1

Microforms

National Archives

Film T825   Reel 35

Research Publications

Film 1890   Reel 9

Pages

x, 1127 pages

Notes

By Charles A. Jenney, Special Agent. There is no population data in this volume, and therefore no table guide is provided.

Decennial year	1890	Dubester 205

Census   Eleventh Census

Volume   Volume XI

Title   Report on insurance business in the United States, Part 2. Life insurance

Publication   Department of the Interior, Census Office; Washington: Government Printing Office

Date   1895

Congress   52d Congress, 1st Session, Volume 50, Part 5

House/Senate   House Miscellaneous Document 340, Part 14

Serial   Serial 3015

Classifications

Supt. of Documents   I 12.5: Bk. 10

Library of Congress   HA201.1890 B. 1 v. 11

card   7-24047

Dewey   q 317.3 Un311 v. 11 pt. 2

Microforms

National Archives   Film T825 Reel 35

Research Publications   Film 1890 Reel 10

Pages   xii, 478 pages

Notes   By Charles A. Jenney, Special Agent. There is no population data in this volume, and therefore no table guide is provided.

<u>Decennial year</u>	1890	Dubester 206

<u>Census</u>   Eleventh Census

<u>Volume</u>   Volume XII

<u>Title</u>   Report on real estate mortgages in the
                             United States

<u>Publication</u>   Department of the Interior, Census Office;
                             Washington: Government Printing Office

Date   1895

<u>Congress</u>   52d Congress, 1st Session, Volume 50,
                             Part 13

House/Senate   House Miscellaneous Document 340, Part 23

Serial   Serial 3027

<u>Classifications</u>

Supt. of Documents   I 12.5: Bk. 17

Library of Congress   HA201.1890 B. 1 v. 12

   card   7-24047

Dewey   q 317.3 Un311 v. 12

<u>Microforms</u>

National Archives   Film T825 Reel 36

Research Publications   Film 1890 Reel H-1

<u>Pages</u>   xi, 943 pages

<u>Maps</u>   Maps and charts

<u>Notes</u>   By George K. Holmes and John S. Lord,
                             Special Agents

This compilation of statistics on real estate mortgages was called
for by the Act providing for the Eleventh Census because of public
interest in the issue. Populist efforts by farmers and other workers
had developed sufficient concern in Congress over the issue of
mortgage debt and foreclosures to make specific provision for such a
study in the Act.

Special agents were appointed to develop the extensive study and to
carry it out. Research was done from local public records, and
covered the entire United States with the exception of Alaska, Indian
Territory and Oklahoma. The introductory pages give precise details
on the method used to obtain the detailed information.

A series of state maps follows page 154 and each one indicates, by
county, the average encumbrance and the average value of a farm acre
for that county. Special studies were made of selected counties, and
data are provided for cities of 100,000.

A table guide for the entire volume would be too extensive. However,
the tables suggested below are included to give indication of the
type of data which might be useful in the study of population.

	United States	States and Territory	Counties
Social and Economic Characteristics			
Farms			
Average encumbrance on an encumbered acre by county, and average value of a farm acre			Maps of all states showing individual counties follow p. 154
Housing			
Average mortgages made between 1880 and 1889	T 19-21	T 19-21	
Numerous other tables on mortgages, value of real estate, and other related subjects throughout the volume.			
Number and amount of real estate mortgages made and number of acres and lots covered, 1880 to 1889			T 105

Decennial year	1890 Dubester 207
Census	Eleventh Census
Volume	Volume XIII
Title	Report on farms and homes: proprietorship and indebtedness in the United States
Publication	Department of the Interior, Census Office; Washington: Government Printing Office
Date	1896
Congress	52d Congress, 1st Session, Volume 50, Part 15
House/Senate	House Miscellaneous Document 340, Part 25
Serial	Serial 3030
Classifications	
Supt. of Documents	I 12.5: Bk. 6
Library of Congress	HA201.1890 B. 1 v. 13
Dewey	q 317.3 Un311 v. 13
Microforms	
National Archives	Film T825 Reels 36 and 37
Research Publications	Film 1890 Reel H-1
Pages	xi, 646 pages
Maps	Illustrations
Notes	By George K. Holmes and John S. Lord, Special Agents

1890   Dubester 207
Volume XIII - Farms and Homes

The study of farms and homes and the indebtedness of families and
their tenure of farms and homes was called for by a special act of
Congress. Extensive efforts had been made by the single-taxer movement members to have a study made of the subject. This volume provides extensive data on all aspects of the subject. Not all tables
are included in the guide below.

Content	Tables	Pages
Introduction	1-6	3-7
Proprietorships	7-23	17-54
Value and encumbrance	24-40	55-100
Interest on encumbrance	41-52	101-134
Objects of encumbrance	53-57	135-160
Description of proprietors	58-91	161-242
General tables	92-164	243-646

References are to table numbers.

	United States	Regions	States and Territories	Counties and Cities
Social and Economic Characteristics				
Families	7	7		13
				28 cities of 100,000
% families on farms or in homes	8	8	8	
By value of farm or home	28-30	28-30		
By tenure	58, 60	58, 60		
Farms				
Tenure	7, 9 10, 14	7, 9 10, 14-15	14	
From 1880	9	9		
By race	61-3	61-3		
By sex	62	62		

333

1890
Volume XIII - Farms and Homes

Dubester 207--
continued

Housing
  Tenure

	7, 11 14	7, 11 14	11,14	11-12 cities of 8000 12- counties of NY and NJ
By race	63-4	63-4		

Immigration
  By decades from 1821 23

Nativity
  % natives resident in
    diffferent state from
    where born   22   22   22

Apportionment, Density, Geography

Density   16   16   16

Foreign data

Farm tenancy in Canada and
  European Countries   p 45-46

| Decennial year | 1890 | Dubester 209 |
| | | separate 210 |

Census   Eleventh Census

Volume   Volume XIV

Title   Report on transportation business in the
                       United States. Part 1. Transportation by
                       land

Publication   Department of the Interior, Census Office;
                       Washington: Government Printing Office

  Date   1894

Congress   52d Congress, 1st Session, Volume 50,
                       Part 11

  House/Senate   House Miscellaneous Document 340, Part 21

  Serial   Serial 3022

Classifications

  Supt. of Documents   I 12.5: Bk. 18

  Library of Congress HA201.1890 B. 1 v. 14, pt. 1

    card   7-24047; 7-19292

  Dewey   q 317.3 Un311 v. 14 pt. 1

Microforms

  National Archives   Film T825   Reel 37

  Research Publications Film 1890   Reel T-1

Pages   viii, 867 pages

Maps   Map

Notes   By Henry C. Adams, Special Agent.
                       Separate: Street railways vii, 195 pages
                       (HE 203. A75)

This volume is divided into two main sections: steam railroad
transportation and street railway transportation. It does not
include any information as to highways or other intercity or intra-
city roads.

Most of the material in the first section on railroads deals with
railroad operations, equipment, finances, earnings, tonnage of commodities and such type of information.

The map following page viii shows the railroad lines and connections
including those with lines in Canada and Mexico.

Useful to the study of population and places may be the details on
locations and names of railroad companies, mileage, number of passenger and sleeping cars, number of employees, miles of passenger service, earnings from local and through traffic, commodities carried by
specific railroads, number of "passengers carried one mile".

The second section on street railways is probably more fruitful for
the study of population. Street railways had just come into their
own in the 1880s, with 49 electric and 7 cable railways having opened
by 1890. Length in miles, number of passenger cars, number of
passengers carried, and number of employees in each city of 50,000
shows the impressive development of this form of transportation in
the development of urban America. Names of individual companies,
length of lines, average fare and number of passengers carried should
prove useful in historical urban studies.

Decennial year	1890	Dubester 211 separates 212-214

Census   Eleventh Census

Volume   Volume XIV

Title   Report on transportation business in the
                          United States. Part 2. Transportation by
                          water

Publication   Department of the Interior, Census Office;
                          Washington: Government Printing Office

  Date   1894

Congress   52d Congress, 1st Session, Volume 50,
                          Part 11

  House/Senate   House Miscellaneous Document 340, Part 21

  Serial   Serial 3023

Classifications

  Supt. of Documents   I 12.5: Bk. 19

  Library of Congress   HA201.1890 B. 1 v. 14, pt. 2

    card   7-24047; 7-19292

  Dewey   q 317.3 Un311 v. 14 pt. 1

Microforms

  National Archives   Film T825 Reel 37

  Research Publications   Film 1890 Reel T-1

Pages   xiii, 532 pages

Maps   Maps

Notes   By Henry C. Adams, Special Agent.
                          Separate: The Pacific Coast. 1893. vii,
                          101 pages; The Great Lakes. 1892. vii, 162
                          pages; Rivers of the Mississippi Valley.
                          1892. vii, 81 pages (HE 203. A 75. 1890)

The main content of this volume deals with equipment, operation, construction, operations, earnings, and expenses of water transportation. There are comparative statistics for the period 1880-1889. In the presentation of this data, there are various statistics on employment: "number making ordinary crews", total wages paid, wages paid per month for various classes of employees such as captains, mates, cooks and bakers, seamen, oilers, deck hands and porters. However, this information is not consistent throughout the volume.

There is also information as to individual ports, including tonnage shipped, sometimes by type of cargo, and by number of passengers. Valuable for any study of individual areas, this volume contains so many specifics that a table guide would be useless. The foldout map facing page xiii is valuable for showing navigable rivers and principal transportation routes along the coasts and on the Great Lakes.

The volume is divided into seven sections:

Contents   Pages

Decennial year	1890	Dubester 216

Census   Eleventh Census

Volume   Volume XV Part 1

Title   Report on wealth, debt, and taxation.
                          Part 1. Public debt.

Publication   Department of the Interior, Census Office;
                          Washington: Government Printing Office

  Date   1892

Congress   52d Congress, 1st Session, Volume 50,
                          Part 2

  House/Senate   House Miscellaneous Document 340, Part 4

  Serial   Serial 3009

Classifications

  Supt. of Documents   I 12.5: Bk. 24

  Library of Congress   HA201.1890 B. 1 v. 15, pt. 1

    card   7-24047

  Dewey   q 317.3 Un311 v. 15 pt. 1

Microforms

  National Archives   Film T825 Reel 38

  Research Publications   Film 1890 Reel 10

Pages   xi, 890 pages

Maps   Maps

Notes   By J. Kendrick Upton, Special Agent.
                          This volume deals with public debt only,
                          including national debt of foreign
                          countries, state, county and municipal
                          debt. Other than a count of population for
                          1890 and 1880 for each county and munici-
                          pality with any debt in order to calculate
                          the amount per capita, there is no popula-
                          tion data. Therefore no table guide is
                          provided.

Decennial year	1890	Dubester 217

Census   Eleventh Census

Volume   Volume XV Part 2

Title   Report on wealth, debt, and taxation.
                          Part 2. Valuation and taxation

Publication   Department of the Interior, Census Office;
                          Washington: Government Printing Office

  Date   1895

Congress   52d Congress, 1st Session, Volume 50,
                          Part 2

  House/Senate   House Miscellaneous Document 340, Part 4

  Serial   Serial 3010

Classifications

  Supt. of Documents   I 12.5: Bk. 25

  Library of Congress   HA201.1890 B. 1 v. 15, pt. 2

    card   7-24047

  Dewey   q 317.3 Un311 v. 15 pt. 2

Microforms

  National Archives   Film T825 Reels 38 and 39

  Research Publications   Film 1890 Reel 10

Pages   vii, 654 pages

Maps   Maps

Notes   By J. Kendrick Upton, Special Agent.
                          This volume attempts to show, under the
                          heading "Wealth of the Nation" the value of
                          all tangible property in the U.S., exclu-
                          sive of Alaska. (The determined total was
                          $65,037,091,197.) Value of real estate and
                          improvements was obtained by county and
                          municipality. There is no population data,
                          and therefore no table guide is provided.

340

Decennial year	1890	Dubester 220

Census   Eleventh Census

Volume   Atlas

Title   Statistical Atlas of the United States, based upon the results of the Eleventh Census.

Publication   Department of the Interior, Census Office; Washington: Government Printing Office

Date   1890

Congress   52d Congress, 1st Session, Volume 50, Part 19

House/Senate   House Miscellaneous Document 340, Part 29

Serial   Serial 3037

Classifications

Supt. of Documents   I 12.2: At 6

Library of Congress   HA201.1890 E

card   10-19233

Dewey   f 317.3 Un311S

Microforms

National Archives   Film T825   Reel 41

Research Publications   Film 1890   Reel 8

Pages   69 pages and 63 colored plates

Maps   Maps

Notes   By Henry Gannett

The Statistical Atlas includes 63 colored plates and in addition to text, numerous diagrams in black and white, each illustrating data obtained from the 1890 Census. A major portion of the information is from population inquiries, but some is from other surveys such as those of religious organizations. There is a great deal of historical information gleaned from earlier Censuses.

The Atlas is very large, and is a handsome publication. Many of the maps illustrate characteristics of the states, and among areas within the states.

	Pages	Plates
Demographic Characteristics		
Aggregate population	11	7
From 1790	16	3-6
States - rank		2
Cities - rank		7
Age	24-27,31	
Race	18	10-11
Sex	24-30	9
Social and Economic Characteristics		
Citizenship		22
Crime - prisoners	36	
Disabilities	36-38	
Education	33	
Employment See occupations		
Families	17	8
Farms	51-57	44-54
Income and property	62	61-62

1890
Statistical Atlas

	Pages	Plates
Institutional population		
Prisoners, juveniles, paupers	36	
Language		
Foreign born unable to speak English		31
Literacy	32	
Nativity	19-22	12-16,22
Native born	23-30	23-31
Foreign born	20,22	17-21
Occupations	45-50	42-43
Paupers	36	
Religion	35	33-40
Transportation	61	59-60
Vital Statistics		
Marital status	31	32
Deaths	39-44	41
Apportionment, Density, Geography		
Density	9,11	
Urban-rural distribution of population	9,15	8
Center of population	10,11	
Geography		
Accessions of territory	9, 51	1

| Decennial year | 1890 | Dubester 221 |

Census   Eleventh Census

Volume   Abstract

Title   Abstract of the Eleventh Census: 1890

Publication   Department of the Interior, Census Office;
                        Washington: Government Printing Office

  Date   1894

Congress   52d Congress, 2nd Session

  House/Senate   House Miscellaneous Document 185, Volume 1

  Serial   In Serial 3229

Classifications

  Supt. of Documents   I 2.2: Ab 81

  Library of Congress   HA201.1890. D1

    card   7-18857

  Dewey   317.3 Un311a

Microforms

  Research Publications Film 1890 Reel 6

Pages   vii, 250, vi pages

Notes   By Caroll D. Wright, Commissioner of Labor
                        in charge. For table guide, see 2d Edition
                        of 1890 Abstract, Dubester 222.

Reprints and facsimiles Arno Press, New York. America in Two
                        Centuries 1976

| Decennial year | 1890 | Dubester 222 |

Census   Eleventh Census

Volume   Abstract

Title   Abstract of the Eleventh Census: 1890,
                        2d Edition Revised and Enlarged

Publication   Department of the Interior, Census Office;
                        Washington: Government Printing Office

Date   1896

Congress   Not a Congressional publication

Classifications

  Supt. of Documents   I 12.2: Ab 82

  Library of Congress   HA201.1890. D2

  Dewey   317.3 Un311A2

Microforms

  National Archives   Film 1890 Reel 40

  Research Publications Film 1890 Reel 6

Pages   xi, 300 pages

Notes   Table guide is for this edition of the
                        Abstract, which is 50 pages longer than the
                        1st Edition, published in 1894. It may be
                        used for each edition with slight change of
                        table and page numbers.

This is the second edition of the 1890 Abstract, and it was revised
and enlarged from the first edition. It was not, however, as the
first edition, part of the Congressional Serial Set. There are 50
more pages, additional tables, and the order is slightly revised.
Otherwise the table guide can be used for both editions of the
Abstract.

Contents	Tables		Pages
Representation in Congress			2
Population		1-35	3-88
Agriculture	A	1-12	90-136
Manufactures	M	1-3	138-160
Fisheries	F	1-2	162-166
Mineral industries		1-4	168-170
Transportation		1-14	172-182
Insurance		1-4	184-190
Wealth, debt and taxation		1-15	192-212
Real estate mortgages		1-7	214-220
Farms and homes: proprietorship and indebtedness	FH	1-22	222-244
Education	Ed	1-6	246-256
Churches	Ch	1-4	258-262
Mortality		1-3	264-274
Insane, Feeble-minded, deaf and dumb and blind	D	1-7	276-284
Crime, pauperism and benevolence	CPB	1-6	286-292
Indian's			294-296
Alaska			298-300

In most tables providing data on states, they are grouped into five
geographical categories. Most data is given by sex and race.
Nativity data is given for whites as native or foreign born, usually
with parental nativity.

	United States	States and Territory	Counties	Cities
Demographic Characteristics				
Aggregate population	1, 2 Cr 3	1,2,3 Cr 3	3	

346

	United States	States and Territory	Counties	Cities
From 1790	p 3			
From 1870	2	2		
From 1880		3	3	4 cities of 8000
Alaska		p 298		
Age	19			
School age, 5 - 20 years	20	20		
Military age, males 18-44 years	20	20		
Voting age, males 21 and over	20,30	20,30		
Employment age, 10 and over	27	27		
Race				10 of 50,000
White and negro	7,13,16	7,13,16		
From 1790	p 5			
Chinese, Japanese, Civilized Indian	9,13	9,13		
Indians	p 294			
Sex	1,11	1,11		10
From 1850	p 4			
From 1870	5	5		

Social and Economic Characteristics

Citizenship		
Foreign born males 21 and over by citizenship status	30	30
Crime		
Prisoners	CPB 3	CPB 3
By race, sex and general nativity	CPB 1	CPB 1
By offense	CPB 3	
Juveniles	CPB 4	CPB 4

Disabilities
  By race, by sex and by
    general nativity
  See page 276

1890
Abstract of the Eleventh Census: 1890

	United States	States and Territory	Counties	Cities
Blind	D 6	D 6		
In one eye only	D 7	D 7		
Deaf but not dumb	D 5	D 5		
Deaf and dumb	D 4	D 4		
Feeble minded	D 3	D 3		
Insane	D 1	D 1		
In asylums	D 2	D 2		
Education				
Students attending school				
By race and general				
nativity	24-26	24-26		
By race and sex	Ed 1-4	Ed 1-4		
	6	6		
Schools	Ed 1-6	Ed 1-6		
Indian Schools	p 295	p 295		
Alaska	p 299	p 299		
Teachers				
By race and sex	Ed 1-4	Ed 1-4		
Employment				
Persons 10 and over				
employed	27	27		
In fisheries - fisherman,				
shoresmen	F 1	F 1		
In manufactures -				
employees and wages				
from 1880	M 1-2	M 1		M 3 of 20,000
In transportation	T 12			
Families				
Number of families and				
persons per family, from				
1870	34	34		
From 1880				35 cities of 50,000
Farms				
Number of farms and average				
size	A 1	A 1		
By tenure	A 2	A 2		
	FH 2,7	FH 2,7		
	13,19	13		
	21-2			

348

	United States	States and Territory	Counties	Cities
Housing				
Number dwellings and persons per dwelling, from 1870	33 FH 1-3	33 FH 1-3		
By tenure	6-8,10 19-22	6-8,10		FH 4 cities of 8,000-100,000 FH 5 cities of 100,000
Institutionalized population				
By race, sex and general nativity				
Benevolent institutions	CPB 6	CPB 6		
Paupers in almshouses	CPB 5	CPB 5		
Prisons and juvenile reformatories	CPB 1-4	CPB 1-4		
Language				
By race, sex and general nativity				
Unable to speak English, 10 years and over	23	23		
Literacy				
Illiterates, by race and general nativity, from 1880	21	21		
By sex, from 1880	22			
Alaska		p 299		
Military				
Veterans and widows, U.S. military	31	31		
Veterans and widows, Confederacy	32	32		
Nativity				
General nativity				
From 1870	6,8,15	6,8,15		10 cities of 50,000
By race	16	16		
By sex	11	11		
By parental nativity	12,17	12,17		

1890
Abstract of the Eleventh Census: 1890

	United States	States and Territory	Counties	Cities
Specific nativity				
By foreign country	14	14		
Percentage foreign born from 1850	p 5			
Foreign parentage	15	15		
Occupations				
Persons 10 and/over employed	27	27		
By occupational groups	28	28		
Specific occupations, by sex	29			
Religion				
Church organizations, members	Ch 1			
By denomination	Ch 2-3			
Alaska		p 299		
Transportation				
Passengers carried on steam railroads by local and through traffic	T2			
Passengers carried on water craft	T 5-8			
Passengers carried on street railways	12	T 12		T 13

Apportionment, Density and Geography

	United States	States and Territory	Counties	Cities
Apportionment				
Representation in Congress from 1880		p 2		
Ratios 1789-1890				

Vital Statistics

	United States	States and Territory	Counties	Cities
See page 264 re registration cities and states				
Deaths				
By cause	V 3	V 3		

350

Abstract of the Eleventh Census: 1890

	United States	States and Territory	Counties	Cities
Number				
By age - under 5 years	V 1-2	V 1-2		V 1
By race and nativity	V 1-2	V 1-2		V 1
By sex	V 1-2	V 1-2		V 1
Rates				p 265
Marital status	18	18		
Alaska		p 299		

Decennial year	1890	Dubester 224
Census	Eleventh Census	
Volume	Compendium, Part I	
Title	Compendium of the Eleventh Census: 1890 Part I. Population	
Publication	Department of the Interior, Census Office; Washington: Government Printing Office	
Date	1892	
Congress	52d Congress, 1st Session, Volume 50, Part 3	
House/Senate	House Miscellaneous Document 340, Part 6	
Serial	Serial 3011	
Classifications		
Supt. of Documents	I 12.2: C73^1	
Library of Congress	HA201.1890 C 1	
card	7-18856	
Dewey	q 317.3 Un311c pt.1	
Microforms		
National Archives	Film T825 Reel 39	
Research Publications	Film 1890 Reel 7	
Pages	cxi, 957 pages	
Maps	Maps	

352

Contents	Tables	Pages
Table of contents		iii
Introduction - Includes considerable material on apportionment, plan of publication of the Eleventh Census, explanation of the use of electronic tabulating machines		ix-xxxiv
Progress of the Nation		xxxv-cxxv
Schedule of 1890 Census questionnaire		cxxviii
Public Laws on the Eleventh Census		cxxx
Population tables	1-28	2-853
Dwellings and Families tables	D1-10	855-914
Statistics of Alaska	A1-4	916-922
Index		923-957

References are to table numbers

	United States	States and Ter'tes	Counties	Minor Civil Divisions	Cities and Places
Demographic Characteristics					
Aggregate population	1 a,b	1 a,b	2	3	4 a,b of 25,000 5 - 2500 6 - 1000
from 1790	1 a,b	1 a,b	2		4 a,b
from 1880				3	5
Alaska		A 1	A 1 Districts		A 2- villages
Age See page cviii School age 5-17, 18-20, 5-20	21 a-i	21 a-i	27		22 25,000 28 2500
Militia age Males 18-44	23	23	27		24 25,000 28

1890
Compendium - Part I

	United States	States and Ter'tes	Counties	Minor Civil Divisions	Cities and Places
Voting age					
Males 21	25	25	27		26
					25,000
					28
Alaska					
Under 5, 5-19, 20-44, 45		A 3,5	A 5		
Race					
See page xcviii	7,11	7,11	19,27	13	17,20
	21,23	21,23			28 of
	25				2500
					22,24
					26 of
					25,000
					28
Specific					
African descent	8	8			17
Chinese	8,12	8,12	14		17
Japanese	8,12	8,12	15		17
Civilized Indians	8,12	8,12	16		17,2
From 1850	11	11			
From 1870			14-16	13	
Alaska		A 1,3-5			A 2
Sex	7,9,	7,9,	19,27		17
	18	18			22 b,c
					of
					25,000
					28 of
					2500
From 1850	9	9			
Alaska		A 1,3-7	A 1		A 2

Social and Economic Characteristics

Citizenship
  Alaska - aliens   A 5

354

	United States	States and Ter'tes	Counties	Minor Civil Divisions	Cities and Places
Employment					
Alaska - white summer employees		A 6	A 6		
Families					
See page cx					
Number families and persons to a family	D 2,7	D 2,7	D 3		D 4 of 2500 D 8 of 25,000
From 1850	D 1	D 1			
By number of families to a dwelling					D 9, 10 100,000
Nativity					
See page lxxxvi					
General nativity	10,18 21,23 25	10,18 21,23	13,19 27		17,20 22,24 26
Alaska		A 1			
From 1850	10	10			
From 1870					26,28
General and parental nativity	7,18 21,23 25	7,18 21,23	13,19 27		20,24 26,28

Apportionment, Density, Geography

Apportionment					
See page x					
Present 1890 and proposed		p 10			
From 1790		p xiv			
Acts		pxi			
Density	1 c	1 c			
See page xliv and page 1					
Density and center of population from 1790					

1890
Compendium - Part I

	United States	States and Ter'tes	Counties	Minor Civil Divisions	Cities and Places

Geographical distribution
  of the population
  See page liii

Places of 1,000 - Table 6
Cities and places of 2,500 - Tables 5, 17, 20, 28 and D 4
Cities of 25,000 - Tables 4 a and b, 22, 24, 26, D 6, D 8
Cities of 100,000 - Tables D 9 and 10

<u>Decennial year</u>	1890	Dubester 225

<u>Census</u>   Eleventh Census

<u>Volume</u>   Compendium, Part II

<u>Title</u>   Compendium of the Eleventh Census: 1890
                         Part II. Vital and social statistics.

<u>Publication</u>   Department of the Interior, Census Office;
                         Washington: Government Printing Office

  Date   1894

<u>Congress</u>   52d Congress, 1st Session, Volume 50,
                         Part 4

  House/Senate   House Miscellaneous Document 340, Part 6

  Serial   Serial 3012

<u>Classifications</u>

  Supt. of Documents   I 12.2: C73^2

  Library of Congress   HA201.1890.C2

    card   7-18856

  Dewey   q 317.3 Un311C2

<u>Microforms</u>

  National Archives   Film T825   Reels 39 and 40

  Research Publications Film 1890   Reel 7

<u>Pages</u>   v, 1062 pages

1890   Dubester 225
Compendium - Part II

Contents	Tables	Pages

	United States	States and Ter'tes Counties	Minor Civil Divisions	Cities and Places

---

Demographic Characteristics

Race	C 1	C 1		
	C 6-18	C 6-18		
	C 21-26	C 21-26		
	E 1-11	E 1-11		
Sex	C 2,3	C 2,3		
	C 14-15	C 14-15		
	C 17-20	C 17-20		
	C 22-23	C 22-23		
	C 25-26	C 25-26		
	E 1-11	E 1-11		

Social and Economic Characteristics

Citizenship

Foreign born males of 21, by citizenship status	FB 4	FB 4		FB 5 of 25,000
Aliens by country of birth by years in U.S.	FB 6,8	FB 6,8		FB 7,9 of 25,000

358

1890
Compendium - Part II

Dubester 225--
continued

	United States	States and Ter'tes Counties	Minor Civil Divisions	Cities and Places
Crime	C 1,2	C 1,2		
Prisoners	3,5	3,5		
See pages 161-169				
Type institution	C 4,6-12	C 4,6-12		
Juvenile prisoners	C 13-15	C 13-15		
Offenses	C 16-20	C 16-20		
Diabilities	D	D	D	
See pages 133-135 and two unnumbered tables for numbers of blind (one or both eyes), deaf, deaf and dumb, feeble-minded and insane				
Statistics for sick and disabled on page 135				
Insane prisoners	C 12	C 12		
Education				
See pages 211-213				
School enrollment	E 1-10	E 1-10		E 11 of 10,000
Teachers	E 1-5	E 1-5		
Employment				
Manufactures in 165 cities				
Average number workers, some classifications, wages				M 1-2
Mineral industries				
Grand total employees, Some classifications				
Institutional population				
See pages 170-176 on Paupers and Benevolent institutions				
See "Crime" above	C 1-20	C 1-20		
Paupers	C 21-23	C 21-23		
Benevolent institutions	C 24-26	C 24-26		

1890   Dubester 225--
Compendium - Part II   continued

	United States	States and Ter'tes	Counties	Minor Civil Divisions	Cities and Places
Nativity	C 1-3 C 6-18 C 21-26	C 1-3 C 6-18 C 21-26			

Specific nativity -
  Foreign born by country
    of birth
	FB 1,4	FB 1,4	FB 3		FB 2,
					5 of
					25,000

Paupers
  See page 170-175
  Note - "outdoor paupers"
    not enumerated in
    1890 Census
	C 21-23	C 21-23			

Religion
  See pages 261-264 for
    church organizations,
    members
	R 1,6-8	R 1,6-8			

Vital Statistics

	United States	States and Ter'tes	Counties	Minor Civil Divisions	Cities and Places

Mortality
  See page 3
  Deaths by age, race, sex,
    general nativity and
    cause for registration
    places
	1-3	1-3	3		1, 3

Cities of 10,000 - Table E 11
Cities of 25,000 - FB 2, 5, 7, and 9

<u>Decennial year</u>	1890	Dubester 226

<u>Census</u>   Eleventh Census

<u>Volume</u>   Compendium, Part III

<u>Title</u>   Compendium of the Eleventh Census: 1890
                              Part III. Population: State or Territory

<u>Publication</u>   Department of the Interior, Census Office;
                              Washington: Government Printing Office

Date   1897

<u>Congress</u>   52d Congress, 1st Session, Volume 50,
                              Part 4

House/Senate   House Miscellaneous Document 340, Part 6

Serial   Serial 3013

<u>Classifications</u>

Supt. of Documents   I 12.2: C73^3

Library of Congress   HA201.1890.C3

card   7-18856

Dewey   q 317.3 Un311C3

<u>Microforms</u>

National Archives   Film T825   Reel 40

Research Publications   Film 1890   Reel 8

<u>Pages</u>   vii, 1150 pages

1890   Dubester 226
Compendium - Part III

Each section contains an introductory essay with unnumbered titles

---

	United States	States and Territories	Cities
Demographic Characteristics			
Aggregate population	23	24	
Age			
See page 188	19,23	20,24-30	22 of 400,000
	25-30	33,39-40	
	33,39-40	54-59	31,41 of 25,000
	54-60	65-69	
	65-69	79	42-45 of 25,000
	79-80	98-99	
	98-99		62,72
	FH 24		

	United States	States and Territories	Cities
Race	19,23	20,24	22
	27-30	27-30	
	32,35-38	32,35-38	101
	47,49-53	47,49-53	
	60,76-78	76-77	
	96-97	96-97	
	FH 22-23		
	FH 25		
	27-28		
Indians			
See page 1115	I 1-4	I 1-4	
Sex	23,26-30	24,26-30	31,41
	33-40	33-38	
	48-60,65	39-40	42-46 of
	73-74	48-59	25,000
	77-92	65,73,75	61 of
	I 1-4	77,79,81	25,000
	M 3-4	83,85,87	62
	FH 21,23	89,91	72
	25-28	I 1-4	95 of
		M 3-5	50,000

Social and Economic Characteristics

Citizenship			
See page 58-	93-94	93	
Education			
See pages 266			
School attendance	32-40	32-40	41
Employment and unemployment			
Employment in			
Express companies	E 5		
Fisheries	F 1,2	F 1,2	
Manufactures	M 1-4	M 1,3,5	
Transportation	T 7		
	TW 3-4		
	8-9		
Unemployed	87,88	87	

	United States	States and Territories	Cities
Farms			
See page 589	A 1-4 FH 1,2 21	A 1-4 FH 1,2	
Housing	FH 1,3-7 21	FH 1,3	FH 4 of 8,000 FH 6 of 100,000 FH 7 outside of cities of 8,000
Language Persons 10 years and over who cannot speak English See page 346	63-69 85,86	63-69 85,86	70-72 of 25,000
Literacy Persons 10 years and over who could read but not write or who could neither read nor write	47-60 83	47,60 83	61 of 25,000 62
Military See pages 572- Soldiers and widows, U.S. and Confederate	96-100	96-100	101 of 25,000
Nativity General and parental nativity	19,23 27,29 34-38,40 47,49-51, 55-57,60 63-64, 66-69 76-78,84 86, 96-97	20,24,27 29,32 34-38,40 47,49-51, 55-57,60 63,64, 66-69 76-77,96-97	22 42,44 70-71
Specific nativity State or territory of birth See pages 3-45	1	1	5 cities of 25,000
By race	2-4	2-4	

1890
Compendium - Part III

	United States	States and Territories	Cities
Foreign born by country of birth	94		
See pages 46-67	89-90	89-90	
Native or foreign parentage			
See pages 68-90	6,28	6,28	16
Foreign parentage	7-15	7-15	17
	91,92	91	
Occupations	73-85	73,75-77	95 of
See pages 374-	87-94,	79,81,83	50,000
	100	85,87,89	
		91,93	

Vital Statistics

	United States	States and Territories	Cities
Marital status	18,81-82	18,81	21 of
See page 115 - "Conjugal condition"			25,000
By age, race, and general nativity	19	20	22 of 400,000

Cities of 8,000 - Table FH 4
Cities of 25,000 - Tables 21, 61, 70, 71, 72, 101
Cities of 50,000 - Table 95
Cities of 100,000 - Table FH 6
Cities of 400,000 - Table 22

Decennial year	1890	Dubester 227

Census   Eleventh Census

Volume   Index to Bulletins

Title   Index to Bulletins. Census Bulletins numbers 1 to 201. Extra Census Bulletins numbers 1 to 21.

Publication   Department of the Interior, Census Office; Washington: U.S. Census Printing Office

Date   1894

Congress   Not a Congressional publication

Classifications

   Supt. of Documents   I 12.2: In2^1

   Library of Congress   HA201.1890.A21

      card   11-26882

   Dewey   317.3 Un311in

Pages   13 pages

Notes   Copy of Index to Bulletins 1-201 follows this page. No copy of the Index to Bulletins 1-380 (Dubester 228) was found at the Library of Congress or the Census Bureau Library in April 1982.

INDEX TO BULLETINS

AGRICULTURE

1

2

ALASKA.

CHURCHES.

3

CHURCHES—Continued.

No.

159   Reformed Church in America, Reformed Church in the United States, Christian Reformed Church, Orthodox Jewish Congregations, Reformed Jewish Congregations, Friends (Orthodox), Friends (Hicksite), Friends (Wilburite), Friends (Primitive), Reformed Presbyterian (Synod), Reformed Presbyterian (General Synod), Reformed Presbyterian Covenanted, Reformed Presbyterian in United States, Associate Church of North America, Associate Reformed Synod of the South, and Spiritualists.

101   Roman Catholic, Greek Catholic (Uniates), Russian Orthodox, Greek Orthodox, Armenian, Old Catholic, and Reformed Catholic.

18   United Presbyterian of North America, Church of the New Jerusalem (Swedenborgian), Catholic Apostolic, Salvation Army, Advent Christian, Evangelical Adventists, Life and Advent Union (Adventists), Seventh-day Baptists, Seventh-day Baptists (German), General Six Principle Baptists, Christian Church South, Schwenkfeldians, Theosophical Society, and Brethren in Christ (River Brethren).

EDUCATION.

Statistics for—

84   Alabama, Colorado, Florida, Georgia, Idaho, Indiana, Kansas, Kentucky, Missouri, Nebraska, Nevada, New Jersey, Tennessee, and 105 Cities.

53   Alaska, Arkansas, Delaware, Illinois, Iowa, Michigan, Minnesota, Mississippi, New Mexico, New York, North Dakota, Oregon, Texas, Utah, Washington, West Virginia, and 42 Cities.

36   Arizona, California, Connecticut, District of Columbia, Maine, Maryland, Massachusetts, Montana, North Carolina, Ohio, Oklahoma, Pennsylvania, Rhode Island, South Carolina, South Dakota, Vermont, Virginia, Wyoming, and 83 Cities.

17   Louisiana, New Hampshire, Wisconsin, and Cities of 10,000 Inhabitants and Over; also, Mormon Schools in Arizona, Idaho, and Utah.

4

FARMS, HOMES, AND MORTGAGES

5

MANUFACTURES.

MINES AND MINING.

PAUPERISM AND CRIME.

POPULATION

8

POPULATION—Continued.

9

TRANSPORTATION.

10

VITAL STATISTICS.

WEALTH, DEBT, AND TAXATION.

EXTRA CENSUS BULLETINS.

AGRICULTURE.

EDUCATION.

FARMS, HOMES, AND MORTGAGES.

INSURANCE.

12

MANUFACTURES.

MINES AND MINING.

POPULATION.

LIST OF BULLETINS BEING PREPARED FOR PRESS.

Annual Interest Charge on Bonded Indebtedness.
Cereal Production—Michigan, Ohio, and Kentucky.
Inmates of Juvenile Reformatories.
Persons of School Age, Males of Militia Age, Males of Voting Age,
    and Citizenship of Foreign Born Males 21 Years and Over, by
    States and Territories.
Population by Color, Sex, and General Nativity—
    Ohio, Indiana, Illinois, Michigan, Wisconsin, and Minnesota.
    Iowa, Missouri, North Dakota, South Dakota, Nebraska, and
      Kansas.
    South Central Division.
    Western Division.
Statistics of—
    Cotton Manufacture.
    Methodist Churches.

EXTRA CENSUS BULLETINS.

Irrigation in Western United States.
Mileage of Railways of the World.
Summary of Church Statistics.
Transportation by Water in the United States.
Vital Statistics of—
    New York and Brooklyn.
    Washington and Baltimore.

Decennial year   1890   Dubester 228

Census   Eleventh Census

Volume   General Reports

Title   Index to Bulletins. Census Bulletins num-
                        bers 1 to 380. Extra Census Bulletins num-
                        bers 1 to 98; corrected to January 1, 1895.

Publication   Department of the Interior, Census Office;
                        Washington: U.S. Census Printing Office

Date   1895

Congress   Not a Congressional publication

Classifications

  Supt. of Documents   I 12.2: In2^2

  Dewey   317.3 Un311 in 2

Notes   No copy of this Index was found at the
                        Library of Congress or the Census Bureau
                        Library in April 1982.

Decennial year	1890	Dubester 229

Census   Eleventh Census

Title   Report on education in the United States

Publication   Department of the Interior, Census Office;
                      Washington, Government Printing Office

Date   1893

Congress   52d Congress, 1st Session

House/Senate   House Miscellaneous Document 340, Part 9

Serial   In Serial 3109

Classifications

Supt. of Documents   I 12.2: Ed8

Library of Congress   L 111.H5. 1890.A

Dewey   7-21972

Microforms   q 317.3 Un 311 ed   q 317.3 Un 311ed

National Archives   Film T825   Reel 26

Research Publications Film 1890   Reel 8

Pages   vii, 141 pages

Notes   By James H. Blodgett, Special Agent
                      Included in Volume I Population, Part 2,
                      Dubester 178. See that volume for table
                      guide.

Tables in this report are also included in Population Volume I Part II.

References are to table numbers except where pages are indicated.

	United States	States and Territory	Counties	Cities

Social and Economic Characteristics

Education
  Aggregate population and
  number attending school,
  from 1850

	United States	States and Territory	Counties	Cities
Aggregate population and number attending school, from 1850	p 18	8		
Enrollment	7, 14-15 19	7-8, 14-15 19	8	22
1840-1880	1-6, 9	1-6, 9-10		
Private Schools	16,20	16,20		
Kindergarten - teachrs, pupils, by sex and race	34	34		
Professional schools	21	21		
Age				
Ages for school census		p 9		
Legal age for attendance		p 8		
Race of students	7,14,16 21	7,11,12 14,16,21	8	22
Sex of students	7,13-14, 16,21	7,13-14, 16,21	6	22
School buildings	p 45	p 45		
Evening schools	p 43	p 43		
Length of term		p 20		
Religious schools by denomination	17 p 41	17 p 41		
Teachers - by race and sex	7,14,17- 18,21	7-8,14 17-18,21	8	22
School finances	23	23		

<u>Decennial year</u>	1890	Dubester 230

<u>Census</u>   Eleventh Census

<u>Volume</u>   General Reports

<u>Title</u>   Report on Social Statistics of Cities in the United States

<u>Publication</u>   Department of the Interior, Census Office; Washington: Government Printing Office

Date   1895

<u>Congress</u>   Not a Congressional publication

<u>Classifications</u>

  Supt. of Documents   I 12.5: So1

  Library of Congress   HA205. A35 1890

    card   25-18811

  Dewey   352.073 Un3r

<u>Microforms</u>

  National Archives   Film T825 Reel 42

  Research Publications   Film 1890 Reel 8

<u>Pages</u>   vii, 137 pages

<u>Notes</u>   By John S. Billings, M.D., Expert Special Agent

1890   Dubester 230
Report on the Social Statistics of Cities

_____

This publication is much more oriented toward governmental services
in cities than the 1880 volume of the same title. Much of the information included would today be part of the Census of Governments
rather than the Census of Population. Many of the data provided are
calculated on a per capita basis.

References are to table numbers.

1890
Report on the Social Statistics of Cities

Dubester 230--
continued

	United States	States	Cities
Demographic Characteristics			
Aggregate population			
Cities of 100,000			8
Cities by population size	1	1	
Number of cities	1	1	
Proportion living in cities	1	1	
From 1880			
Social and Economic Characteristics			
Housing			
Number dwellings, number persons per dwelling			63
Transportation			
Miles of paved road, by size of city	14-17		64-65
Street lighting	19-20		21,23-24
Suburban travel - number passengers, commuters, daily trains			62, 74
Apportionment, Density, Geography			
Density by size of city	5-6		
by ward - 25 cities of 100,000			8
For 326 cities			63
Vital Statistics			63
Death rate by density			7
By ward, 25 cities			8
Foreign Data			
Dwellings and density - European and U.S. cities			9-11

| Decennial year | 1890 | Dubester 231 |

Census   Eleventh Census

Volume   Special Report

Title   Special Census Report on the occupations of
                     the population of the United States

Publication   Department of the Interior, Census Office;
                     Washington: Government Printing Office

Date   1896

Congress   52d Congress, 1st Session, Volume 50,
                     Part 17

  House/Senate   House Miscellaneous Document 340, Part 27

  Serial   Serial 3032

Classifications

  Supt. of Documents   I 12.2: Oc1

  Library of Congress HB2595.A3.1890

  Dewey   317.3 Un311 oc

Microforms

  Research Publications   Film 1890 Reel 8

Pages   127 pages

Notes   A special report. Not a "final volume".

386

1890   Dubester 231
Special Report on Occupations

_____

This report was submitted to Congress before the completion of the
final volumes of the Eleventh Census, even though it was not completed until late 1896. The lengthier report on occupations was
eventually to become part of Volume I Part II - Population. That
volume was published a year later, and the section on occupations
encompassed some 525 pages in addition to nearly a hundred pages of
introductory material.

The first 29 pages of this Special Report include summary tables and
essays on each of the characteristics presented in the main tables.
There is no table of contents or index.

Some tables in this Report give specific occupations. Others group
occupations into five categories:

   Agriculture, fisheries and mining
   Professional service
   Domestic and personal service
   Trade and transportation
   Manufacturing and mechanical industries

Data is for the United States as a whole, and for states and territories.

Contents   Tables   Pages

Letter transmitting the Report and indicating
   contents, also listing plans for publication
   of final reports.   1
Statistics of occupations. Essay and summary
   tables. Explanation of occupational groups   3-29
Tables   1-16   30-127

_____

                                    United   States and
                                    States   Territories
_____

Social and Economic Characteristics

Employment and unemployment
   Unemployed, by length of time
      unemployed
      By usual occupation, by sex
         Groups of occupations   11   11
         Specific occupations   12

	United States	States and Territories
Language		
Persons unable to speak English, by sex		
In occupations, by groups	15	15
In specific occupations		
By race and general and parental nativity	16	
Literacy		
Illiterate persons engaged in gainful occupations, by sex		
In occupations, by groups	13	13
In specific occupations, by race		
By race and general and parental nativity	14	
Occupations		
By age, by sex		
Persons in occupational groups	7	7
Persons in specific occupations	8	
By race		
By general and parental nativity	4	4
By sex	5	5
By specific occupation	6	
By sex		
Persons in occupational groups	1	1
Persons in specific occupations	2	3
By general and parental nativity,		
By race		
Persons in occupational groups	5	5
Persons in specific occupations	6	
By marital status,		
By sex		
Persons in occupational groups	9	9
Persons in specific occupations	10	

Decennial year	1890	Dubester 232

Census   Eleventh Census

Volume   General Reports

Title   Vital statistics of Boston and Philadelphia,
                        covering a period of six years ending May
                        31, 1890

Publication   Department of the Interior, Census Office;
                        Washington: Government Printing Office

  Date   1895

Congress   Not a Congressional publication

Classifications

  Supt. of Documents   I 12.2: B65

  Library of Congress   HB3527.B7A4.1890

  Dewey   q 312 Un32B

Microforms

  National Archives   Film T825   Reel 41

  Research Publications Film 1890   VS-I

Pages   vii, 269 pages

Notes   By John S. Billings, Expert Special Agent
                        Information for this volume, Vital Statis-
                        tics for Boston and Philadelphia, also
                        applies to the two succeeding volumes for
                        District of Columbia and Baltimore, and New
                        York City and Brooklyn.

This volume, and the two succeeding ones on New York City and
Brooklyn and on the District of Columbia and Baltimore follow almost
identical formats. Statistics are provided for a six year period
ending on May 31, 1890, and are limited to deaths.

Data on deaths are given by cause, and are crosstabulated by age,
race, sex, nativity, parental nativity and by birthplace of mother.
For purpose of comparison of demographic and occupational data for
the two cities tables on age, race, marital status and on occupations
are provided in each volume.

Decennial year	1890	Dubester 233

Census   Eleventh Census

Volume   General Reports

Title   Vital statistics of New York City and
                          Brooklyn covering a period of six years
                          ending May 31, 1890

Publication   Department of the Interior, Census Office;
                          Washington: Government Printing Office

Date   1894

Congress   Not a Congressional publication

Classifications

  Supt. of Documents   I 12.2: N42y

  Library of Congress   HB1357:N5A4 1890

    card   07-18860

  Dewey   q 312 Un32N

Microforms

  National Archives   Film T825 Reel 41

  Research Publications   Film 1890 Reel VS-1

Pages   vii, 529 pages

Notes   By John S. Billings, Expert Special Agent
                          See Vital Statistics for Boston and
                          Philadelphia, Dubester 232, for details on
                          this volume.

Decennial year	1890	Dubester 234

Census   Eleventh Census

Volume   General Reports

Title   Vital statistics of the District of Columbia and Baltimore, covering a period of six years ending May 31, 1890

Publication   Department of the Interior, Census Office Washington: Government Printing Office

Date   1893

Congress   Not a Congressional publication

Classifications

     Supt. of Documents   I 12.2: D63

     Library of Congress   HB 1355.D6b.A4

        card   7-18859

     Dewey   q 312 Un32D

Microforms

     National Archives   Film T825   Reel 41

     Research Publications   Film 1890 VS 1

Pages   vii, 241 pages

Maps   Maps and diagrams

Notes   By John S. Billings, Expert Special Agent See Vital Statistics for Boston and Philadelphia, Dubester 232, page 2, for details on this volume.

<u>Decennial year</u>	1890	Dubester 235

<u>Census</u>   Eleventh Census

<u>Volume</u>   General Reports

<u>Title</u>   Tabular statements exhibiting the popula-
                          tion of each state and the apportionment of
                          members of the House of Representatives
                          from 332 to 375 under the Eleventh Census
                          of the United States: 1890

<u>Publication</u>   Washington: U.S. Census Printing Office

  Date   1890

<u>Congress</u>   Not a Congressional publication

<u>Classifications</u>

  Supt. of Documents   I 12.2: Ap

  Library of Congress   JK 1341.A3.1890

  Dewey   317.3 Un311Ap

<u>Microforms</u>

  Research Publications   Film 1890 Reel 8

<u>Pages</u>   32 pages

<u>Notes</u>   Printed at the request of the Chairman of
                          the House Committee on the Eleventh Census

1890   Dubester 235
Population of Each State and the Apportionment of
Members of the House of Representatives

This is a November 1890 document from the Superintendent of the
Census transmitting the final population counts for the states and
territories.

The letter also describes the time needed to develop the final counts
in earlier censuses, and includes tables for apportionment of representatives with a House of 332 to 375 members.

Contents

	United States	States and Territory
Demographic Characteristics		
Aggregate population	p 3	p 3
Apportionment, Density, Geography		
Apportionment		
Alternate apportionments for 332 to 375 seats	p 8-25	p 8-25

<u>Decennial year</u>	1890	Dubester 237
<u>Census</u>	Eleventh Census	
<u>Volume</u>	Census Bulletins	
<u>Title</u>	Census Bulletins, numbers 1-380	
<u>Publication</u>	Washington: U.S. Census Printing Office	
Date	1889-1894	
<u>Congress</u>	Not a Congressional publication	

<u>Classifications</u>

Supt. of Documents	I 12.3: 1-380
Library of Congress	HA 201.1890.A1
Dewey	317.3 Un311B8
<u>Pages</u>	Various pages

<u>Notes</u>

"Preliminary results as contained in the Eleventh Census Bulletins . . . " Indexed in Dubester 227 and 228; however, no copy of 228 has been located. Bound copies may be found of these preliminary results in the Census Bureau Library. For information in these bulletins, see final volumes of the 1890 Census.

Decennial year   1890   Dubester 238

Census   Eleventh Census

Volume   Census Bulletins

Title   Population by minor civil divisions as returned at the Eleventh Census, June 1, 1890

Publication   Washington: U.S. Census Printing Office

  Date   1891

Congress   Not a Congressional publication

Classifications

  Supt. of Documents   I 12.2: P812

  Library of Congress   HA 201.1890.A32

  Dewey   317.3 Un311mi

Microforms

  Research Publications   Film 1890 Reel 6

Pages   Various pages

Notes   By Robert P. Porter
Bound volume of 54 unnumbered bulletins, one for each state

Decennial year	1890
Census	Eleventh Census
Volume	Census Bulletins
Title	Population by color, sex, and general nativity, with school, militia, and voting ages as returned at the Eleventh Census, June 1, 1890
Publication	Washington: U.S. Census Printing Office
Date	1893
Congress	Not a Congressional publication

Dubester 239

Classifications

Supt. of Documents	I 12.2: P81
Library of Congress	HA 201.1890.A32
card	5-19332+
Dewey	317.3 Un311 p81

Microforms

Research Publications	Film 1890 Reel 6
Pages	Various pages
Notes	Bound volume of bulletins.

Decennial year   1890   Dubester 240

Census   Eleventh Census

Volume   Census Bulletins

Title   Manufactures in cities

Publication   Washington: U.S. Census Printing Office

  Date   1892

Congress   Not a congressional publication

Classifications

  Supt. of Documents   I 12.2: M

  Library of Congress   HA 201.1890.M1

  Dewey   317.3 Un311m

Microforms

  Research Publications   Film 1890 Reel M-I

Notes   Bound volume of 96 bulletins numbered 158-
                          310. For final volume, see Dubester 194,
                          Report on Manufacturing Industries; sta-
                          tistics of cities.

Decennial year	1890	Dubester 241
Census	Eleventh Census	
Volume	Extra Census Bulletins	
Title	Extra Census Bulletins numbers 1-98	
Publication	Washington: U.S. Census Printing Office	
Date	1891-1895	
Congress	Not a congressional publication	

Classifications

Supt. of Documents	I 12.7: 1-98
Library of Congress	HA 201.1890.A2
card	7-18861
Dewey	317.3 Un311ex
Pages	Various pages

Notes

"Numbered Extra Census Bulletins with additional material incorporated in the final reports." Index to numbered Extra Census Bulletins found in volume at Census Bureau Library. No table guide is provided.

<u>Decennial year</u>	1890	Dubester 242

<u>Census</u> Eleventh Census

<u>Volume</u> Extra Census Bulletins

<u>Title</u> The five civilized tribes in Indian
territory: The Cherokee, Chickasaw,
Choctaw, Creek, and Seminole Nations

<u>Publication</u> Washington: U.S. Census Printing Office

Date 1894

<u>Congress</u> Not a Congressional publication

<u>Classifications</u>

Supt. of Documents I 12.7: In21

Library of Congress E 78.I5 U25

card 7-18863

Dewey q 970.4 Un 3f

<u>Microforms</u>

Research Publications Film 1890 Reel 6

Library of American
Civilization LAC 40051

<u>Pages</u> vii, 79 pages

<u>Maps</u> Maps

<u>Notes</u> I 12.2: D71 is report on lawsuit in equity
to restrain publication of this report.
This bulletin and the one following are
included in the Library of American
Civilization ultramicrofiche collection.

1890   Dubester 242
Extra Census Bulletin - The Five Civilized Tribes
in Indian Territory

Contents   Pages

	Indian Territory	Individual Tribes
Demographic Characteristics		
Aggregate population	4	4-10 52,56,63
Age	4-6	58
Race Numerous comments regarding white and black persons living among tribes and in Indian Territory throughout this Bulletin	1,4-61	4-7
Sex	4-7	4-7
Social and Economic Characteristics		
Citizenship	7,9,33	56,65
Crime and administration of Justice Includes information regarding jurisdiction of tribal and U.S. agencies	1,7,9,21	37,45,52-3 64,68,69
Disabilities and health	60	
Education	7,8,13-16	59,61,65,70
Employment	11-12	59,63,70

1890
Extra Census Bulletin - The Five Civilied Tribes

	Indian Territories	Individual Tribes
Farms	1,8,10 11	48,51,54,58 69
Housing	1,13	41,48,59,69

Income and property
  Annuities to tribes and
    individual incomes
	1,7,12 13,19,25	37,41,47,55 57,60,68

Language	13,41,50	
Literacy	7	

Military
  Indian-U.S. wars, Union and
    Confederate service of Indians
    in Civil War
	24,27,29 31	42,47

Paupers Tribal care for own poor	13	
Publications and libraries	7, 13	65

Religion
  Indian practices and Western
    religions
	1, 16-19	39,49,61 63,66-67

Slavery
  Indian ownership of slaves prior
    to emancipation
	7	40,54

Transportation	13,32	51,57,65 69

Apportionment, Density, Geography

| Geography
  Description of lands, treaty lands | 2,10,22 32 | 34,42,51 57,62,68 |
| Vital Statistics | 13 | 53,58 |

Decennial year	1890 Dubester 243
Census	Eleventh Census
Volume	Extra Census Bulletins
Title	Indians. Eastern band of Cherokees of North Carolina
Publication	Washington: U.S. Census Printing Office
Date	1892
Congress	Not a Congressional publication

Classifications

Supt. of Documents	I 12.7: In2^3
Library of Congress	E 99.C5.U3
card	8-14410
Dewey	970.3 D71 I

Microforms

National Archives	Film T 825 Reel 42
Research Publications	Film 1890 Reel 6
Library of American Civilization	LAC 40051
Pages	24 pages
Notes	By Thomas Donaldson, Expert Special Agent This is the only one of the four Bulletins on Indians which appears on the National Archives film. It is also included in the Library of American Civilization collection.

1890   Dubester 243
Extra Census Bulletin - Indians, Eastern Band of
Cherokees of North Carolina

	Eastern Band of Cherokees - Pages

Demographic Characteristics

Aggregate population   7
   From 1850 - shown to be increasing   8

Economic and Social Characteristics

Citizenship   5, 7
   Indians taxed, vote in North Carolina
   Citizens of U.S. and of states of NC,
      Ala, Ga, Tenn, Ky, Va; incorporated
      into white population elsewhere;
      Indian Territory

Crime and courts
   Lack of crime among Cherokees   8,14,15

Disabilities and Health   8

Education   7,9,12,13,15
   Aid to schools   7
   Students by age and sex, teachers by race
      and sex, attendance, buildings,
      expenses, curriculum   9

Farms   8,11-13

Housing   11-13

Income and property   7,9,17
   Annuities to tribe; individual incomes

Literacy   7,15
   Written language

404

1890
Extra Census Bulletin - Indians, Eastern Band of
Cherokees of North Carolina

Dubester 243--
continued

	Eastern Band of Cherokees - Pages

Military
  Union soldiers and widows, Confederate
    soldiers
	21

Occupations Farming, lumbering, day labor, miscellaneous	5,7,11
Religion	13-14

Apportionment, Density, Geography

Apportionment - Representative population, Indians taxed	7

Geography
  Residence in NC, Ala, Ga, Tenn
  Treaty lands
	5,10,11-13
	17-20

Vital Statistics

Birth - minimal number illegitimate births	15

1890   Dubester 244
Extra Census Bulletin - Indians. The Six Nations
of New York

	The Six Nations and Seneca Reservation

Demographic Characteristics

Aggregate population, from 1798 — 6

Race - American Indians
  The Six Nations of New York: Cayugas, Mohawks (Saint Regis), Oneidas, Onondagas, Senecas, Tuscaroras — 19-23
  Historical outline — 19-23,72-76

Social and Economic Characteristics

Citizenship — 80

Crime and courts — 4

Disabilities
  Statistics of cripples, and acute and chronic and other diseases — 7, 71

Education — 9-10,63-70

Employment
  Industries of the Six Nations — 49-51

Families
  Marriage and the Indian home — 54-62

Farms — 14-15,49-51

Government — 33-41

Housing — 13-14,54-58

406

1890
Extra Census   Bulletin - Indians.   The Six Nations   Dubester 244--
of New York   continued

	The Six Nations and Seneca Reservation
Income and Property	
Value of houses and household effects	13, 55
Annuities	77-78,80-81
Institutionalized population	
The Thomas Orphan Asylum	67-68
Language	3,9,70
Military	
Union soldier and sailors	16-17
Occupations	
Statistics of occupations, professions	11
Industries	49-51
	52-53
Social life	8-9,42-48
	59-62

Apportionment, Density, Geography

Geography
   Reservations and locations,
      New York and Pennsylvania
      from 1721   11-14,24-32

Vital Statistics   6-8,71

Births   7
Deaths   7
Marriages and divorces   8
Life tables   8

<u>Decennial year</u>	1890	Dubester 244

<u>Census</u> Eleventh Census

<u>Volume</u> Extra Census Bulletins

<u>Title</u> The Six Nations of New York: Cayugas,
Mohawks (Saint Regis), Oneidas, Onondagas,
Senecas, Tuscaroras

<u>Publication</u> Washington: U.S. Census Printing Office

Date 1892

<u>Congress</u> Not a Congressional publication

<u>Classifications</u>

Supt. of Documents I 12.7: In2^3

Library of Congress E 99.17 B U5

card A-11-1193

Dewey q 970.3 D71 In

<u>Microforms</u>

Research Publications Film 1890 Reel 6

<u>Pages</u> vii, 89 pages

Decennial year	1890	Dubester 245

Census   Eleventh Census

Volume   Extra Census Bulletins

Title   Moqui Pueblo Indians of Arizona and Pueblo
                          Indians of New Mexico

Publication   Washington: U.S. Census Printing Office

  Date   1893

Congress   Not a Congressional publication

Classifications

  Supt. of Documents   I 12.7: In2^4

  Library of Congress   E 99.H7 U5

    card   7-18865

  Dewey   q 970.3 D71

Microforms

  Research Publications   Film 1890 Reel 6

Pages   vii, 136 pages

Maps   Maps and photographs

Notes   By Thomas Donaldson, Expert Special Agent

1890   Dubester 245
Extra Census Bulletin: Moqui Pueblo Indians of
Arizona and Pueblo Indians of New Mexico

Contents   Pages

Moqui Pueblos of Arizona

Demographic Characteristics

Aggregate population   8,9,15
  1583-1890   45-48,92
    Age   7,15,45
                                                       92
  Sex   92

Social and Economic Characteristics

Citizenship - Citizens of the U.S. by treaty   9-10

Crime - Administration of justice   11

Disabilities and Health   19,28,95

Education   36-37,45,
                                                       94-95

Employment - Commerce, Handiwork   8

Families - Pueblo life   10,95

Farms - Subdivision of lands, water supply   5,42,43

Housing - the Pueblos in 1890   6,16,
                                                       47-48
          Land and town holdings   9

1890
Extra Census Bulletin: Moqui Pueblo Indians of
Arizona and Pueblo Indians of New Mexico

Income & Property	46,95
Language	15,45,93
Literacy	45,93
Military - Prisoners in 1892	39
Occupations	45,92-93
Religion	17-19

Apportionment, Density, Geography

Geography
   Lands, Ancient Pueblos, Water supply, description of
      Pueblos throughout the volume

5,15
42-43,51

Vital Statistics

Births, Deaths

95

TERMINOLOGY USED IN THIS VOLUME

Age--Generally inquiries made by the Census were simply "age?" In 1870 and 1880 the inquiry was "age at last birthday," and in 1890 the question was changed to "age at nearest birthday." For the first time, in 1870, the number of months since birth was asked for a child born during the census year, thus enabling development of birth statistics.

In the First Census, only ages of white male heads of families was taken, and that in just two categories--16 and above, and below 16. By 1800, the categories were increased, and eventually the census enumerated the age of each person: females, colored persons and slaves. Data for the latter was generally grouped in larger categories than for whites in the printed reports.

In later years, age data was published, by sex, in connection with school statistics, in an effort to determine the number of persons in school in proportion to the potential school population. This was referred to as School Age. Age of males in what was termed the natural militia, generally 18-45, referred to as Military Age, was also published. Numbers of males over 21, as citizens and as non-citizens, was published as Voting Age.

Aggregate Population--total population

Apportionment--Article I, Section 3 of the United States Constitution states that: "Representatives and direct taxes shall be apportioned among the several States which may be included within the Union, according to their respective numbers, which shall be determined by adding to the whole number of free persons, including those bound to service for a term of years, and excluding Indians not taxed, three-fifths of all other persons. The actual enumeration shall be made within three years after the first meeting of the Congress of the United States, and within every subsequent term of ten years, in such manner as they shall by law direct . . . "

This is the basis of the Census. The results of the decennial enumeration provided a count for determining the number of representatives for each state, generally referred to as apportionment. Prior to the passage of the 13th and 14th Amendments, it was necessary to count slaves separately to determine the "representative population" or the "Federal numbers."

Center of population--Throughout most of its history, the Census has calculated the movement of population by designating a center of population--a point where a north-south line crosses an east-west line, with one half the population on each side. The center of population has of course generally moved west, and somewhat south.

412

Citizenship--Inquiries on United States citizenship did not appear until 1820, when an inquiry was made as to the "foreigners not naturalized." A similar inquiry was made in 1830, after which the question disappeared for several decades. In 1850 and 1860 there was a question on place of birth, asking for name of state, territory or country. However, there was no reference made to citizenship. In 1870, the schedule called for "male citizens of the U.S. 21 years and upwards. No direct question on citizenship appeared in 1880. In 1890, in addition to "number of years in the United States," there were two direct inquiries: "Whether naturalized" and whether naturalization papers have been taken out." Inquiries on citizenship were thus limited to 1820, 1830, 1870 and 1890.

Conjugal condition--Term used for marital status during the Nineteenth Century.

Color--Term color rather than race is used on census schedules from 1850 through 1890. Prior to that, the inquiries referred to "free white" and "free colored" persons and slaves. In this volume, the term "color" is used interchangeably with race. See also race.

Crime--The first census question relating to crime was used in 1850 when there was an inquiry as to "whether a "member of the household was a convict." The same schedule was used in 1860. No such inquiries were made in 1870 and 1880 on the population questionnaires. However, in 1880, a number of separate schedules were used, including one for "Inhabitants in prison." Considerable data was developed from that schedule, and published in a final volume. In 1890, the population schedule once again used a question "Whether a prisoner, convict," and the enumerator was referred to a special schedule which made several inquiries on prisoners, crimes, and imprisonment.

Some final volumes include the names of individual prisons and jails. The 1880 and 1890 separate volumes include considerable demographic data on prisoners and those in juvenile reformatories. The 1890 publications on Indians include information on crime and the administration of justice in Indian areas.

Density--Population per land area, usually stated as persons per square mile.

Disabilities--Beginning with 1830, the year of the first preprinted schedules, inquiries as to disabilities of individuals were made by the Census. The first schedule called for the listing of the number in each family who were blind and the number who were deaf and dumb, the latter categorized by age groups. In 1840, an inquiry on "insane and idiots" was added, and whether they were supported "at private or public charge." In 1850 and 1860 both free and slave schedules had columns for listing those disabled in the four categories, and similar inquiries were made in 1870. The 1880 schedule included a section entitled "Health" with the first question "is the person (on

the day of the enumerator's visit) sick or temporarily disabled so as
to be unable to attend to ordinary business or duties? If so, what
is the sickness or disability? "Seven supplemental schedules were
provided for the "Defective, dependent and dilinquent" classes.
These included numerous questions on place where the person was
located, history of attacks, type of restraints, and name of
establishment where institutionalized. A complete volume was published as a result of expanded inquiries on separate schedules. For
the first time, the deaf were distinguished from deaf-mutes in 1890.

Education--No question was used before 1840. In that year, an
overall column entitled "Schools &c." provided spaces for the number
of persons in each household attending universities and colleges,
academies and grammar schools, or primary and common schools. A
seventh column inquired as to the "number of scholars at public
charge." No later census inquired in such detail.

The schedules for 1850 through 1890 limited their questions to the
names of persons who attended school within the year. However, special inquiries were apparently made to schools to obtain data about
pupils, teachers and school finances, thus producing considerable
detail on education for those years. Data for pupils and teachers is
generally tabulated by sex, race and nativity.

Employment and unemployment--The 1820 Census inquired as to how many
persons were employed in agriculture, in commerce, and in manufactures. Later censuses expanded a great deal on employment and
occupations. No differentiation is made in this volume between
employment and occupation. See Occupation for greater detail.

Unemployment was the subject of inquiry only in 1880 and 1890, when
there was a question as to number of months unemployed during the
census year. This inquiry was to be made of only those who had listed
a gainful employment in the previous inquiry.

Family--From the First Census, enumeration of persons has been based
on households. Through 1840, only the name of the head of the household was recorded, and the other members were counted only. By 1850,
when the name of every person was to be listed, the first two columns
were entitled "Dwelling Houses--numbered in the order of visitation"
and "Families--numbered in the order of visitation." This index makes
no differentiation between "families" and "households."

By 1880, and again in 1890, the inquiry was made as to the relationship of each person to the head of the family--"whether wife, son,
daughter, servant, boarder or other." By 1890, the schedule had
dropped the word "Inhabitants" and changed to "Family schedule."

Farms--Information on the number of persons engaged in farming and
the number and size of farms is included in this index because of the
large number of persons engaged in agriculture during the Nineteenth
Century. As early as 1820, inquiries were made as to the number of

persons in agriculture, as well as in commerce and in manufacturing. Although there was no such question in 1830, one reappeared in 1840, and inquiries have continued throughout the Census. By 1860, a separate volume on agriculture was published in the final reports with considerable data on farms and their production. In 1870 agricultural data was included in the volume on Wealth and Industry, and in 1880 and 1890 separate volumes were again published.

Foreign Data--Considerable information about foreign countries was published in the U.S. Census, particularly in the years 1850 through 1870. The population of major foreign cities, vital statistics, sex ratios, data on educational institutions and libraries, emigration, and other such data were sought out and used for comparison with those of the United States. This information was generally included in the introductory chapters of volumes for comparison with American information, and is noted in this volume because of its potential value to anyone doing research for the period involved.

Geography--In an effort to enumerate the population, it has been necessary for the Census to devote considerable attention to geography. It is essential to establish boundaries of states and territories as well as minor civil divisions to determine and describe the location of population. A great deal of definitive geographical data is therefore included in Census volumes. Volume I of the 1870 Census provides an extremely valuable section on the historical geography of states and the United States.

Health--See disabilities

Housing--From the First Census, population data has been collected by households. Thus there is ample information throughout on housing. By 1850, the number of dwellings and the number of families were published in the final reports, often with the number of persons to a dwelling. In addition, there are other sources of information on housing. In 1890 there were questions on farms and homes and on tenure (rental or owned with or without a mortgage). The 1860 Slave Schedule had a question on the number of slave houses, and the 1890 Indian Schedule had several inquiries on Indian housing, the results of which appeared in the final reports.

Immigration--The population census itself could not of course develop immigration statistics. However, in the early census volumes, considerable data from other government documents was included as to immigration in early years. These data are frequently found in introductory chapters of population volumes. Data is provided by sex and by occupation as well as country from which persons had emigrated.

The 1820 and 1830 Census counted "Foreigners not naturalized" without reference to former nationalities. Then, beginning in 1850 and 1860, place of birth, including states and territories as well as foreign countries, was asked. In 1870, there were columns for indicating whether the father or mother was of foreign birth. Not until 1900, outside the scope of this index, was year of immigration and number of years in the United States asked.

Income--Although there were no specific questions addressed to income in the Nineteenth Century, information on wages appears in connection with employment or farm sales through most of the Century.

Indians--Article I Section 2 of the United States Constitution, which called for the enumeration of the population to determine the number of representatives each state would send to Congress, specifically excluded "Indians not taxed." Therefore Indians were generally not included in the Census. As Indians gradually became integrated in white communities they presumably paid taxes and were counted in the population. They were referred to in census volumes as "civilized Indians." Special schedules were used for the enumeration of Indians in both 1880 and 1890, and a very complete volume was published in 1890 with details on the Indian population in each state and territory.

Institutionalized Population--Both the 1880 and 1890 Censuses made use of special schedules for what were called "Defective, dependent and delinquent classes." In 1880 these included the disabled, homeless children, individuals in prison, and paupers and indigent inhabitants in institutions, poor houses and asylums. In 1890 were added schedules for the insane (not included with other disabilities in 1880), school statistics for the deaf, a schedule for persons in benevolent institutions, and one for soldiers homes. Results of these inquiries were published in separate volumes in both 1880 and 1890. Prior to those years, statistics on prisoners and other institutionalized persons were incorporated in the main population volumes. See also "Crime" and "Paupers."

Language--The question "Able to speak English? If not, the language or dialect spoken" was asked only in 1890. The resulting data was crosstabulated by demographic and social characteristics. No data was published in the final volumes as to the language spoken by those unable to speak English. In several 1890 volumes on Indians, there is some information on language.

Literacy--The first inquiry on literacy appeared in 1840, as to the number of persons of 20 years of age who could not read and write. The question was continued with each decade. By 1870, separate inquiries were made as to those who could not read and those who could not write, the form of inquiry continued in 1880 and 1890. Published data generally are crosstabulated by age, race, sex, and nativity.

Marital Status--An inquiry as to marital status was made only in 1880 and 1890, as was one on relationship to the head of the household. However, each census between 1850 and 1890 had a place to check whether married during the past year.

Migration--This term is not used in this index. To search for data on internal migration, or immigration from other countries, use information shown under the term nativity.

Military age--See Age

Natural Militia--A term used to indicate the number of males of certain ages, usually 18-45, who were potentially capable of providing military service.

Nativity--The place of birth--state, territory or country--was asked on each census from 1850 through 1890. Nativity in this index is referred to as general nativity meaning native or foreign born, or specific nativity referring to the place of birth, i.e. specific state, territory or foreign country.

In addition, the 1870 questionnaire asked whether the father or mother of each person was of foreign birth, and the 1880 and 1890 qustionnaire asked for their places of birth. These questions are referred to in this index as parental nativity.

Results of data from questions on place of birth are published extensively in the final reports, with many crosstabulations such as by sex and by occupation. It should be noted, however, that most such data is for whites only.

Occupations--Information on occupations, employment and industry appears under the term Occupations in this index. In 1820, the first inquiry on occupations was made, as to whether persons were engaged in agriculture, commerce or manufactures. Later censuses expanded on such inquiries. By 1850, the profession, occupation, or trade of each person, male or female of 15 years, was asked. The 1820 and 1840 inquiries were precise, but later censuses asked each individual to describe his or her occupation, and it was up to the Census Office to categorize the answers once received, for inclusion in the final volumes. Final volumes for 1850 through 1890 provide totals for occupational groups, as well as for specific occupations. Data are frequently crosstabulated by sex, race and general nativity.

Paupers--This is a Nineteenth Century term which can simply not be translated. Coming from the French pouvre and the Spanish pobre, a 1907 Webster's defines a pauper as a "poor person, particularly one so indigent as to depend on the parish or town for maintenance." The 1850, and 1860 questionnaires inquired whether any member of the household was a pauper. The 1870 Census dropped the question, but the 1880 Census had a separate schedule for paupers and indigent inhabitants in institutions, poor houses, or asylums, or boarded at public expense in private homes, as well as a schedule for "homeless children." In 1890, there was a schedule for "statistics of benevolence containing some 47 separate questions. Detailed data on paupers appears in separate volumes in both 1880 and 1890 final reports.

Population--The number of inhabitants.

Prisoners - See crime and institutionalized population.

Private Charge--Paid for by non-governmental sources.

Progress of the Nation--A term frequently used in the Ninetenth Century census volumes. It provides insight into the thinking of the census takers and those compiling the information into the final volumes.

Property--Inquiries concerning property were limited to 1850, 1860, and 1890. Value of real estate owned was the question in 1850, and in 1860 personal estate was added. No question was asked on property in 1870 and 1880, but as a result of the efforts of the "Single Taxers" and the concern over debts, a great deal of attention was devoted to home and farm tenure and encumbrances in 1890. A separate schedule was used for mortgaged farms and homes. Two volumes were published in the final reports, Farms and Homes and Real Estate Mortgages as the result of this schedule. The 1890 special schedule for Indians also called for statements of property, and several of the volumes on Indians provide data on the subject.

Public Charge--Paid for from government funds.

Publications--Several final census volumes include information about newspapers and periodicals. Information is tabulated by circulation and by subject and frequency of publication. A special study was made for the 1880 Census which resulted in a major section of one volume, entitled History and Present Condition of the Newspaper and Periodical Press of the United States, with a catalogue of the Publications of the Census Year. With over 40 pages, this volume is a useful source of historical information on newspapers and periodicals, and also on the cities in which they were published.

Race and Condition--In the First through the Eighth Census, 1790 through 1860, race was always tied to condition: i.e. free or slave. In 1850 and 1860 there were separate schedules for "Free inhabitants" and "slave inhabitants." The latter schedule had fewer inquiries.

In the First Census, race and condition were categorized as "free whites, all other free persons, and slaves." From 1800 through 1830, the categories were whites, "all other free persons except Indians not taxed" and slaves. In 1840, the schedule called for free white persons, free colored persons and slaves.

In 1850 and 1860 the Free Inhabitants schedule called for white and colored, and the slave schedule inquired as to color. By 1870, following the end of slavery, the inquiry "color" provided choices of white, black, mulatto, Chinese and Indian. The 1880 schedule was the same, and in 1890, the terminology "quadroon," "octaroon," and "Japanese" were added.

Data resulting from the inquiries were usually published in the same terms, except all non-whites were often placed together as "colored" in single tables, frequently with footnotes showing the number of Chinese, Japanese, and Indians.

418

See also Indians.

Religion--Although no question on religion was asked in a population
enumeration, inquires were made to religious organizations as to the
number of their members or communicants, church edifices and accommodations, and finances, and were published in 1850, 1860 and 1870
final reports. In addition, a complete volume, with considerable
detail, was published in 1890 in a volume entitled Churches. Some
statistics on publications also provide details on denominational
periodicals. In addition, some of the descriptions of Indians and
Alaskans refer to their religion. Today, presumably inquiries to
religious organizations and publication of results would be considered unconstitutional under the First Amendment.

School age--See Age

Sex--In the First Census, only the sex of free whites was published.
By 1820, free colored persons were counted and by 1830, slaves were
likewise counted by sex. Most census data was tabulated by sex
throughout the Nineteenth Century. This includes data on age, race,
and most social and economic characteristics.

Slavery--Information on slavery is contained in each census from 1790
through 1860. Details as to the number of slaves, and their age and
sex is shown under Race and condition in this index. In the earliest
years, inquiries about slaves were less detailed than those about
free inhabitants. Inquiries were made to slave owners, not to slaves
themselves. In 1850, a separate schedule was used for slaves and
reused in 1860. Inquiries as to age, sex and color (black or mulatto)
were made, as well as the number of slaves manumitted and the number
of fugitives. Throughout the period of slavery, the final volumes
gave details as to the proportion of slaves to free inhabitants.

Unemployment--See Employment

Voting age--See Age

Territories--At the First Census, land beyond the boundary of the
States was designated Territory Northwest of the River Ohio and
Territory South of the River Ohio. At each succcessive census, new
designations of territories had occurred. Reference should always be
made to the map preceding information of each census to determine the
territorial designation at the time of the enumeration.

In some census volumes, territories are listed at the end of the
states, and in some volumes, or even in the same volume, they are
sometimes interspersed among the states.

Transportation--Although transportation is somewhat beyond the scope
of this volume, there are occasional places where transportation data
is useful for the study of population, and therefore it is indexed in
this publication. Locations of railways, street railways and canals
are frequently precisely noted in census volumes.

Vital Statistics--Census or enumeration usually refers to a count of persons living on a certain date. Vital statistics usually refers to a count of events: births, deaths, marriages and divorces. Mortality statistics, a count of deaths during the year preceding the census day, began in 1850. A separate schedule was used when someone in the household had died during the year. This procedure continued through 1890. Statistics of deaths were published in great detail in the census final volumes. By 1890, there are four volumes totaling over 4000 pages on the statistics of deaths; only a handful of pages on births was included in the four volumes.

Births were never recorded in connection with the census as such, but some data on age was recorded from 1790, gradually expanding to the entire population. Beginning in 1870, the month of birth was recorded, providing data for vital statistics records.

"Married within the year?" was also a new question in 1850, continued through 1890, but results of the inquiry were never included in the census reports in the same detail.

Divorce appeared on the schedules only in connection with marital status in 1880 and 1890. Thus no statistics on the event of divorce were developed by the Census, but number of divorced persons appears in tables entitled conjugal conditions.

Vital statistics are no longer a function of the Census, as such events are recorded by the state or local governments at the time of occurrence, in most cases on a form recommended by the Federal government. The Census remains a count of persons, not of events.

STATES AND TERRITORIES AS THEY APPEAR
IN CENSUS VOLUMES 1970 - 1890

	Organized as Territory	Appears as Territory	Admitted as State	Appears as State
Alabama	March 3, 1817	1790 See Georgia 1800 See Georgia and Mississippi T. 1810 See Mississippi Territory	12-4-1819	1820
Alaska	Purchased 1867 Organized as Territory 1912	1880 1890	1-3-1959	1960
Arizona	Feb. 24, 1863	1860 See New Mexico Territory 1870 Arizona T. 1880 Arizona T 1890 Arizona T.	2-14-1912	1920
Arkansas	March 2, 1819	1820 1830	6-15-1836	1840
California	--	--	9-9-1850 Compendium includes 1852 state census	1850
Colorado	Feb. 28, 1861	1860 See Utah and New Mexico T. 1870 See also Utah, Nebraska, and Kansas Territories	8-1-1876	1880
Connecticut	Original State	--	--	1790
Dakota Territory	March 2, 1861	1860 1870 1880	North and South Dakota	
Delaware	Original State	--	11-2-1889	1790
District of Columbia	Formal March 30, 1791	Appears alternately as territory or among states	Virginia portion receded 7-9-1846	1800

	Organized as Territory	Appears as Territory	Admitted as State	Appears as State
Florida	March 30, 1822	1830 1840	3-3-1845	1850
Georgia	Original State	--	--	1790
Hawaii	June 1900	--	8-21-1960	1960
Idaho	March 3, 1863	1870 Idaho T. 1880 Idaho T.	7-3-1890	1890
Illinois	March 1, 1809	1790 - See Territory NW of River Ohio 1800 Indiana T.	12-3-1818	1820
Indiana	July 4, 1800	1800 Indiana T. 1810 Indiana T.	12-11-1816	1820
Indian Territory	Indian Removal Act of 1830	--	As Oklahoma 11-16-1907	1910
Iowa	July 3, 1838	1830 See Michigan Territory 1840 See Iowa T.	3-3-1845 Readmitted enlarged boundaries 12-28-1846	1850
Kansas	May 30, 1854	1860 Kansas T.	1-29-1861	1860
Kentucky	--	1790 See Territory SW of River Ohio	6-1-1792	1790
Louisiana	--	1810 See Territory of Orleans and Louisiana T.	4-30-1812	1820
Maine	--	Governed by Massachusetts prior to statehood, but appears as Maine in 1790, 1800, 1810	3-15-1820	1790
Maryland	Original State	--	--	1790
Massachusetts	Original State	--	--	1790

	Organized as Territory	Appears as Territory	Admitted as State	Appears as State
Michigan	June 30, 1805	1790 See Territory NW of River Ohio 1800 See Territory NW of River Ohio 1810 Michigan T. see also Indiana T. 1820 Michigan T. 1830 Michigan T.	1-26-1837	1840
Minnesota	March 3, 1849	1830 See Michigan Territory 1840 See Iowa T. 1850 See Minnesota Territory	5-11-1858	1860
Mississippi	April 7, 1798	1790 See Georgia T. 1800 See Georgia and Mississippi T.	12-10-1817	1820
Missouri	Dec. 7, 1812	1820 Missouri T.	8-10-1821	1830
Montana	May 26, 1864	1870 Montana T. 1880 Montana T.	11-8-1889	1890
Nebraska	May 30, 1854	1860 Nebraska T.	3-1-1867	1870
Nevada	March 2, 1861	1860 See Utah T.	10-31-1864	1870
New Hampshire	Original State	--	--	1790
New Jersey	Original State	--	--	1790
New Mexico	Dec. 13, 1850	1850 New Mexico T. 1860 New Mexico T. 1870 New Mexico T. 1880 New Mexico T.	1-6-1912	1920
New York	Original State	--	--	1790
North Carolina	Original State	--	--	1790
North Dakota	See Dakota Territory March 2, 1861	1840 See Iowa T. 1850 See Missouri and Minnesota T. 1860 See Dakota T. 1870 See Dakota T. 1880 See Dakota T.	11-2-1889	1890

	Organized as Territory	Appears as Territory	Admitted as State	Appears as State
Ohio	--	1790 See Territory NW of River Ohio 1880 See Territory NW of River Ohio	11-29-1802	1910
Oklahoma	May 2, 1890	1890 Oklahoma T. Also see Indian Territory	11-16-1907	1910
Oregon	Aug. 14, 1848	1850 Oregon T.	2-14-1859	1860
Orleans Territory	1804	1810 Orleans T.	As Louisiana 4-30-1812	1820
Pennsylvania	Original State	--	--	1790
Rhode Island	Original State	--	--	1790
South Carolina	Original State	--	--	1790
South Dakota	See Dakota Territory March 2, 1861	1840 See Iowa T. 1850 See Missouri and Minnesota T. 1860 See Dakota T. 1870 See Dakota T. 1880 See Dakota T.	11-2-1889	1890
Tennessee	--	1790 See Territory Sw of River Ohio	6-1-1796	1800
Territory Northwest of the River Ohio	1787	1790	Became States of Ohio Illinois Indiana Michigan Wisconsin and part of Minnesota	
Territory Southwest of the River Ohio	1790	1790	Became States of Kentucky and Tennessee	

	Organized as Territory	Appears as Territory	Admitted as State	Appears as State
Texas	--	--	12-29-1845	1850
Utah	Sept. 9, 1850	1850 Utah T.	1-4-1896	1900
Vermont	--	--		1790
Virginia	Original State	Parts ceded to District of Columbia from 1800 to 1840 were receded on 1846 to Virginia		
Washington	March 2, 1853	1850 See Oregon T. 1860 Washington T. 1870 Washington T. 1880 Washington T.	11-11-1889	1890
West Virginia	Set off from Virginia Dec. 31, 1862	1790 - 1860 see Virginia	6-19-1863	1870
Wisconsin	July 3, 1836	1790 See Territory NW of River Ohio 1800 See Indiana T. 1810 See Illinois T. 1820 See Michigan T. 1830 See Michigan T. 1840 Wisconsin T.	5-29-1848	1850
Wyoming	July 25, 1868	1870 Wyoming T. 1880 Wyoming T.	7-10-1890	1890

Dates on organization of territories and admission of states from the Eleventh Census 1890, Compendium Part I, Table 4 (Dubester 224), the same volume in which maps of states and territories for 1790 to 1890 are found.

The best source I have found for state boundaries and various territorial changes is in the Eighth Census 1870, Volume I, pages 571-592 et seq.

CONGRESSIONAL SERIAL SET VOLUMES
WHICH INCLUDE CENSUS DATA

Census Year	Serial Set	Congress Session	Volume	House or Senate	Number	Census Volume	Dubester Number
1830	221	22d 1st	6	House Doc	263	5th Bk 2	21
1840	376	26th 2d	2	Sen. Doc	32	6th -	(28)
1840	402	27th 2d	2	H Ex Doc	76	-	(29)
1850	686	32d 2d	-	H Misc Doc	Unnumb'd	7th Bk 1	30
1850	805	33d 2d	13	H Ex Doc	98	7th Bk 2	32
1850	984	35th 2d	10	S Ex Doc	39	7th -	31
1860	1137	37th 2d	9	H Ex Doc	116	8th Prelm	41
1860	1202	38th 1st	-	H Misc Doc	Unnumb'd	8th Bk 1	37
1860	1203	38th 1st	-	H Misc Doc	Unnumb'd	8th Bk 2	38
1860	1204	38th 1st	-	H Misc Doc	Unnumb'd	8th Bk 3	39
1860	1205	38th 1st	-	H Misc Doc	Unnumb'd	8th Bk 4	40
1870	1473	42d 1st	-	H Misc Doc	Unnumb'd	9th Bk 1	45
1870	1474	42d 1st	-	H Misc Doc	Unnumb'd	9th Bk 2	49
1870	1475	42d 1st	-	H Misc Doc	Unnumb'd	9th Bk 3	52
1870	1476	42d 1st	-	H Misc Doc	Unnumb'd	9th Com 'pm	57
1880	1968	46th 3rd	18	H Ex Doc	65	10th Appt	155
1880	2059	47th 1st	2 pt 1	H Misc Doc	64 pt 1	10th Com 'pm pt 1	153
1880	2060	47th 1st	24 pt 2	H Misc Doc	64 pt 2	10th Com 'pm pt 2	153
1880	2129	47th 2d	13 pt 1	H Misc Doc	42 pt 1	10th V 1	61
1880	2130	47th 2d	13 pt 2	H Misc Doc	42 pt 2	10th V 2	63
1880	2131	47th 2d	13 pt 3	H Misc Doc	42 pt 3	10th v 3	75
1880	2132	47th 2d	13 pt 4	H Misc Doc	42 pt 4	10th v 4	82
1880	2133	47th 2d	13 pt 5	H Misc Doc	42 pt 5	10th v 5	88
1880	2134	47th 2d	13 pt 6	H Misc Doc	42 pt 6	10th v 6	98
1880	2135	47th 2d	13 pt 7	H Misc Doc	42 pt 7	10th v 7	105
1880	2136	47th 2d	13 pt 8	H Misc Doc	42 pt 8	10th v 8	107
1880	2137	47th 2d	13 pt 9	H Misc Doc	42 pt 9	10th v 9	112
1880	2138	47th 2d				10th maps	-
1880	2139	47th 2d	13 pt 10	H Misc Doc	42 pt 10	10th v 10	113
1880	2140	47th 2d	13 pt 11	H Misc Doc	42 pt 11	10th v 11	117
1880	2141	47th 2d	13 pt 12	H Misc Doc	42 pt 12	10th v 12	118
1880	2142	47th 2d	13 pt 12	H Misc Doc	42 pt -	10th plates	118
1880	2143	47th 2d	13 pt 13	H Misc Doc	42 pt 13	10th v 13	119
1880	2144	47th 2d	13 pt 14	H Misc Doc	42 pt 14	10th v 14	122

Census Year	Serial Set	Congress Session	Volume	House or Senate	Number	Census Volume	Dubester Number
1880	2145	47th 2d	13 pt 15	H Misc Doc	42 pt 15	10th v 15	123
1880	2146	47th 2d	13 pt 16	H Misc Doc	42 pt 16	10th v 16	125
1880	2147	47th 2d	13 pt 17	H Misc Doc	42 pt 17	10th v 17	134
1880	2148	47th 2d	13 pt 18	H Misc Doc	42 pt 18	10th v 18	141
1880	2149	47th 2d	13 pt 19	H Misc Doc	42 pt 19	10th v 19	142
1880	2150	47th 2d	13 pt 20	H Misc Doc	42 pt 20	10th v 20	144
1880	2151	47th 2d	13 pt 21	H Misc Doc	42 pt 21	10th v 21	145
1880	2152	47th 2d	13 pt 22	H Misc Doc	42 pt 22	10th v 22	146
1890	3008	52d 2d	50 pt 1	H Misc Doc	340 pt 1	v 7	199
1890	3009	52d 2d	50 pt 2	H Misc Doc	340 pt 4	v 15 pt 1	216
1890	3010	52d 2d	50 pt 2	H Misc Doc	340 pt 4	v 15 pt 2	217
						Compendium	
1890	3011	52d 2d	50 pt 3	H Misc Doc	340 pt 6	pt 1	224
1890	3012	52d 2d	50 pt 4	H Misc Doc	340 pt 6	pt 2	225
1890	3013	52d 2d	50 pt 4	H Misc Doc	340 pt 6	pt 3	226
1890	3014	52d 2d	50 pt 5	H Misc Doc	340 pt 14	pt 1	204
1890	3015	52d 2d	50 pt 5	H Misc Doc	340 pt 14	v11 pt 2	205
1890	3016	52d 2d	50 pt 6	H Misc Doc	340 pt 15	v10	202
1890	3017	52d 2d	50 pt 7	H Misc Doc	340 pt 17	v 9	201
1890	3018	52d 2d	50 pt 8	H Misc Doc	340 pt 18	v 1 pt 1	177
1890	3019	52d 2d	50 pt 8	H Misc Doc	340 pt 18	v 1 pt 2	178
1890	3020	52d 2d	50 pt 9	H Misc Doc	340 pt 7	v 8	200
1890	3021	52d 2d	50 pt 10	H Misc Doc	340 pt 20	v 5	188
1890	3022	52d 2d	50 pt 11	H Misc Doc	340 pt 21	v 14 pt 1	209
1890	3023	52d 2d	50 pt 11	H Misc Doc	340 pt 21	v 14 pt 2	211
1890	3024	52d 2d	50 pt 12	H Misc Doc	340 pt 22	v 6 pt 1	193
1890	3025	52d 2d	50 pt 12	H Misc Doc	340 pt 22	v 6 pt 2	194
1890	3026	52d 2d	50 pt 12	H Misc Doc	340 pt 22	v 6 pt 3	195
1890	3027	52d 2d	50 pt 13	H Misc Doc	340 pt 23	v 12	206
1890	3028	52d 2d	50 pt 14	H Misc Doc	340 pt 24	v 3 pt 1	181
1890	3029	52d 2d	50 pt 14	H Misc Doc	340 pt 24	v 3 pt 2	182
1890	3030	52d 2d	50 pt 15	H Misc Doc	340 pt 25	v 13	207
1890	3031	52d 2d	50 pt 16	H Misc Doc	340 pt 26	v 2	179
1890	3032	52d 2d	50 pt 17	H Misc Doc	340 pt 27	Spec Rpt	231
1890	3033	52d 2d	50 pt 18	H Misc Doc	340 pt 28	v 4 pt 1	184
1890	3034	52d 2d	50 pt 18	H Misc Doc	340 pt 28	v 4 pt 2	185
1890	3035	52d 2d	50 pt 18	H Misc Doc	340 pt 28	v 4 pt 3	186
1890	3036	52d 2d	50 pt 18	H Misc Doc	340 pt 28	v 4 pt 4	187
1890	3037	52d 2d	50 pt 19	H Misc Doc	340 pt 29	Atlas	220
1890	3229	53rd 2d	1	H Misc Doc	185	Abstract	

EXPLANATION OF ROMAN NUMERALS

An explanation of Roman numerals is included here because of the frequency of their use both as page numbers and as table numbers in the Nineteenth Century census volumes.

Roman numerals are easy to understand if one thinks of someone having to carve them in stone during the time of the Roman Empire. Nearly all Roman numerals are made from straight lines to make the cutting easier. Also, the shortest number of digits as possible is used to make the least work and take the least space.

The basic rule is to begin with the symbol for the largest number and to add the smaller ones to the right. A number following a number adds to its value. A smaller number preceding one of the higher value subtracts from it.

Today, both upper and lower case is used in type for Roman numerals. Frequently introductory pages in a book are numbered in lower case, and tables are numbered in upper case. Some of the census volumes indexed in this book use both upper and lower case Roman numerals.

Explanation

Arabic	1	5	10	50	100	500	1000
Roman							
Upper case	I	V	X	L	C	D	M
Lower case	i	v	x	l	c	d	m

Examples

Arabic	Upper Roman	Lower Roman	Arabic	Upper Roman	Lower Roman
1	I	i	20	XX	xx
2	I	ii	23	XXIII	xxiii
3	III	iii	24	XXIV	xxiv
4	IV	iv	25	XXV	xxv
5	V	v	29	XXIX	xxix
6	VI	vi	30	XXX	xxx
9	IX	ix	35	XXXV	xxxv
10	X	x	40	XL	xl
11	XI	xi	45	XLV	xlv
12	XII	xii	49	IL	il
13	XIII	xiii	50	L	l
14	XIV	xiv	57	LVII	lvii
15	XV	xv	59	LIX	lix
16	XVI	xvi	75	LXXV	lxxv
17	XVII	xvii	101	CI	ci
18	XVIII	xviii	405	CDV	cdv
19	XIX	xix	1001	MI	mi
20	XX	xx	1982	MCMLXXXII	mcmlxxxii

NATIONAL ARCHIVES AND RECORDS SERVICE

Films of Population Schedules
1790 through 1890

Decennial Census	Microfilm Number	Number Reels
1790	M 637 - Original schedules	12 reels
	T 498 - Schedules as published by the Library of Congress, 1907-1908	3 reels
1800	M 32	52 reels
1810	M 252	71 reels
1820	M 33	142 reels
1830	M 19	201 reels
1840	M 704	580 reels
1850	M 432	1009 reels
1860	M 653	1438 reels
1870	M 593	1748 reels
	M 132 - Schedules for some Minnesota counties	13 reels
1880	T 9	1454 reels
	T 734-T780 - Soundex Index to the 1880 Population Schedules	2367 reels
1890	M 407 - Those few 1890 Population Schedules which survived a 1921 fire	3 reels
	M 496 - Index to the surviving schedules	2 reels
	M 123 - Special schedules of Union veterans and widows of Union veterans of the Civil War	118 reels

Source: General Services Administration, National Archives and Records Service. Federal Population Censuses, 1790-1890: A catalog of microfilm copies of the schedules, 1977.

STATE CENSUSES

Anyone searching for census information from the Nineteenth Century should be aware of the fact that in some cases, state as well as federal census data may be available. The word _may_ cannot be overemphasized.

During the Nineteenth Century, some states took no state census at all, either during their territorial periods or after admission as states. Others made one or more enumerations, but some or all of the reports or the completed schedules are missing. Other states did make enumerations and have a number of state census reports and original schedules available. Among those states which have written reports of their census counts, some also have available for research the original schedules completed by the enumerators. Some such schedules have been filmed by the National Archives and Records Service, such as those of the Colorado state census of 1885.

Henry J. Dubester, who was chief of the Census Library Project at the Library of Congress, and on whose work on Decennial Census Publications this volume is based, also prepared "An annotated bibiography of censuses of population taken after the year 1790 by States and Territories of the United States "which was jointly published by the Bureau of the Census and the Library of Congress in 1948, and entitled State Censuses.

State Censuses is based in part on a survey begun by the Bureau of the Census in 1941, but discontinued during World War II. Dubester supplemented responses to the survey with materials he found in the Library of Congress after the War. He limited the volume to censuses which attempted to count the entire population, as opposed, for example, to school censuses.

Dubester's volume includes references both to published reports and to the original schedules which were still available. The body of the volume makes reference to the constitutional and statutory prosions of the various states which did provide for a state census, under what authority they were to be made, and the years in which they were actually undertaken. Where Dubester found them in the Library of Congress, he indicated classification numbers. The appendix of his volume includes information as to whether the original schedules were then available, and in which state agency or library they might be found.

In his preface, Dubester states that "The information contained in the correspondence from official and semiofficial State sources in answer to the original Census Bureau inquries is often contradicted by the existence of published materials which indicate rich histories of census activities. Furthermore the lack of official information extends not only to the existence of State censuses but also to whether the

430

original schedules and returns have survived. Thus the present
bibliography is doubtlessly incomplete and even inaccurate in some
details, and therefore any attempt at a comprehensive coverage for
all of the United States must be tentative." He then requested additional information from those who could add to his bibliography.

In the nearly thirty-five years since State Censuses was published,
there have doubtless been searches, even successful searches, for
early census material made in individual states. Given the interest
in the quantitative study of history, in local history, in genealogy,
and in the development of better records of state documents, some
additional records of state censuses must surely have been found.
Apparently there has not however been any later comprehensive study
of all states since that done by Dubester.

For some time I had looked forward to meeting the person who had
made such bibliographical order out of early census material, and in
the Spring of 1982 had the opportunity to meet with Dr. Dubester. As
the authority on the subject, I assumed that he would be knowledgeable
about any efforts to make such a study. In our conversation I found
that he knows of none, and I have been unable to discover any through
library sources.

The listing below, therefore, is basically a shortened list of the
state censuses cited in the 1948 Dubester volume. It should be of
some assistance to those searching for information about a certain
state, and should encourage them to read the original Dubester
citations. Then they will no doubt wish to make inquiries of the
State Archives, Library or Historical Society to learn whether any
discoveries of additional state material has been found since the
publication of State Censuses.

STATE CENSUSES AND ORIGINAL SCHEDULES
LISTED IN DUBESTER "STATE CENSUSES"

1790-1890

State	Years of state censuses	Page on which cited	Appendix page original schedules cited
Alabama		1	
Alaska	--		
Arizona	1864 T 1866 T	2	67
Arkansas	1854	2	

California
  (Results of California
  state census of 1852 are
  included in U.S. Census
  Compendium for 1850,
  published in 1854
	1852	3	67

Colorado	1861 T 1885	3	
Connecticut	no record		
Delaware	no record		
District of Columbia	1803 1807 1818 1867 1878 1885 1888 1894 1897	4	
Florida	1825 1845 1855 1885 1895	7	67
Georgia	1824	10	67

State	Years of state censuses	Page on which cited	Appendix page original schedules cited
Hawaii	--		
Idaho	1863 T	11	
Illinois	1810 T 1818 T 1820 T 1835 T 1840 T 1845 T	11	67
Indiana	1801 T 1815 T	13	
Iowa (See also Wisconsin Territory)	1836 T 1838 T 1847 1849 1854 1856 1859 1862 1865 1867 1869 1873 1875 1885 1895	14	68
Kansas	1855 T 1859 T 1875 1885 1895	20	69
Kentucky		23	
Louisiana	1853 1858	23	
Maine	no record of a state census		
Maryland	no record of a state census		

State	Years of state censuses	Page on which cited	Appendix page original schedules cited
Massachusetts	1837	24	69
	1840		
	1850		
	1855		
	1865		
	1875		
	1885		
	1895		
Michigan	1827 T	29	70
	1834 T		
	1837		
	1845		
	1854		
	1864		
	1874		
	1884		
	1894		
Minnesota	1849 T	33	70
	1857 T		
	1865		
	1875		
	1885		
	1895		
Mississippi	1816 T	35	35
	1840		
	1880		
Missouri	1817 T	37	70
	1821		
	1824		
	1828		
	1832		
	1836		
	1840		
	1844		
	1852		
	1856		
	1860		
	1864		
	1868		
	1876		

State	Years of state censuses	Page on which cited	Appendix page original schedules cited
Montana		41	
Nebraska	1854 T	41	
	1855 T		
	1856 T		
	1874		
	1875		
	1876		
	1877		
	1878		
	1879		
	1882		
	1883		
	1884		
	1885		
Nevada	1861 T	42	
	1875		
New Hampshire	no record of a state census		
New Jersey	1855	43	70
	1865		
	1875		
	1885		
	1895		
New Mexico	no record of a state census		
New York	1795	45	70
	1801		
	1807		
	1814		
	1821		
	1825		
	1835		
	1845		
	1855		
	1865		
	1875		
	1892		
North Carolina	no record of a state census		
North Dakota	1885 T	51	71

State	Years of state censuses	Page on which cited	Appendix page original schedules cited
Ohio	--	52	
Oklahoma	--	52	
Oregon	1845 T 1849 T 1865 1875 1885	53	71
Pennsylvania	no record of a state census		
Rhode Island	1865 1875 1885 1895	54	71
South Carolina	1868 1875	57	
South Dakota See also North Dakota	1885 T	58 51	72
Tennessee	1805 1812 1819 1826 1833	60	
Texas	1847 1848	60	
Utah	1851 T 1895 T	61	
Vermont	no record of a state census		
Virginia	no record of a state census		
Washington	no record of a state census		
West Virginia	no record of a state census		

436

State	Years of state censuses	Page on which cited	Appendix page original schedules cited
Wisconsin	1836 T	62	72
	1838 T		
	1846 T		
	1947 T		
	1855		
	1865		
	1875		
	1885		
	1895		
Wyoming	--	65	73

T after year of census indicated territorial status at that date

BIBLIOGRAPHY

This entire publication is based on the work of Henry J. Dubester, Chief of the Census Library Project at the Library of Congress during the 1940s. Publications resulting from that project were jointly published by the Bureau of the Census and the Library of Congress Reference Service.

U.S. Department of Commerce, Bureau of the Census, and U.S. Library of Congress, Reference Department. Census Library Project. Henry J. Dubester. Catalog of U.S. Census Publications, 1790-1940. Washington, Government Printing Office: 1950.

State Censuses: An annotated bibliography of censuses of population taken after the year 1780 by States and Territories of the United States. Washington, U.S. Government Printing Office: 1948.

U.S. Department of Commerce, Social and Economic Statistics Administration, Bureau of the Census. Bureau of the Census Catalog of Publications, 1790-1972. Washington, Government Printing Office: 1974. This publication includes the entire text of the 1790-1940 catalog.

U.S. Department of Commerce, Social and Economic Statistics Administration, Bureau of the Census. Population and Housing Inquiries in U.S. Decennial Census, 1790-1970. Working Paper 39. Washington, Department of Commerce: 1973.

U.S. Department of Commerce, Bureau of the Census. Twenty Censuses: Population and Housing Questions, 1790-1980. Washington, Government Printing Office: 1978.

United States Senate. 56th Congress, 1st Session, Document 194. The History of the United States Census, prepared for the Senate Committee on the Census by Carroll D. Wright, Commissioner of Labor, assisted by William C. Hunt, Chief Statistician, Twelfth Census. Washington, Government Printing Office: 1900.

MICROFORM COLLECTIONS AND INDEXES THERETO

U.S. General Services Administration, National Archives and Records Service.

Records of the Bureau of the Census. Record Group 29. Publications of the Bureau of the Census, 1790-1916. Film T 825 42 rolls. Roll list (mimeographed.)

438

<u>Federal Population Censuses, 1790-1890: A catalog of microfilm copies
of the schedules</u>. Washington, National Archives Trust Fund Board:
1977.

Research Publications, Inc. <u>Bibliography and Reel Index: A guide to
the Microfilm Edition of United States Decennial Census
Publications: 1790-1970</u>. Woodbridge Connecticut, Research
Publications: 1975.

Library Resources, Inc. <u>The Microbook of American Civilization</u>. <u>The
Library of American Civilization</u>. Chicago, Library Resources:
1971.

Evans, Charles. <u>American Bibliography</u>. New York, Readex Microprint
Corporation. Opaque.

Sabin, Joseph. <u>Bibliotheca Americana</u>. New York, Readex Microprint
Corporation. Opaque.

Sowerby, E. Millicent. <u>U.S. Library of Congress. Jefferson Collection</u>.
Compiled with annotations by E. Millicent Sowerby. Washington,
Library of Congress: 1952-1959.

Useful as a source for determining names of counties enumerated in each
census:

Stemmons, John "D." <u>The United States Census Compendim, A Directory of
Census Records, Tax Lists, Poll Lists, Petitions, Directories, Etc.
Which can be Used as a Census</u>. Logan, Utah, Everton Publishers,
Inc., 1973.

UNION LIST OF LIBRARY HOLDINGS

The purpose of the following section is to aid the library using this volume in developing a list of specific locations of each census volume referred to here, and to note the method of classification of that volume in that library.

Census reports are classified under at least three different classification systems: the Superintendent of Documents, the Library of Congress, and the Dewey or Universal Decimal Classification. For the decennial censuses taken in 1850 through 1890, the census reports were also published as Congressional documents, and carry those numbers in the Congressional system as well as Serial Set notations. In addition, a few of the early volumes appear in the Evans, Sabin and Sowerby collections, and others appear in the Library of American Civilization ultramicrofiche series.

The National Archives and Record Service in 1974 filmed the entire Dubester collection through 1890. These films are designated in Record Group 29, Series T825, Reels 1-42. They have been made available at each of the Regional Centers of the National Archives and Records Service. In addition, Research Publications has filmed the reports and has published a reel index.

Libraries lacking some Census volumes, and that would include most of us, may wish to note here which library in their state or region holds individual volumes. This union list provides a place to record that information. A complete union list of holdings within a borrowing area could be developed with the use of the following pages. This would not be an easy task. Most of the major decennial volumes may be found, but the smaller, more obscure pieces may only be available in the Washington area. Some do not seem to be available even there. It is our hope that by the time this volume is in print, Michener Library will have been able to copy all the pieces now lacking in our collection.

Since libraries may be reluctant to lend census volumes, some of which are becoming very fragile indeed, it may be necessary to use the union list and the table finding guides to request that certain tables be copied by a holding library. For that reason, the guides in this volume have been burdened with excessive detail.

It is the intent of this publication to make easier access of census materials, even, or particularly, where the user cannot have the volumes he or she needs directly in front of them.

440

Union List of Libraries

<u>Library A</u>

Library

Address

Librarians   Phone

<u>Library B</u>

Library

Address

Librarians   Phone

<u>Library C</u>

Library

Address

Librarians   Phone

<u>Library D</u>

Library

Address

Librarians   Phone

<u>Library E</u>

Library

Address

Librarians   Phone

Union List of Libraries Holding Census Volumes

Holding Library and Classification
of Volume by Dubester Number

Census Year	Library A	Library B	Library C	Library D	Library E
1790					
D 1					
D 2					
D 3					
D 4					
D 5 Connecticut Maine Maryland Massachusetts New Hapshire New York North Carolina Pennsylvania Rhode Island South Carolina Vermont Virginia					
D6					
1800					
D8					
1810					
D 10					
D 11					
1820					
D 15					
D 16					
1830					
D 19					

442

D 20

D 21

1840 _____

D 24

D 25

D 26

D 27

1850 _____

D 30

D 31

D 32

D 331

D 332

D 34

1860 _____

D 37

D 38

D 39

D 40

D 41

1870 _____

D 45

D 49

D 52

D 55

D 57

443

1880 _____

D 61

D 63

D 75

D 82

D 89

D 98

D 105

D 107

D 112

atlas

D 113

D 117

D 118

D 119

D 122

D 123

D 125

D 134

D 141

D 142

D 144

D 145

D 146

D 153

444

D 155

D 156

D 157

D 158

D 159

D 160

D 161

D 162

D 163

D 164

D 165

D 166

D 168

1890 _____

D 177

D 178

D 179

D 181

D 182

D 184

D 185

D 186

D 187

D 188

D 193

D 194

D 195

D 199

D 200

D 210

D 202

D 204

D 205

D 206

D 207

D 209

D 211

D 216

D 217

D 220

D 221

D 222

D 224

D 225

D 226

D 227

D 228

D 229

D 230

D 231

D 232

D 233

446

Guide to Volumes—By Dubester Number

Column groupings by census year: **1790** (2, 5) · 6 · **1800** (8, 10) · **1810** (15) · **1820** (16) · **1830** (19, 20, 21) · **1840** (24, 25, 26, 27, 29) · **1850** (30, 31, 32, 33, 34) · **1860** (37, 38, 39, 40, 41) · **1870** (45, 49, 52, 55, 57) · **1880** (61, 63, 75, 82) · 89,98 · 105 · 107 · 112 · 113

Demographic Characteristics

	2	5	6	8	10	15	16	19	20	21	24	25	26	27	29	30	31	32	33	34	37	38	39	40	41	45	49	52	55	57	61	63	75	82	89,98	105	107	112	113
Aggregate Population	●	●		●	●	●		●	●	●	●			●		●	●	●	●		●					●	●	●	●		●	●	●		●	●	●		
Historic from 1790								●						●		●	●	●	●		●					●	●	●			●	●							
Age	●	●		●	●	●		●	●	●	●		●	●		●	●	●			●					●		●	●		●	●						●	
Race and Condition	●	●	●	●	●	●		●	●	●	●			●	●	●	●	●	●		●					●	●	●			●	●			●		●		
Sex	●	●		●	●	●		●	●	●	●			●		●	●	●			●					●	●	●			●	●							

Social and Economic Characteristics

	2	5	6	8	10	15	16	19	20	21	24	25	26	27	29	30	31	32	33	34	37	38	39	40	41	45	49	52	55	57	61	63	75	82	89,98	105	107	112	113
Citizenship						●		●	●		●																				●								
Crime																		●	●							●		●			●	●							
Disabilities								●	●		●			●		●		●	●	●							●		●		●	●							
Education											●			●		●			●							●		●			●	●				●			
Employment and unemployment						●	●				●		●	●		●	●	●		●				●	●	●		●	●	●	●				●	●	●	●	●
Families	●	●	●	●										●		●					●					●		●			●	●							
Farms																●		●	●				●	●	●		●		●			●	●			●	●		
Housing																●		●		●				●			●				●	●	●		●		●	●	●
Immigration																●		●	●	●				●	●				●										
Income and property													●					●	●					●	●			●				●	●	●	●			●	●
Institutionalized population																●																							
Language																																				●			
Literacy											●		●			●			●							●		●	●	●									
Military											●			●	●	●										●													
Nativity																●		●	●	●	●					●		●	●	●									
Occupations							●				●		●	●		●		●	●		●						●	●	●	●	●								
Paupers																		●	●							●		●			●	●							
Publications and Libraries																●		●	●					●	●	●					●	●				●			
Religion																●		●	●					●			●		●	●						●			
Slavery	●	●		●	●	●		●	●	●	●			●		●		●	●		●	●	●	●												●			
Transportation																						●		●	●									●					

Apportionment, Density, Geography

	2	5	6	8	10	15	16	19	20	21	24	25	26	27	29	30	31	32	33	34	37	38	39	40	41	45	49	52	55	57	61	63	75	82	89,98	105	107	112	113
Apportionment						●		●	●		●					●		●	●	●						●	●				●	●							
Density																●		●	●							●	●	●	●	●				●					
Geography																●		●	●								●			●				●					

Vital Statistics

	2	5	6	8	10	15	16	19	20	21	24	25	26	27	29	30	31	32	33	34	37	38	39	40	41	45	49	52	55	57	61	63	75	82	89,98	105	107	112	113
Births																●		●			●						●		●										
Deaths																●		●	●	●	●					●	●		●					●					
Marriages and Divorces																●		●		●																			

Foreign Data

	2	5	6	8	10	15	16	19	20	21	24	25	26	27	29	30	31	32	33	34	37	38	39	40	41	45	49	52	55	57	61	63	75	82	89,98	105	107	112	113
Foreign Data																●		●	●	●	●					●	●	●					●	●	●			●	●